THE REVOLUTION IN
ETHICAL THEORY

THE REVOLUTION IN
ETHICAL THEORY

BY

GEORGE C. KERNER

1966

OXFORD UNIVERSITY PRESS

NEW YORK AND OXFORD

PREFACE

My first aim in this book has been to trace and to make intelligible the radical change that ethical theory has undergone during the course of the present century. I have tried to put the fundamental issues into clearer light. The present-day radical reorientation in moral philosophy is part of the new general outlook on the Anglo-American philosophical scene. The close connexion between contemporary ethical theory and the more broad philosophical issues, such as that concerning the nature of language, will therefore be evident throughout our discussions. However, my direct concern has been with ethical theory. My second aim has been to inquire where future progress may lie. I have tried not only to take stock of the work done so far but also to carry moral philosophy a step further. The social pressure on the moral philosopher for getting results is greater than on his colleagues. Hence, he is likely to be anxious to reach definite conclusions, to round off his doctrines and to make them at least appear final. It is perhaps for this reason that the twentieth-century revolution in ethical theory has been plagued by the threat common to all revolutions—the premature emergence of new orthodoxies. Instead of offering a new rival doctrine of my own, I have therefore sought to clarify the significance of recent developments and to make suggestions which, I hope, will help to prepare the way for future progress.

I wish to thank all those who, over the years, have fostered my interest in and have taught me what I know about ethics and philosophy in general. My gratitude is due particularly to Henry S. Leonard, William Callaghan, and Henry D. Aiken. As far as the book is concerned more directly, it is evident that very little of it is really original. Many of the points I make have been made before although not exactly in the same manner or with the same emphasis. I have learned a great deal from everyone whom I mention in the text and in the footnotes and, needless to say, most of all, from the four authors whom I discuss extensively. I have drawn heavily on the late J. L. Austin and tried to apply some of his ideas, as I have understood them, to moral philosophy. R. M. Hare has read an earlier version of the manuscript and his penetrating and generous comments have resulted in numerous improvements. Of course, the reader must not assume that therefore he will find here an authorized account of Hare's views and may dispense with consulting his own text. In order to comment on some twentieth-century moral philosophers, I have had to summarize their arguments. I hope I have done this fairly. But I have intended my book to be a stimulus rather than a substitute for studying the works which I discuss in it. The late Arnold Isenberg helped me to see several things in a better perspective. Ronald Suter has saved me from a number of obscurities. Bruce Buchanan, Peter List, and Peter Meloney have been helpful in eliminating slips and typing errors. For the various shortcomings, which no doubt remain, I am of course alone responsible.

A Michigan State All-University Research Grant has provided funds for typing.

The most frequent references are identified as follows:

PE: G. E. Moore, *Principia Ethica*, Cambridge University Press, 1903.

EL: Charles L. Stevenson, *Ethics and Language*, Yale University Press, 1944 (Oxford University Press paperback edition, 1960).

PRE: Stephen Toulmin, *An Examination of the Place of Reason in Ethics*, Cambridge University Press, 1950.

LM: R. M. Hare, *The Language of Morals*, Oxford University Press, 1952.

FR: R. M. Hare, *Freedom and Reason*, Oxford University Press, 1963.

GEORGE C. KERNER

East Lansing
August 1964

CONTENTS

INTRODUCTION   1

I. G. E. MOORE   5
   1. The Indefinability of 'Good'   5
   2. Goodness as a Property—a Quandary   8
   3. The Open Question Argument   16
   4. Supervenience and Evidence   21
   5. Sense and Reference and Performative Force   25
   6. Moore's Views on Moral Reasoning   32
   7. Moore's Later Views on Moral Reasoning   35

II. CHARLES L. STEVENSON   40
   1. The Two Types of Meaning   40
   2. The Basic Inadequacy of Stevenson's Theory of Meaning   45
   3. Dependent Emotive Meaning   52
   4. Independent Emotive Meaning—Meaning as Impact   58
   5. General Principles and "Persuasive Definitions"   64
   6. The Paradoxical Character of Stevenson's Theory of Moral   73
     Reasoning
   7. Stevenson on Validity   76
   8. The Insufficiency of "Giving Reasons"   83
   9. The Extravagance of "Persuasion"   88
   10. Stevenson's Dilemma and Subsequent Developments   91

III. STEPHEN TOULMIN   97
   1. The New Approach   97
   2. The Theory of "Good Reasons"   102
   3. Truth and Validity   107
   4. The Function of Moral Discourse   112
   5. Toulmin's Thesis is not a Logical Thesis   116
   6. Science and Ethics, Toulmin's Thesis as a Moral Recom-   127
     mendation

CONTENTS

IV. R. M. HARE   138

1. Imperatives and "Phrastics" and "Neustics"   138
2. Criteria of Application, Performative Force, and Kinds of Meaning   150
3. Prescriptivity, Criteria, and Reasons   160
4. Logic and Moral Reasoning   170
5. Decisions and Principles   175
6. Hare's Further Thoughts on Moral Reasoning   182

V. SUMMING UP AND LOOKING AHEAD   197

1. Towards the Proper Method   197
2. Reasons and Linguistic Performances I   202
3. Reasons and Linguistic Performances II   212
4. Expressions of Feelings, Decisions, and Moral Argument   216
5. Criteria, Evaluative Proof, and Moral Reasoning   224
6. The Variety of Performative Force and Moral Reasoning   230
7. Conclusion and the Task Ahead   239

INDEX   253

THE REVOLUTION IN
ETHICAL THEORY

INTRODUCTION

IT has become a commonplace that the problems of moral philosophy are not the same as those problems which, as a matter of course, confront us in moral life. Underlying this common belief is not just the view that philosophical questions relating to morality are more general and far-reaching than questions which ordinarily arise in moral practice. Rather, this belief is rooted in the more radical idea that some of the problems of moral philosophy are different in kind from those problems which confront the moral agent or, on a larger scale, the moralist.

In its sharpest and also exaggerated form the distinction between moral problems and the problems which belong specifically to ethical theory is sometimes put as follows. The language of ethical theory is different in logical type from the language of morals. The language of morals is of the first type: it deals with the questions of what things are morally good and what men are morally obliged to do. The language of ethical theory, on the other hand, is of a logically higher type: it deals with the meaning and structure of the language of the first type. The problems of ethical theory are thus not problems of morals but of moral language; in short, they are "meta-ethical".

This way of putting the matter may suggest that the specific task of the moral philosopher is to develop a formal system, that is, to stipulate the rules of an artificial or ideal language of morals. But setting down the rules of an artificial language can justifiably be called moral philosophy only if that artificial language bears a recognizable resemblance to the language ordinarily used in discussing and settling moral problems. How else would one know that one's artificial language or system is applicable to moral problems? But what is to count here as a recognizable resemblance? In order to be able to make a comparison between an artificial language and the natural language of morals, we must have some clear idea about the nature of the latter. And this is a question on which no general agreement has yet been reached. On the contrary, it is this question—that of the nature of ordinary moral language—which at present predominates in the minds of moral philosophers.

Consequently, if we wish to separate out these issues of contemporary moral philosophy which are not directly concerned with moral conduct or appraisal, we must guard against identifying them with problems of abstract system building. By ethical theory we must mean, essentially, the logical analysis of ordinary moral language—in other words, an investigation into the nature of the terms and modes of reasoning which are actually employed in discussing and settling moral issues in practice.

The historical development that led to this present-day conception of moral philosophy had its beginning in G. E. Moore's *Principia Ethica*. Since the publication of that work in 1903 many of the most interesting issues which have been raised in ethics have been, in a broad sense, logical ones: those concerning the analysis of moral terms, judgements, and modes of reasoning. Besides G. E. Moore, the authors who have made major contributions to the development of moral philosophy in this direction have been Charles S. Stevenson, Stephen Toulmin, and R. M. Hare. By examining the work of these men we can get a good picture of the novel issues and methods introduced into ethical theory in the twentieth century.

The idea which epitomizes these revolutionary changes is the distinction, for the first time drawn explicitly by Stevenson, between two types of meaning of moral judgements—evaluative and descriptive. This distinction, although it contains a grain of truth and was historically prompted by good reasons, led to new problems. We shall see that the paradoxical and inadequate character of much of recent ethical theory arises from this distinction and the rigidity with which it has been drawn. The general tendency has been to conceive of moral language as possessing a *kind of meaning* of its own which makes it absolutely unlike descriptive or factual language. I shall argue that the whole matter is more complicated. To say that moral judgements exemplify a special kind of meaning is seriously misleading. On one level of meaning—on the level of sense and reference—these judgements are absolutely like all other speech-acts. What distinguishes moral judgements from other speech-acts, such as factual statements, is rather what, following Austin, I shall call their performative force or use.[1] In order to appreciate this point, excursions into the philosophy of language in general will prove necessary. As linguistic performances[2] moral judgements are governed by conventions which tie them to emotions, attitudes, decisions, and actions in ways that are essentially different from those found in language when used for discoursing more directly about matters of fact. Due to these conventions moral language is a complicated and subtle, but often confusing, organon for reasoning relating to moral choice and responsibility. But this does not mean that moral language contains a kind of meaning all of its own. In fact, we shall see that it is the widespread belief in the existence of this special kind of meaning that has been responsible for the fact that a wholly satisfactory theory of moral reasoning has not yet been developed. If we realize that moral judgements are different from utterances of a roughly speaking descriptive kind not on account of a special kind of meaning but on account of their characteristic performative force or forces, a more adequate account of moral reasoning becomes possible. The currently popular doctrine of the bifurcation of meaning is too crude, it has led to an exaggerated view concerning the difference between moral judgements and factual statements and has created a spurious logical gulf between them. If we are to understand how description and evaluation—facts and values—are logically connected, a more subtle and unified conception of language is needed. The outlines of such a conception have been developed by J. L. Austin. By making use of his ideas we shall, first of all, gain a clearer view of the forms of moral argument which have been discussed most widely by twentieth-century ethical theorists. Second, we shall be able to see how and to what extent such forms of argument are really logically possible. And finally, we shall come to the recognition of an additional form of moral reasoning which, although often very central in practice, has received very little attention in recent ethical theory.

In the course of this book we shall build up to these conclusions

---

[1] I shall explain my use of the term 'performative force' below; it may not be quite identical with how Austin himself sometimes used it.

[2] My use of this Austinian expression is also explained below.

gradually, by first meeting our authors largely on their own terms, by learning from them and by bringing out their relative strengths and weaknesses. They all believed that they were describing and analysing the ordinary use and meaning of moral terms and judgements and the ordinary forms of moral reasoning. Nevertheless, they arrived at different and conflicting conclusions. Consequently, if fidelity to actual practices in moral discourse is to be the criterion of correctness of an ethical theory, not all of the theories offered by these writers could be true. In fact we shall discover that none of their theories can be said to have brought out quite adequately and precisely the logical features of ordinary moral language. At the same time, each of these theories does succeed in emphasizing some important facts about that language.

It will become evident that although the ethical theories which we shall examine do not constitute the easily assimilable parts of a total picture of moral language, neither do they always represent mutually exclusive alternatives. The air of total incompatibility between different theories of moral language is often created by the assumption that it is the task of the ethical theorist to specify *the* meaning of moral judgements. If this assumption were abandoned, we would realize that we are not forced to take our pick from among the ethical theories offered in the twentieth century, nor when all of them, taken singly, prove unsatisfactory, to develop a totally new alternative. Ethical theory need not be an attempt to construct a doctrine which, once and for all, tells us what moral discourse is, but only a continued attempt to clarify the varieties of moral utterances. Work is already being done in this spirit. Moral philosophers are getting to be less and less concerned with defending an existing or propounding a new doctrine concerning the meaning of ethical terms. There is more and more interest in the variety of ways in which language reflects our concern with actions and their justification. But these investigations are still too scattered, heterogeneous, and tentative. By tracing and evaluating the revolutionary forces of the recent past, a clearer sense of direction may become possible. And then there is always the reactionary who believes that the revolution is already complete and is concerned only with fortifying the position reached so far. My aim has also been to dispel his dogmatism.

I

G. E. MOORE

1. *The Indefinability of 'Good'*

ONE of the most famous as well as controversial assertions in twentieth-century philosophy has been G. E. Moore's claim that the term 'good' is indefinable. Practically everyone is by now agreed that this claim, at least in the way in which Moore himself conceived of it, is either absolutely false or hopelessly obscure. But it is also generally agreed that Moore's thesis was tremendously important and influential and that if it did not exactly constitute in itself a revolution in ethical theory, then it at least had a great deal to do with its eventual occurrence. What interests us, therefore, is what can be found in it in the light of subsequent developments. We shall be less concerned with the questions of whether that claim is true or false and what it was exactly that Moore himself meant by it. But of course these matters will have to come in also.

What then is involved in the claim that the term 'good' is indefinable? Moore himself must have felt that its meaning was far from self-explanatory and devoted many pages to an effort to clarify it. There are two points which he hastened to make in an attempt to ward off possible misunderstanding. First, he pointed out that he was not claiming that the term 'good' is indefinable in a purely verbal sense. Second, he said that in maintaining that 'good' is indefinable he was saying something about the "object or idea" that is designated by the word 'good' (*PE*, 5–8). Let us look at these two points. By a verbal definition of the term 'good' he meant an account of how people as a matter of fact generally use that term (*PE*, 6). And such an account, he was readily willing to grant, is quite possible to be given. We of course can describe the sense which the word 'good' has in English. But he denied that anything along these lines would be of philosophical interest: it would not take us beyond pure lexicography. A dictionary definition, he held, would not disprove his claim about the indefinability of the term 'good'. Such a definition would only tell us how a certain word is used in a given language by identifying what Moore called the "object or idea" for which the word stands without really telling us anything about that object or idea, without giving us what Moore called an "analysis" of it.

One wonders whether Moore was quite fair to dictionaries and whether there always is a sharp distinction between a purely verbal definition—an account of how people use a word—and an analysis of an object or idea. It is perhaps true that a foreign language dictionary can usually give us only verbal knowledge. We can benefit by a definition in a foreign language dictionary only if we are already familiar with and know the thing in question—we merely do not know the word for it. There are cases in using a monolingual dictionary where the situation may be exactly the same: we run into an unknown word, look it up and have increased our knowledge of words but not of the world or of ideas. Very often, however, when we look up a word in a dictionary we may very well be after knowledge about the world and ideas: we have some notion of the sort of thing or idea that the word designates but the notion is vague, incomplete, and uncertain. In those cases we can no longer say that our trouble is merely linguistic or verbal. It is true that we cannot hope to get complete knowledge on a subject from a dictionary, but then it is still a beginning. And surely, no definition of *any* kind can give us complete information about anything. Whether we are gaining merely verbal knowledge from a definition is a matter of degree which depends on the information that is already available to us and the purposes that we have in mind. Surely there are states of ignorance where an account of how people use a word, except perhaps when it is an account to be found in an abridged foreign language dictionary, can help us gain more than anything that can be plausibly called mere verbal knowledge. It can very well tell us something about objects and ideas as well.

Does all this disprove Moore's contention that the term 'good' is indefinable? It would seem so. We have seen that all that can be plausibly maintained is that the difference between a verbal definition (an account of how people use a word) and a definition that instructs us about objects and ideas is only that of degree and relative to the amount of information already at hand and to the purposes for which the definition is used. And a verbal definition, Moore himself admitted, is capable of being given for the term 'good'. Hence, if there is no real difference between verbal and, let us say "real" definitions, it would seem to follow that the term 'good' *is* definable. But fortunately the truth and falsity of Moore's thesis is not, as we said, what we are most anxious about. Besides, we have not yet mentioned another point that forms a very important part of what is involved in that thesis. Before we turn to that, however, there are two things to notice in connexion with what we have said so far.

First, the above argument would show not only that the term 'good' is definable but also that any term whatsoever is. An account of how people generally use it can be given of any term. Therefore there would not be any indefinable terms. This may sound paradoxical: we certainly talk of indefinable terms. But of course on the basis of the above argument we do not have to say that no term can be *taken* as indefinable. We may decide not to define a term in a given context, but that does not mean that it could or would not ever or anywhere be defined. A term may not be definable in a context or system, but then one may be found or already exist in which it is definable.

Second, only a part of a full account of how people generally use a word is what is traditionally meant by a definition. A definition is traditionally thought of as that which gives the "meaning"—specifies the sense (intension) and the referent (extension), or perhaps both—of a term. But an account of how a word is generally used may also include something else: the description of the role that a term plays in language, that is, of the kind of speech-act or linguistic performance in which it characteristically figures.[1] An account of how a term is generally used might thus concentrate on the question 'What sort of act does one characteristically perform

---

[1] Ludwig Wittgenstein and J. L. Austin were largely responsible for giving the philosophical concern with language this direction. "Speech-act" and "linguistic performance" are Austin's terms and they will receive a great deal more attention below.

in using the term?' rather than on the question 'What does the term refer to or what is its sense?' Writers who followed Moore came to be interested more and more in the first of these questions as it relates to the term 'good' and other ethical terms and the quest for a traditional definition was largely abandoned.

2. *Goodness as a Property—a Quandary*

Let us now turn more directly to the second point that Moore made in his effort to make it plain what he meant by the claim that the term 'good' is indefinable. That point, as we said, was that he was concerned with the "object or idea" that the word 'good' designates. Moore held that it was due to the unanalysable character of this object or idea that the term 'good' is indefinable. Now the phrase "object or idea" is puzzling. It seems clear that for him that whole phrase referred to good or goodness as a property, but goodness as a property and goodness as an idea are certainly distinct. Goodness as a property would belong, *in rerum natura*, to certain things, acts, and persons. The idea of goodness, on the other hand, could not be said to belong to or characterize anything in the same sense.

In Moore's own work the difference between ideas and properties or attributes is blurred. Perhaps his phrase "object or idea" merely provides stylistic variety. We need not try to decide this issue. It is plain that Moore was a "Platonist", that for him the word 'good' stood for an entity of some sort and that according to him it was the simple and unanalysable nature of that entity that made the term 'good' indefinable. It is Moore's "Platonism" and his belief in the ultimate simplicity of goodness as a kind of entity that has made his views outdated and unpalatable to many. We must now turn to these matters. We shall see eventually that there are considerable portions of Moore's doctrine that can be interpreted without any reference to goodness as an entity.

Moore's thinking about the simplicity of goodness and the type of knowledge which he therefore deemed possible of the goodness of something is clearly related to the manner in which the Logical Atomists came to think of ultimate simples and our knowledge of them. The trouble with the sort of knowledge that we can acquire from dictionaries by learning how a word is generally used is not that it would be necessarily merely verbal and not knowledge about objects or ideas. But that sort of knowledge would be second hand. In many cases this would not matter and due to the limits of our experience is inevitably so. Now Moore seems to have thought that with goodness it does matter a great deal. As a matter of fact, for him, second-hand knowledge about goodness was no knowledge at all. We *must* have first-hand acquaintance with what the term 'good' refers to, we must intuit it, or we would simply lack knowledge of it altogether. It is for this reason that the term 'good' is indefinable. But why is second-hand knowledge about goodness no knowledge at all? The answer that Moore gave was: because goodness is absolutely simple. A description of an object, that is, an indirect report about it, is genuinely informative only as long as the object in question is complex, has various parts which are related to one another in a certain way. But, so Moore's thought went, if the object is absolutely simple it can only be named or pointed to. And goodness, for Moore, was one such absolutely simple object.

The notion of ultimate simples has fallen into disrepute as the whole programme of Atomism has. For our purposes it would be uninteresting to review the reasons for this. The notion of the simplicity of goodness never won very many adherents and would probably not have won any at all had not the idea that at least one task of philosophy is analysis and that analysis is the discovery of the ultimate simple elements of experience or of reality once enjoyed the vogue it did. A moment's reflection shows how utterly fantastic and incredible it is to think of goodness as something simple. Goodness, like reality, is one of the most complex and variegated concepts that there is. Think of the innumerable *sorts* of things that are good and innumerable *sorts* of reason there are for saying that something is good (cf. Aristotle's arguments against Plato's Form of the Good, *Nicomachean Ethics*, Book I). One of the ironies of the history of philosophy is that although there have been other writers who have also claimed that the term 'good' is indefinable, they have done so on the ground that goodness instead of being too simple is too complex.

It cannot be denied that the belief that the term 'good' refers to an entity and that that entity is simple played an essential role in Moore's ethical theory. And in so far as Moore's views do rest on this belief, they are full of difficulties and puzzles. However, there are considerable portions of Moore's doctrine which can be interpreted as not depending on the assumption that goodness is a kind of entity. In fact, Moore's way of formulating his points and arguments often makes no reference to goodness as a property or attribute. And it is these parts of his doctrine and these ways of arguing that formed the starting-point for much of the subsequent development in twentieth-century moral philosophy.

It is not necessary to think of the idea of goodness as an idea of an entity: even if there were no such thing as the property of goodness, we could still think about goodness and therefore have an idea of it. We also have an idea of, say, negation, but one would not say that it is an idea of some entity. The same idea or concept can be conveyed by different inscriptions and utterances of a word or of related words. An idea or concept is what is "common" to a range of instances of using a word or expression; yet this does not mean that it constitutes an extra-linguistic entity. Rather, an idea or concept is a manner or mode of thinking and talking, and to think of it is to think of the rules which govern the use of a word or several related words in language.

It is in this linguistic way that writers who succeeded Moore tended to think of and discuss ethical concepts. They abandoned the notion, still lingering strongly in Moore, that goodness is an entity of some sort. If we think of goodness as an entity we are then led to think of it either as an objective property belonging to or having a place in the object (this was Moore's own view), or as a subjective property characterizing or having a place in the subject (this was by and large the view that Moore was anxious to refute). This framework of thought, which of course has had a long history in moral philosophy, came to be abandoned by Moore's successors. The abandonment of the notion of moral properties opened new avenues for ethical thought and brought with it a surge of original and promising writing. In fact, it produced what may be called a revolution in ethical theory. And, as we continue our examination of Moore's views, we shall see that this development was initiated to a considerable extent by Moore's own wrestling with the problems that arose from conceiving of goodness as a sort of entity, as a "non-natural property" as he called it.

Moore said, then, that in claiming that the term 'good' is indefinable, he was concerned to say something about the object or idea which that term stands for, in other words, about goodness as a property or attribute. We saw that it is not necessary to think of the idea of goodness as an idea of a property and that in the subsequent ethical thought the notion of goodness as a property was in fact abandoned. We also mentioned that this abandonment of ethical properties was to a considerable extent motivated by the outcome of Moore's own labours. In fact it was envisaged as a definite possibility in his own later work. In *Principia Ethica*, Moore argued that if the term 'good' is indefinable, it followed that the property of goodness is a property of a special kind. In the course of his career Moore adopted and subsequently abandoned several ways of describing the nature of this property. He found none of these ways fully satisfactory and in his latest writings he expressed doubt as to whether goodness is a property at all and adumbrated an altogether different way of dealing with the problems of ethical terms. We shall now turn to these matters in detail.

In *Principia* Moore both likened and contrasted goodness and yellowness. He said that goodness is like yellowness by being a simple property, but unlike yellowness by being a non-natural property. But what *are* non-natural properties and how are they to be distinguished from natural properties? Moore confessed that the problem is difficult if not insoluble. In *Principia* he proposed the following test for deciding whether a property is natural or non-natural: If we can imagine a property "as existing *by itself* in time", then that property is a natural property; if not, then the property is a non-natural property (*PE*, 41). But, as C. D. Broad pointed out, no properties or characteristics can be said to exist in time *by themselves*.[1] Broad's point seemed to Moore quite justified and he agreed that no distinction between natural and non-natural properties

[1] C. D. Broad, 'Certain Features in Moore's Ethical Doctrines', in *The Philosophy of G. E. Moore*, Schilpp, ed., Evanston and Chicago, 1942.

could be drawn along these lines.[1] The fact that Moore ever proposed the above "test" shows that the whole notion of non-natural properties was perfectly extraordinary from the very start. Moore could not have arrived at his non-naturalism by having first noticed that there are non-natural properties. What he must have noticed first were no doubt certain logical differences between the behaviour of the predicate 'good' and predicates like 'pleasant', 'desired', &c. In order to account for these differences, he invented non-natural properties so as to fit the whole matter into the familiar object–property pattern.

It seems that Moore himself had felt uneasy about his explanations concerning non-natural properties in *Principia* long before Broad published his criticism. In an essay which appeared in 1922[2]—twenty years before the publication of Broad's criticism—Moore attacked the problem in a new way. What he succeeded in giving was merely a "vague expression of the difference" he felt there to be between natural and non-natural properties or, as he called them now, intrinsic values. In that essay Moore wrote:

To say that a kind of value is "intrinsic" means merely that the question whether a thing possesses it, and in what degree it possesses it, depends solely on the intrinsic nature of the thing in question. (*Philosophical Studies*, p. 260.)

He went on to explain the concept of intrinsic value by pointing out that the above definition involves two things: (1) "that it is impossible for what is strictly *one and the same* thing to possess that kind of value at one time, or in one set of circumstances, and *not* to possess it at another" (p. 19); and (2) that "it is *impossible* that of two exactly similar things one should possess it and the other not" (p. 261). Two things can therefore differ in their intrinsic value only if they differ in their intrinsic natures. If their intrinsic natures are the same, they must necessarily possess the same intrinsic value. But this raises the question:

What is meant by the words "impossible" and "necessary" in the statement: A kind of value is intrinsic if and only if, it is *impossible*

---

[1] G. E. Moore, 'A Reply to My Critics', in *The Philosophy of G. E. Moore*, Schilpp, ed.

[2] 'The Conception of Intrinsic Value', in G. E. Moore, *Philosophical Studies*, London, 1922.

that X and Y should have different values of the kind, unless they differ in intrinsic nature; and in the equivalent statement: A kind of value is intrinsic if and only if, when anything possesses it, that same thing or anything exactly like it would necessarily or *must* always, under all circumstances, possess it in exactly the same degree. (Ibid., p. 265.)

Moore considered three possibilities. The first possibility was that the necessity in question is mere "factual necessity". In this case to say that it is impossible for two things which are exactly alike or have the same intrinsic nature not to possess the same intrinsic value or to possess it in different degrees, would be merely to say that there is or ever was or ever will be only one such thing which possesses the intrinsic value in question. But the necessity in question must not be confined to what actually is or was or will be the case; it must, according to Moore, also involve what could be the case or could have been the case or could become to be the case. Moore therefore rejected this first possibility as being insufficient.

The second possibility which Moore listed was that the necessity in question is "causal necessity". In that case, to say that something is an intrinsic value is to say that if a thing possessed it, it is causally necessary that any other thing which is exactly like it possesses it also. But the necessity envisioned by Moore was such that it would have to obtain also in a universe governed by causal laws quite different from those of our universe.

Finally, he considered the possibility that the necessity in question is "logical necessity". Logical necessity is exemplified, according to Moore, by a statement like 'Whatever is a right-angled triangle is a triangle' (ibid., p. 271). But it seemed to him that this was not the required kind of necessity either. He did not think that "it can be deduced from any logical law" (ibid., p. 272) that if a given object possesses a certain intrinsic value, then anything exactly like that object would also possess that intrinsic value. The attempt to clarify the notion of goodness as a property through the notion of intrinsic value thus also proved unsuccessful.

It is hard to say whether the first of the possibilities considered by Moore suggests a philosophically interesting alternative. Surely not exactly as Moore himself formulated it. It is also doubtful that

Moore considered the second possibility which he listed as constituting a realistic choice for any philosopher. However, it does seem in some ways like the alternative which Stevenson indeed came to choose. We shall see that the fact that our beliefs concerning the properties of an object often causally or psychologically necessitate our calling the object good receives a great deal of attention in Stevenson's theory. The third possibility is the most interesting and crucial one for Moore. Moore rejected it because accepting it would have (1) eradicated the difference between non-natural properties (or intrinsic values) and at least some natural properties, (2) made his own position indistinguishable from at least some forms of naturalism, and (3) been inconsistent with the claim that the term 'good' is indefinable.

The important point that Moore insisted on in his paper on "Intrinsic Value" was that goodness must be viewed as a dependent or supervenient property: its presence in an object depends or supervenes upon the intrinsic nature of that object. But what is the nature of this supervenience or dependence remained an extremely obscure and puzzling matter. What intrinsic natures or what natural intrinsic properties go with what intrinsic values is, according to Moore, not discoverable by empirical methods. All statements of the form 'X is good' are non-empirical and *a priori*. But this, he claimed, does not make them analytic in the sense that from a statement that a certain thing has such and such an intrinsic nature, it would logically follow that that thing is good.

Statements like 'This is good' were thus said to be synthetic, but not empirical; *a priori*, but not analytic. They came to be located in what seemed to be a logical and epistemological no-man's-land. According to Moore, statements of the form 'X is good' were both synthetic and *a priori*, but this in terms of current views was a paradox and at least in need of further explanation. For other writers there were two possible ways out of this predicament. The one was to try to keep the usual classification of legitimate statements, to assume that it is exhaustive, and to deny that moral judgements are "cognitively meaningful". The other possibility was to insist that moral judgements are logically and epistemologically quite respectable, but to claim that the usual categories are too restrictive when applied to moral judgements and therefore themselves in need of revision. The first of these alternatives was wholeheartedly embraced only by the Logical Positivists. The thesis of the cognitive meaninglessness of moral judgements was worked out with great clarity and consistency by such writers as A. J. Ayer[1] and enjoyed a considerable vogue as a part of the general doctrine of Logical Positivism. But the paradoxical and stark character of that thesis did not allow it to remain the last word. The second alternative proved, in the end, to be the more fruitful one. It led to the more productive developments in ethical theory.

After these failures, Moore tried a completely different way of explaining the difference which he felt there must be between terms like 'yellow' and terms like 'good'. In his essay on "Intrinsic Value" he had remarked:

Intrinsic properties seem to describe the intrinsic nature of what possesses them in a sense in which predicates of value never do. (*Philosophical Studies*, p. 274.)

He admitted that this way of putting the matter also only "vaguely expresses" the kind of difference in question. He thought that so long as we are unable to specify the relevant sense of the word 'describe' this account too remains inadequate. He therefore came to believe that the fundamental question concerning ethical terms is perhaps not the question: 'What kind of properties do they denote?' but the question: 'Do they denote any properties at all?'[2] These two ideas, (1) that ethical terms or predicates do not describe objects, and (2) that it is possible that goodness is not a property at all, were not worked out in any detail by Moore himself, but other writers found them extremely provocative.

Thus, on Moore's own showing, the notion of ethical properties brought with it insuperable difficulties. To consider terms like 'good' as denoting or standing for certain properties makes it possible to view ethical theory as a purely descriptive and neutral study, its aim being to bring out the features of an objectively and independently existing "world". The correctness of a proposed

---

[1] See his *Language, Truth and Logic*, chapter vi, first published in 1936.

[2] G. E. Moore, 'A Reply to My Critics', in *The Philosophy of G. E. Moore*, Schilpp, ed., pp. 591–2.

ethical theory would be the correspondence between the statements of the theorist and the features of that world. The criteria for choosing between alternative theories in ethics would be just as neutral and objective as those used in, say, astronomy. To this ideal Moore tenaciously adhered. At the same time, through his keen analytic sense he also made us aware of its pitfalls.

3. *The Open Question Argument*

In explaining the meaning of his contention that the term 'good' is indefinable Moore did then, undoubtedly, make reference to goodness as a kind of entity. But it also became clear, through his own labours, as we have seen, that goodness as a property is an extremely obscure concept. Fortunately, not the whole of Moore's doctrine concerning the nature of ethical terms rests on that concept. In particular, his method of arguing for the claim that the term 'good' is indefinable—his now very famous Open Question Argument—does not really in any essential way depend on the assumption that goodness is a property. Thus although the notion of goodness as a property came to be largely abandoned, the Open Question Argument in various guises and modifications has become a stock-in-trade in the moral philosophy of the twentieth century. Our next task is therefore to examine that argument as it was put forth by Moore himself and to see how it can be interpreted as not requiring the assumption that goodness is a property. In fact, we shall discover that only by interpreting that argument in that way can we appreciate what is valid and important in it.

Moore claimed that if the term 'good' is not indefinable and does not denote something simple, we are left with two alternatives: that term either denotes something complex or it is void of meaning altogether. He wrote:

In fact, if it is not the case that "good" denotes something simple and indefinable, only two alternatives are possible: either it is a complex, a given whole, about the correct analysis of which there may be disagreement; or else it means nothing at all, and there is no such subject as Ethics. . . . There are, in fact, only two serious alternatives to be considered, in order to establish the conclusion that "good" does denote a simple and indefinable notion. It might possibly denote a complex, as "horse" does; or it might have no meaning at all. (*PE*, 15.)

How should one interpret the above passage? What sort of simplicity and complexity is Moore talking about? Is he talking about the simplicity and complexity of concepts ("logical" simplicity and complexity) or of objects and entities (physical, spatial, chemical, psychological, &c., simplicity and complexity)? The following passage seems to force us to decide in favour of the latter interpretation:

> When we say . . . 'The definition of horse is "A hoofed quadruped of the genus Equus"' . . . we may mean that a certain object, which we all of us know, is composed in a certain manner: that it has four legs, a head, a heart, a liver etc., etc., all of them arranged in definite relations to one another. It is in this sense that I deny good to be definable. I say that it is not composed of any parts, which we can substitute for it in our minds when we are thinking of it. We might think just as clearly and correctly about a horse, if we thought of all its parts and their arrangements instead of thinking of the whole: we could, I say, think how a horse differed from a donkey just as well, just as truly, in this way, as we now do, only not so easily; but there is nothing whatsoever which we could so substitute for good; and that is what I mean, when I say that good is indefinable. (*PE*, 8.)

Was Moore comparing horses, the animals, with goodness as a property?[1] If we decided for this interpretation we could give no clear sense to what Moore might have meant. A television set can be said to be complex, and a piece of wire something simple. A dance is complex, a pose simple. An organism is complex, a cell simple. It would be easy to think of other such pairs of opposites, but in each case there would be an implicit reference to a wider or narrower class of comparison. And it seems that a horse and the property goodness could not both fit into any such class. We are therefore, I think, left with the first interpretation.

[1] Cf. Morton White, *Toward Reunion in Philosophy*, Cambridge: Harvard University Press, 1956 (Oxford University Press), pp. 184–5 and John Wisdom, *Interpretation and Analysis in Relation to Bentham's Theory of Definition*, London: K. Paul, Trench, Trubner & Co., 1931.

We must interpret the two passages just quoted as dealing with the simplicity and complexity of concepts and not of things or entities of any sort. What Moore was saying then, is that the concept of a horse is complex, whereas the concept of goodness is simple. If we considered the whole of Moore's theory as dependent on the assumption that goodness is a property, that is, a sort of entity just like a horse is, criticisms could be found all too easily. But we might fail to see the full force of his views. Let us then formulate the first alternative to the indefinability of the term 'good' mentioned by Moore as the assertion that the concept of goodness is a complex concept. If the concept of goodness is complex, it can be analysed into its components, and the term 'good' could be defined. The definiens would disclose or exhibit the complexity of the concept of goodness which lies hidden in the definiendum. It would indicate the concepts which are the different parts or components of the concept of goodness and their relations to one another. But in order that the resulting definition be a correct definition, this is all that it may do. The analysans—that is, the concepts and their manner of combination which are described by the definiens—must in all other respects be indistinguishable from the analysandum, that is, from the concept of goodness. Moore claimed that such a definition or analysis could never be found and tried to prove his claim by what is now known as his Open Question Argument:

To take, for instance, one of the more plausible, because one of the more complicated, of such proposed definitions, it may easily be thought, at first sight, that to be good may mean to be that which we desire to desire. Thus if we apply this definition to a particular instance and say 'When we think that A is good, we are thinking that A is one of the things which we desire to desire,' our proposition may seem quite plausible. But, if we carry the investigation further, and ask ourselves 'Is it good to desire to desire A?' it is apparent, on a little reflection, that this question is itself as intelligible, as the original question 'Is A good?'—that we are, in fact, now asking for exactly the same information about the desire to desire A, for which we formerly asked with regard to A itself. (*PE*, 15–16.)

In accordance with our decision to interpret the part of Moore's theory which we are now considering as involving assertions only about concepts but not about properties, we may take his second alternative to the indefinability of 'good' as being simply that there is no concept of goodness. In two places he seems to have meant just this.[1] But it is perhaps preferable to formulate this alternative as saying that the concept of goodness is simple, but not *sui generis*, not different in kind from all other simple concepts. In the Table of Contents to *Principia* he himself summarized this alternative as the assertion that: "There is no notion at all *peculiar* to Ethics" (*PE*, xiv, italics mine). The essential difference between Moore's two alternatives is just that while in the first the concept which is said to be indistinguishable from the concept of goodness is "a complex", in the second it is itself unanalysable and simple. This difference did not, however, alter Moore's method of refutation. Whatever such simple concept be chosen, we can always ask the Open Question. As an example Moore discusses the concept of pleasure:

It is very easy to conclude that what seems to be a universal ethical principle is in fact an identical proposition: that if for example, whatever is called 'good' seems to be pleasant, the proposition 'Pleasure is the good' does not assert a connection between two different notions, but involves only one, that of pleasure, which is easily recognized as a distinct entity. But whoever will attentively consider with himself what is actually before his mind when he asks the question "Is pleasure (or whatever it may be) after all good?" can easily satisfy himself that he is not merely wondering whether pleasure is pleasant. (*PE*, 16.)

Now it may be granted that the Open Question Argument is convincing with respect to these two particular examples mentioned in the last two passages I have quoted. We must admit that it does show that the concept of desiring to desire as well as the concept of pleasure are not indistinguishable from the concept of goodness. It may be granted further that this argument is effective in regard to many, or most, or all definitions of the concept of goodness offered in the past. But, the objection may be raised, how do we know that this argument would work in absolutely all cases? Why is it not possible that a complex concept could be found which is

[1] In the passage quoted on pp. 16–17 above from *Principia Ethica* and on p. 16 of the same work.

such that if it is put in the place of 'desire to desire' in the question 'Is it good to desire to desire A?' that question would no longer be "as intelligible" as the question 'Is A good?' Or, similarly, why could a simple concept not be found which is such that if put in the place of 'pleasure' in the question 'Is pleasure after all good?' it would make that question just as trivial as the question 'Is pleasure pleasant?' I do not think that any definite and satisfactory answer can be given to these questions. At the same time, it seems to be true also that no *a priori* reasons can be given for believing that a definition of the term 'good' *can* be found which is immune to the Open Question. The only proof that could be offered for this belief would be actually to give such a definition or to point to one which already exists.

The Open Question Argument, although it is a useful device for testing any definitions of the term 'good' which may be actually proposed, does not then prove that a search for such definitions is in principle wrong-headed. Moore believed that it did prove this very thing. Thus he went on to argue:

And if he will try this experiment [i.e. the Open Question] with each suggested definition in succession, he may become expert enough to recognise that in every case he has before his mind a unique object, with regard to the connection of which with any other object, a distinct question may be asked. Every one does in fact understand the question "Is this good?" When he thinks of it, his state of mind is different from what it would be, were he asked "Is this pleasant, or desired, or approved?" It has a distinct meaning for him, even though he may not recognise in what respect it is distinct. Whenever he thinks of "intrinsic value," or "intrinsic worth," or says that a thing "ought to exist," he has before his mind the unique object—the unique property of things—which I mean by "good". (*PE*, 16–17.)

In the above passage Moore seems to regard the Open Question merely as a heuristic device through which the nature of goodness as a unique *property* is made evident. If, however, we keep in mind the difficulties attending the notion of goodness as a property, the above passage will lack force. To reintroduce moral properties into Moore's theory at this point would lead into another impasse. If we took the term 'good' as referring to goodness as a property, we should formulate a requirement for the correctness of a definition of that term as follows:

(1) The property to which the definiens refers must be identical with the property goodness.

Correspondingly, we should say that Moore's contention that the term 'good' is indefinable ultimately rested on the assertion that:

(2) No property, other than goodness itself is identical with goodness.

And, we should say further, the Open Question is a method by which the truth of (2) is proved or made evident. But (2) is a tautology and cannot serve as the reason for any significant claim. Therefore, if the assertion that the term 'good' is indefinable is to be significant, that is, to be able to conflict with such assertions as 'Good is pleasure' or 'Good is what we desire' it could not rest on statement (2). And consequently, if the function of the Open Question is to show that it does rest on that statement, that question would be as good as useless.

In order to prevent Moore's theory of the indefinability of the term 'good' from becoming a tautology, we have tried in this section to interpret it as independent of the assumption that goodness is a property. But we have now seen that we can do this only if we regard Moore's Open Question Argument as a valuable aid in testing definitions of the term 'good' that have been or might be offered, and not as a proof that to seek such definitions must be given up altogether as a completely wrong-headed and impossible task.

4. *Supervenience and Evidence*

We have seen that when Moore likens the term 'good' to the term 'yellow' and contrasts it with the term 'horse', he is guilty of a confusion. Perhaps, if both goodness and yellowness are properties or qualities they can be compared with regard to their simplicity, but in no case can goodness be compared with a horse along the same lines. Whatever the simplicity of goodness as a property or attribute may be (and of yellowness, for that matter), it cannot be contrasted with the complexity of a horse as a physical or biological object.

Let us agree then that Moore is comparing the *concepts* 'goodness', 'yellowness', and 'horseness' as indicated respectively by the predicates 'good', 'yellow', and 'horse'. What Moore really must have had in mind in calling the first two simple and the third complex was the idea which was to become shortly a commonly held epistemological doctrine—namely, that certain predicates are attributed to objects on the basis of bottom-level experience or direct acquaintance, whereas others are attributed to objects only on the basis of direct experience *plus* interpretation and inference. Being a horse or horsehood is something complex because we do not directly see or otherwise perceive a horse but only certain colours and shapes arranged in a certain way (or perhaps coloured patches: we need not go into the minutiae of that doctrine) which we then interpret as an instance of horsehood. Yellowness, on the other hand, is simple since we do perceive it directly.

Now even if we accept this epistemological dichotomy, there is bound to be some hesitation with regard to how to deal with goodness in terms of it. Moore himself argued, as we saw, that an object is good or has intrinsic value always by virtue of other characteristics which it has. Goodness depends on other properties in a way in which yellowness does not. Its attribution, just as that of horsehood, is thus also in some sense indirect. At the same time, in terms of the epistemological view which seems to have been operating in Moore's thought, there is a difference betweeen goodness and horsehood as well. From the complete set of appropriate sense-reports (we shall not concern ourselves with the much debated question whether there ever *is* such a complete set) it would analytically follow that the object in question is a horse and from a partial set it would analytically follow that the object in question is probably a horse ('This is a horse' or any "physical object statement", as proponents of this epistemological theory say, is an "empirical hypothesis").

Now the naturalist who, as Moore put it, holds that goodness is an "analysable whole", would say that all this is equally true of goodness. But, of course, Moore disagreed. For him, the statement

'This is good' (or the statement 'This is probably good') never analytically follows from any other statement or group of statements. The naturalist claims that there are some statements of the form 'If this is X, Y, Z, then this is good' (or 'If this is X, Y, Z, then this is probably good') which are analytic. For Moore, statements of that form, although they are *a priori* and express necessity, are always synthetic. In other words, statements of the form 'X is good' rest, according to Moore, always on a form of perception, never on inference. For him, the evidence for a statement of the form 'X is good' is direct and perceptual, not indirect and inferential.

From these considerations it becomes evident that the intuitionist like Moore is caught between the horns of a dilemma. On the one hand he certainly wants to assert that goodness is a dependent or supervenient or consequential property. Surely it does not make sense to say that two objects x and y are exactly alike in all other respects but x is good whereas y is not. On the other hand, the intuitionist also wants to assert that this dependence of goodness on other properties is not analytic but itself synthetic and discovered through a special mode of perception called intuition. We attribute goodness to objects not on the basis of perception plus logical inference, but on the basis of a special kind of seeing by which we become directly aware of the necessary connexion between goodness of an object and its good-making characteristics. But then, the question arises, in what sense can the attribution of goodness be said to rest on evidence? It seems that in spite of all the talk about supervenience—the dependence of goodness on other properties—the attribution of goodness is for the intuitionist a matter of mystery: one just sees that something is good or that it is not and that is the end of the matter.

The concept of supervenience as the intuitionist understands it is incompatible with the concept of evidence. To say that goodness is a supervenient property is to say that it is impossible that although two given objects are exactly similar in all other respects, one of them is good while the other is not. And yet we saw that Moore insisted that the impossibility in question is neither logical (analytic) nor causal impossibility. The dependence or supervenience of goodness on other properties is a necessary connexion, but it is neither logical nor causal. Now when we speak of evidence it is either one or the other type of necessity that we have in mind. We say that X, Y, Z constitute evidence for G when there is an analytic statement of the form 'If A is X, Y, Z, then it is G', in other words, when X, Y, Z are the sort of thing we mean by G. And we say also that X, Y, Z constitute evidence for G when there is a causal law or empirical generalization of the form 'If A is X, Y, Z, then it is G.'[1] But Moore's views on how the goodness of an object depends on the other properties of that object do not allow us to view these properties as evidence for goodness on either the analytic or the causal model.

Moore's views thus have an epistemological foundation which is full of puzzles. Goodness is not known on the basis of either direct or indirect evidence. The evidence cannot be indirect, since there is no logical inference. It cannot be direct, since goodness is a supervenient property. We know that something is good through perception alone, but this perception must be of a peculiar kind: it involves somehow a 'because' or 'therefore' clause since goodness always depends on other properties present in an object.

It was this epistemological unorthodoxy on Moore's part which was not the least of the reasons that led to dissatisfaction with Moore's theory and to a widespread rejection of it. If statements of the form 'X is good' are not known through direct perception as ordinarily understood nor through indirect, inferential evidence, how then *are* they known? It became clear that the traditional notions that all adjectives designate properties and that language consists essentially of descriptive statements were inadequate to provide an explanation. Part and parcel of these traditional notions was the epistemological theory that properties are either simple or complex depending on whether our knowledge of their belonging to an object is either direct perception or indirect evidence, that is, direct perception plus analytic inference. Moore made use of this whole conceptual framework, but his own conscientious and penetrating discussions made it evident that this framework, when applied to moral discourse, is a strait jacket.

---

[1] Cf. P. F. Strawson, 'Ethical Intuitionism' in Sellars and Hospers, *Readings in Ethical Theory*, New York: Appleton, Century, Crofts, Inc., 1952.

5. *Sense and Reference and Performative Force*

The new developments in ethical theory went hand in hand with radical revisions in modes of philosophical thought in general. One of these revisions, that concerning the nature of language, will occupy our attention in a preliminary way in this section. We shall see that here too Moore had anticipated, although in an obscure and cryptic way, an idea which became of paramount importance with later writers. These writers have, in effect, made us see that in trying to discover the nature of a concept, there are really two distinguishable questions to consider concerning a word or group of similar words. The first question refers to the criteria according to which certain words or expressions are applied; the second, to what we are *doing*, that is, what sort of act we are performing, when we use those words or expressions. The first of these questions is concerned roughly with what has been traditionally called the meaning of expressions, that is, with their sense and reference. But philosophers now have come to realize that there is another equally important question to consider; that relating to the different uses to which expressions are put in our utterances or speech-acts. The traditional preoccupation with the first of these questions has been due to the fact that people have seen the paradigm of language in descriptive discourse. And it is true that with regard to descriptive discourse the question of criteria of application, of sense and reference, is the most interesting and important question. With regard to moral language, however, an equally crucial matter to consider is the sort of linguistic performance or conventional speech-act we engage in when we use a certain form of words.

It is possible to overemphasize this last point and in discussing moral language neglect sense and reference altogether. We shall see that the fact that an adequate analysis of moral concepts must pay attention to both criteria of application and use is not yet generally appreciated. Nor has it yet become quite clear what it is to talk about the *uses* of moral terms, of the sorts of linguistic acts we perform when we are engaged in moral discourse. The three major works in contemporary ethical theory which we shall subsequently examine are, although written in the revolutionary style, one-sided and confused in one way or another. As our discussion progresses, one of our major tasks will be to try to point out and to eliminate this one-sidedness and confusion. In this section I shall only mark the distinction between criteria of application and performative force or use in a preliminary way and shall attempt to show that it was foreshadowed in Moore's work.

Conventions that determine the correct application of terms are not the same as the conventions that determine uses, that is, the nature of the acts we perform when we utter sentences in which those terms figure. Thus two words or expressions might have the same sense and reference but nevertheless what we are saying, that is, doing, when we are using one of them can be different from what we are saying or doing when we are using the other. And a person may know whether or not two expressions have the same application without knowing whether or not they have the same use. He would then know the criteria of application of those words, but he would not know what parts or roles are played by those words in language. He would be able to use them in a manner which, outwardly, might pass for correct, but he would be doing so only mechanically and as a mere matter of routine. He would be using language in a parrot-like fashion and would not realize why, on an occasion when he is applying a word correctly, that is, in accordance with the right criteria, his utterance may nevertheless be deemed inappropriate. The following are some examples of pairs of expressions with regard to which what I have just said is easily seen to be the case: 'give birth'—'spawn', 'merchant'—'peddler', 'wealth' —'mammon', 'father'—'papa'. For each of these pairs of terms the criteria of application are at least sometimes the same, but in using the second term in each of these pairs we would quite likely be doing something quite different from what we would be doing in using the first. In order to be clear about such terms we must therefore pay attention to two questions:

(1) What are its criteria of application?
(2) What is its characteristic role, function, or use?

Actually the whole study of concepts through the analysis of language is of course more complicated; further distinctions must be observed and further questions must be raised. Criteria of application are either criteria of reference or criteria of sense. It is through criteria of reference or demonstrative conventions that I will know what individual item or items in the world are singled out by someone's speech-act. And it is through descriptive criteria or conventions governing sense that I will know what non-individual item or items, that is, universals, are singled out and hence what is said about individual items or how they are characterized.[1] Complications may arise. Some words in language, such as 'it' and 'this' may lack criteria of sense and others, such as 'if' and 'because' may lack criteria of application of either sort. Perhaps the latter have only "syntactical" meaning. But the trouble in ethical theory has been mainly over the question of the descriptive criteria or the criteria of sense of words like 'good'. Fortunately, we may therefore ignore such complications.

Furthermore, the expression 'role, function or use' is ambiguous. (1) To use a word or expression is to use it as part of a vocabulary and as subject to certain rules of grammar or syntax; it is to use it as part of a language. (2) Applying a word to an item or items in reality, either individual or repeatable, i.e. universal, is also to use it. Criteria or rules of use are in this sense criteria of application. They may be also called semantical rules. But uses in senses (1) and (2) enter into and are ancillary to (3) the use of an expression in the performance of full speech-acts such as describing, stating, praising, warning, promising, commending, approving, &c.[2] The rules of grammar and application do not yet fix the force or point of an utterance. I will have to observe further conventions if my intended speech-act is not to misfire or to be taken for what it is not. Now one of the most significant developments in recent ethical theory has been to pay increased attention to the use of such terms as 'good' in this third sense. Moral philosophers now

[1] Cf. J. L. Austin, *Philosophical Papers*, Oxford University Press, 1961, pp. 89–90.
[2] The above distinctions overlap largely with those made by Austin in his *How to Do Things with Words*, Oxford University Press, 1962. See particularly pp. 91 ff. (1) is what Austin calls a 'phatic' act, (2) what he calls a 'rhetic' act. I have left out his 'phonetic' act, although for the sake of completeness we could say with Austin that to use a word or expression is also, or first of all, "to perform the act of uttering certain noises". (1) and (2) plus the 'phonetic' act constitute what Austin calls the 'locution', (3) is what he calls the 'illocution'.

typically ask: What is the force or point of such utterances as
'This is good' or 'You ought to do that'? But we must be clear
about the proper meaning of this question. Language may be used,
and this would give us a still further sense or senses of the expression
'the use, role or function of a word', not only for the performance of
conventional acts but (4) for causally producing real effects on the
minds and actions of men.[1] The point of my utterance may be to
startle someone or to calm him or what not, that is, causally make
him feel or act in a certain way. I may choose and use an expression
with such an aim in mind. We shall see that it is extremely important
to distinguish this causal sense of 'use' from the third sense of 'use'
mentioned above. For example, to say that the point of my utterance
was to startle someone is not at all the same sort of thing as to say
that the point of my utterance was to warn him. Warning someone
involves rules or conventions in a way in which startling him does
not; the former is a form of communication whereas the latter is not.

The distinctions we have made are of great importance for ethical
theory and we shall be making use of them again in our subsequent
discussions. As we shall see, a great deal of trouble has arisen in
recent ethical theory from a failure always to keep the various
senses in which we can be said to be using language apart from
one another. In order to facilitate our not falling into the same trap,
let us review what we have said and develop some terminology.

(1) To use language is to use *a* language, that is, a structure or
system with its own formation rules which must be followed in
order to produce well-formed expressions or sentences, that is,
concatenations of expressions. No special problems have arisen in
recent ethical theory in this connexion. As we said in the Introduction, moral philosophers are at the present not concerned with the
development of an artificial language of morals with its own grammar and vocabulary but with the analysis of ordinary language in
moral contexts. The problems of moral philosophy on this level are
therefore simply the problems of correct English or Italian and so on.

(2) To use language is to single out items in reality. Let us say
that to use language in this sense is to *apply* words and expressions

---

[1] To use language in this further sense is to use it for performing what Austin
calls the 'perlocution'.

and that a sentence or a speech-act will thus have a *sense* and a *reference*. The rules of language or the linguistic conventions which govern sense are *criteria of sense*, those governing reference, *criteria of reference*; taken together, these will form *criteria of application*. They may be also called semantical rules. Sometimes we shall find it useful to restrict 'meaning' to sense and reference, as it is done traditionally, but we shall also recognize a wider meaning of 'meaning'.

(3) To use language is to perform a *speech-act* or act of communication. A (full) speech-act possesses besides sense and reference (and vocabulary and syntax) a *performative force* or *use*. Performative force or use is governed by *pragmatic rules* or conventions which connect expressions not with items in reality but with the occasions of their utterance and may commit the speaker in various ways. Meaning, in a broad sense, is constituted by sense and reference *and* performative force.[1]

(4) To use language is causally to affect the minds and conduct of men. This *causal use* of language has psychological and social effects which must be distinguished from meaning. There are no linguistic rules governing the causal use of language although the causal laws that operate here may give rise to rules of, say, effective propaganda.

The subject matter of the present chapter demands that we pay particular attention to the distinction between (2) and (3), between sense and reference and performative force, between the criteria of application and the pragmatic rules of use. In the next chapter we shall be concerned a great deal with the distinction between (3) and (4), between the performative use and the causal use of language.

We have said that the distinction between criteria of application or sense and reference and performative force or use came into prominence, although confusedly and in various forms with

---

[1] 'Performative force' is Austin's term. He often uses also 'illocutionary force' to mark the same thing. Sometimes Austin may give the impression that performative force belongs only to what he calls 'performative' or 'performatory' utterances which he contrasts with 'constatives'. As I use the term, 'performative force' belongs to *any* speech-act although not all speech-acts are (explicit) performatives. I shall discuss what Austin calls 'performative utterances' or 'performatives' below.

subsequent writers, and that it was not observed in an explicit form by Moore himself. Nevertheless, the roots of this distinction lie in Moore's writings. In his "A Reply to My Critics" he listed three requirements which a correct analysis of a concept must fulfil:

(a) Nobody can know that the *analysandum* applies to an object without knowing that the *analysans* applies to it, (b) nobody can verify that the *analysandum* applies without verifying that the *analysans* applies, (c) any expression which expresses the *analysandum* must be synonymous with any expression which expresses the *analysans*. (p. 663.)

Requirements (a) and (b) are concerned with criteria of application; requirement (c) however, seems to go beyond this. Could it be that synonymy, for Moore, meant sameness of use? In view of the above passage, the claim that the term 'good' is indefinable or unanalysable is seen to be more complex than it would otherwise appear. It is significant that he listed (c) as an *added* requirement, not covered by (a) and (b). By synonymy he must have clearly meant something more than sameness of sense and reference. So we are perhaps not reading too much into the above passage if we take it to suggest that besides sense and reference, there is another matter to be considered, when we are investigating the nature of a given term and comparing it with others. Two terms may be indistinguishable as far as requirements (a) and (b) are concerned—they may both have the same sense and reference, the same criteria of application—but it could still be the case that they do not express one and the same concept because they may not be "synonymous". Moore nowhere discussed what he meant by synonymy, and hence we cannot know with certainty whether my suggestion that he meant by it sameness of use is justified. But since he does mention synonymy as something additional to sense and reference, this interpretation seems entirely natural: what other additional matters, besides performative use, would there be to consider regarding a term once its sense and reference have been determined?

Writers who followed Moore came to pay more and more attention to the use rather than the "meaning" of expressions which figure conspicuously in moral discourse. The characteristic question for them to ask was not 'How, if at all, is the term "good" and other ethical terms to be defined?' but rather 'What are we doing, what sort of act are we performing, when we use ethical terms?' But, as we shall see, they have not always been clear about what this latter question properly means. They have assumed that the characteristic use to which moral terms are put lends them a separate and peculiar kind of meaning in the full, or perhaps rather indiscriminate, sense of that term. Thus instead of the valid distinction between sense and reference and performative use, they have drawn an exaggerated and invalid distinction between two kinds of meaning—evaluative and descriptive—and said that moral terms possess meanings of both of these kinds. We shall see that this bifurcation of meaning has been responsible for a great deal of fumbling and unnecessary paradox. One has seen rightly that ethical terms are not predominantly descriptive. But this does not mean that those terms possess a special kind of meaning or contain two kinds of meaning existing side by side. What it does mean is that they have a distinctive performative use or force and that it is this, rather than a total kind of meaning, that distinguishes them from descriptive terms.

We have seen that in his later writings Moore came to doubt that the term 'good' and other ethical predicates describe the objects to which they are applied. But, he thought, *if* words like 'good' are not descriptive, they would have no criteria of application and a person using these terms would then be "asserting nothing whatever that might be true or false".[1] Such a conclusion appeared to Moore too paradoxical and he therefore refused to abandon his initial belief that ethical terms are descriptive. It seems that subsequent writers were equally impressed by the paradoxical character of the conclusion which seemed to follow from the belief that ethical terms are not descriptive. The way in which they tried to soften the paradox was to say that terms like 'good' are in part descriptive but in part non-descriptive, in part governed by criteria of application but in part not, and that moral judgements are therefore in part capable of being true and false but in part not. They came to believe that in moral judgements there are two meanings existing alongside one another and that each moral

---

[1] *The Philosophy of G. E. Moore*, Schilpp ed., p. 542; see also pp. 535–54.

judgement is really two propositions in one joined together by what seemed like a mere coincidence. The valid distinction between criteria of application and use was exaggerated and became the invalid distinction of two types of meaning. And this exaggerated distinction brought with it, under a different guise, the same problem to which Moore was unable to find a satisfactory answer. For Moore the insoluble problem was: since goodness is a dependent or supervenient property, what then is the nature of this dependence? How does the presence of certain other properties in an object make it necessary that goodness is also present in it? What is the connexion between these two sorts of property? For those who instead of kinds of property began to talk of kinds of meaning the problem became: How are evaluative and descriptive meanings connected, how does evaluation depend on description? And again no fully satisfactory solution was capable of being found.

6. *Moore's Views on Moral Reasoning*

Moore maintained that before we can know what sort of reasons may support moral judgements, we must become clear about moral terms. He said that "we can never know on what *evidence* an ethical proposition rests, until we know the nature of the notion which makes the proposition ethical" (*PE*, 142-3). But since, as we saw, he held that goodness is an unanalysable and unique concept, it followed that statements like 'This is good' rested on no evidence whatever: they could not be arrived at through any process of argument or reasoning. Just as the term 'good' turned out to be indefinable, statements like 'This is good' turned out to be incapable of being supported by reasons. They were found to be "synthetic", "self-evident", and incapable of being "logically deduced from any other proposition" (*PE*, 143).

Thus, in one sense, for Moore there was no such thing as ethical argument. At least one type of moral judgement, that which is concerned with the goodness or intrinsic value, cannot be inferred from any other statement. Judgements of that type rest on direct perception, direct perception of a peculiar sort, but perception nevertheless and not argument. If one person says 'This is good' and the other says 'No, this is not good', all they can do in the end in order to find out who is right, is to look more closely, to refer the matter once more to direct experience. This experience Moore called intuition. And the term 'intuition' was, as we saw, intended to cover more than is involved in sense experience and at the same time to exclude the intrusion of logical steps.

We saw also that, for Moore, goodness was a dependent or super-venient property. An object is good always only *because* it has certain "good-making" properties. If an object A has properties X, Y, Z, then it *necessarily* is good. But the words 'if', 'then', and 'necessarily' do not indicate here a logical connexion. What exactly is the nature of this necessary connexion Moore was, however, unable to explain even to his own satisfaction. And an explanation was clearly needed since the necessity in question, whatever it was, was not of one of the ordinarily recognized varieties. Moore claimed that the truth of statements of the form 'X is good' did not depend on my intuiting that X is good. It is not the intuition that makes such a statement true. What makes it true is presumably the necessary connexion that exists between the natural good-making characteristics of X and its goodness. But in practice all we have to go by are our intuitions. Thus Moore's theory represents a practical disagreement concerning goodness as an impasse in which reasons come to an end. In this intuitionism shares an unfortunate feature with subjectivism. For the subjectivist, there is no appeal beyond feelings and attitudes; for the intuitionist, there is no appeal beyond intuitions. Moore's attempt to explain the nature of moral reasoning thus seems to have ended in a failure. To refer the matter to intuition was ultimately just as unsatisfactory as the attempt to clarify moral terms by the notion of non-natural properties.

Moore tried to soften the paradox that in moral matters there is no reasoning or argument possible and that it is all a matter of intuitive awareness in the following way. Judgements about good-ness or intrinsic value, he pointed out, are not the only kind of moral judgement. In fact, the question 'What things are good?' was, according to him, not a question belonging to what he called "practical ethics". Practical ethics, he held, is rather concerned with the question, 'What ought we to do?' (*PE*, 146). And, he held, to settle this, as opposed to the former question, does involve argument and reasoning.

Moore's theory in *Principia* was that "the assertion 'I am morally bound to perform this action' is identical with the assertion 'This action will produce the greatest possible amount of good in the Universe'" or with the assertion "The whole world would be *better*, if this action be performed, than if any possible alternative were taken" (*PE*, 147). Consequently, he said, answers to questions like 'What am I morally bound to do?' or 'What ought I to do?' as opposed to answers to questions like 'Is this good?' are capable of proof. According to Moore, answers to questions of the former sort are not self-evident or intuitive, and he emphasized that he was not an intuitionist in the sense of holding that we simply intuit what is right or what we ought to do.

We need not concern ourselves with details. The essence of what Moore said was that ethical argument consists in exhibiting a chain of cause-effect relations. To know that a given act is our duty is to know that such and such are the effects of that act and that these effects possess greater goodness than the effects of any possible alternative act. But we can only prove or argue in favour of the fact that such and such *are* the effects of a possible action and its alternatives. We cannot prove or argue that these effects are good or bad or that they are good or bad in such and such a degree. For the latter question, as we saw, no argument is possible. Therefore, if we set ourselves the question, 'What are the criteria by which it can be judged whether a piece of ethical reasoning is correct or incorrect, valid or invalid?' the answer is that we must first be clear about the kind of question we are considering. If the question turns out to be one like 'Is this good?' there are neither criteria nor validity, since there is no argument. If, on the other hand, the question turns out to be about our duty or what is right or what we ought to do, the criteria for the validity of our argument are those of the type of reasoning by which statements about causes and effects are appraised.

Do we have now an adequate account of moral reasoning, of how moral judgements are justified by arguments? It would seem not. All this talk about causes and effects has not really taken us beyond the intuitionist's paradox. Clearly, arguments concerning causes and effects are not part of moral reasoning proper. They can be merely a preliminary to it. In some broad sense there is no harm in saying that reasoning about causes and effects is relevant to moral matters. After all, what is said to be morally good or bad, right or wrong, is always something in the world, an experience, a thing or an event, having its place in one way or another in a causal nexus. In that sense no one would deny the relevance of causal inferences to ethics. The causal properties of experiences, things, and events are, we may grant, among their good-making or right-making characteristics. The real problem is, however, what is the sort of inference and argument, that leads from such characteristics to goodness or rightness? And as far as this problem is concerned, Moore's answer remained the paradoxical one that there is no such inference and no such argument.

7. *Moore's Later Views on Moral Reasoning*

The theory of *Principia* was, however, not the only theory of moral reasoning that Moore offered. In his later writings he came to believe that there are not one but two unanalysable ethical concepts and that they are logically equivalent to one another. He abandoned the view that 'ought' could be defined in terms of 'good' or that the concept of moral obligation could be analysed in terms of the concept of intrinsic value. He no longer insisted on the identity of certain ought-statements with certain statements of intrinsic value, but only on logical equivalence between them. In *Ethics*, he gave two propositions, one containing the concept of obligation, the other the concept of intrinsic value and said that these statements are logically equivalent although not identical. The two propositions were:

(1) It would be better that A should exist quite alone than that B should exist quite alone.
(2) Supposing we had to choose between an action of which A would be the sole effect, and one of which B would be the sole effect, it would be our duty to choose the former rather than the latter. (p. 39.)

Finally, in his "A Reply to My Critics", he listed a number of pairs of propositional functions in order to formulate the relation of logical equivalence which, he now held, holds between the concepts of intrinsic value and moral obligation. His formulations of these equivalencies are quite complicated and lengthy and I shall quote only one of them:

Each of the five functions enumerated below under A, namely,

A. "If any state of affairs

$$\left.\begin{array}{l} \text{has} \\ \text{ever had} \\ \text{ever will have} \\ \text{were to have} \\ \text{had had} \end{array}\right\} \text{the natural intrinsic property } \phi, \text{ it}$$

$$\left.\begin{array}{l} \text{is} \\ \text{was} \\ \text{will be} \\ \text{would be} \\ \text{would have been} \end{array}\right\} \text{intrinsically good"}$$

follows from the function

B. "If there had been or was an agent who, before any world existed, knew that, if he chose, he could create a world which would have the natural intrinsic property ϕ, knew also that he could make this choice, and knew finally that if he did not make it *no world at all would ever exist*, then it *would have been or was the duty* of this agent, provided he did not think it would be wrong to make it, to make this choice."
And also B follows from each of the five functions enumerated under A. (pp. 608-9.)

Other equivalences that Moore gave are not any briefer or less complicated and they all make reference to a possible or hypothetical agent.

These new views differed significantly from those expressed in *Principia*. They still contained the notion that some moral judgements are self-evident, but now they were no longer claimed to be exclusively of the form 'X is good'. Both kinds of moral judgement, judgements of intrinsic value and judgements of moral obligation, were now capable of being the conclusions of an argument. Nevertheless, in order to prove a judgement of one of these types we must have a judgement of the other type as a premise which is accepted as self-evident. The self-evident or intuitive starting-point in a moral argument is sometimes a judgement of intrinsic value, sometimes a judgement concerning the moral obligation of an agent "existing before any world existed". A further difference was that no judgements of moral obligation were now said to be identical with any judgements of intrinsic value. Certain statements containing the concept of moral obligations are said to be merely logically equivalent with certain statements containing the concept of intrinsic value.

It would seem then that according to his theory, once the question of relevant cause-effect relations has been settled, we can still speak of drawing inferences and conducting an argument. By virtue of the equivalences formulated by Moore, there will be certain judgements of moral obligation which follow, may be inferred, from certain judgements of intrinsic value and vice versa. Moral reasoning would thus consist in using Moore's equivalences as rules of inference. But what, it must be asked, do these rules really have to do with moral reasoning? Moore feared that some people might think that the equivalences he listed are fantastic, but he believed that "something like" each of those statements "is really true" (p. 610). And since he also claimed that he was concerned with moral terms and judgements as they are actually used (p. 570), he must have thought that these statements, or something like these statements, are "really true" in the sense of accurately reflecting the concepts of moral obligation and goodness as we actually use them. But this is certainly false. As it became gradually clear through the efforts of other writers, in ordinary moral discourse statements of the form 'X is good', 'A ought to do Y', and others like them, are characteristically used to perform such acts as praising and blaming, commanding, commending, prescribing, advising, approving, and many others. It has also become clear that moral judgements as they are actually used have thus an intimate connexion with decision, intention, and choice, a feature which they do not share with speech-acts of a more theoretical sort such as describing, stating, and informing. There is more and more emphasis on the fact that moral judgements are practical judgements. It is this discovery, or rediscovery, about moral discourse which I shall discuss in detail in subsequent chapters. We are interested in defending or criticizing moral judgements in the course of making up our mind about what to do. And by accepting or rejecting a moral judgement we have implied something about our decisions and intentions. These facts are not recognized in Moore's theory.

Suppose that it is intuitively self-evident that anything possessing a given "natural intrinsic property" ϕ, is "intrinsically good". On the basis of Moore's statement of equivalence which we quoted above, I can then arrive at the conclusion that:

If there had been or was an agent who, before any world existed, knew that, if he chose, he could create a world which would have the natural intrinsic property ϕ, knew also that he could make this choice, and knew finally that if he did not make it *no world at all would ever exist*, this it *would have been or was the duty of this* agent, provided he did not think it would be wrong to make it, to make this choice. (See p. 36 above.)

But how could that conclusion be part of my trying to make up my mind concerning what I should now or ever do? It may *make* me decide in one way rather than in another in a given case. Beliefs about the sort of "agent" that Moore described in the above passage may psychologically influence our conduct. But this would all depend on the sort of persons we happen to be. Someone who knows what kind of person I am may be in a position to predict what I shall do in a given case if I tell him that I believe that 'If there had been or was an agent, &c.' It may also be the case that there are certain "normal" attitudes and intentions that people can be expected to have when they believe that 'If there had been or was an agent, &c.' But certainly, by expressing such beliefs, we would not be implying, logically, anything concerning our own decisions and intentions. There are no conventions by reference to which we can say that a person who expresses a belief of this sort and then does not act in a certain way when the occasion offers itself has misled us by his words. By claiming that an agent of Moore's hypothetical kind has an obligation a man has not committed himself to anything since he, after all, does not exist before any world existed, nor does he always know whether, if he chose, he could bring X into existence and whether it is the case that if he did not bring X into existence nothing else would exist at all, nor is he likely to know any other similar thing which Moore mentioned.

As we are not in the same position as the possible agent who would exist before there was any world and since we do not have the type of knowledge he might have, our uttering or consenting to statements which are instances of the propositional functions which Moore lists would be idle since doing so would not imply anything about our own intentions and decisions. But when we engage in passing moral judgements and in reasoning about them, our aims are practical. We seek to influence conduct. Exactly how we should view the connexion between moral discourse and conduct is a large topic which we shall develop gradually as we come to more recent authors.

II

CHARLES L. STEVENSON

1. *The Two Types of Meaning*

MOORE had made it clear that moral discourse cannot be regarded simply as a part of empirical discourse. His Open Question Argument, as we have seen, although it does not demonstrate the impossibility of a naturalistic approach in ethics in principle, does constitute a powerful weapon against all the known varieties of naturalism. In one form or another this argument has been used to point out basic difficulties in all existing naturalistic systems. It would, however, be a mistake to assume that the battle has therefore been won on the side of non-naturalism in the sense in which Moore conceived of that term. It is rather that these terms—'naturalism' and 'non-naturalism'—coined and largely given sense by Moore, are passing out of usage as designations of two warring philosophical camps. It is very hard to classify writers like Stevenson, Toulmin, Hare, and many others as either naturalists or non-naturalists. The Moorean labels simply no longer apply. In at least one sense all these writers are opposed to both naturalism and non-naturalism as conceived by Moore. If one were to look for a label to designate the work of all these philosophers, 'non-descriptivism' would probably be the most appropriate one. We saw that in his late career Moore also turned into something like a hesitant non-descriptivist. But in most of his writings he was a descriptivist, just as his foes, the naturalists, were. For the classical naturalist, *and* for Moore, the term 'good' and other value-terms were descriptive terms, designating either objective or subjective properties or relations. The only questions were: 'What kind of properties—natural or non-natural—do terms like "good" designate?' and 'What sort of facts—natural or non-natural—do sentences like "This is good" describe?'

Moore's arguments were convincing in so far as the negative

side of his doctrine went: moral properties are not, or very likely not, natural properties and moral facts are not, or very likely not, natural facts. But on the positive side, as we saw, his success was meagre: what *are* non-natural facts and properties and what is the connexion between them and their natural counterparts, were questions to which he had no clear answers. Moore's efforts to throw positive light on the meanings of moral terms and the nature of moral arguments resulted in a failure. He himself came to suspect that the whole trouble lies deeper: perhaps there are no moral facts and properties and perhaps moral terms are not descriptive terms at all. This was the possibility that was taken seriously by other writers. They hoped in this way to save what was valid in Moore's doctrines and, at the same time, avoid the impasse to which those doctrines had led in Moore's own hands. What made Moore's results particularly disturbing was the implication that moral language is not practical. Any theory that contradicted the obvious fact that moral discourse is intimately connected with action, attitudes, intentions, and decisions was bound to call forth a reaction. Such a reaction was first provided by Stevenson. For him, the connexion between moral judgements and human behaviour and attitudes was the most conspicuous feature of moral language. We shall see that Stevenson's account of this connexion was ultimately unsatisfactory but his theory did draw attention to many important and long neglected facts about moral discourse.

Stevenson claimed that moral terms and judgements have two kinds of meaning. These two kinds of meaning were to be identified more or less accurately by what he called the "working models":

(1) "This is wrong" means *I disapprove of this; do so as well.*
(2) "He ought to do this" means *I disapprove of his leaving this undone; do so as well.*
(3) "This is good" means *I approve of this; do so as well.* (EL, 21.)

Stevenson believed that the first kind of meaning is rendered quite precisely and clearly by the declarative clauses in each of the three working models. Moral terms and judgements, he said, have partially the same kind of meaning as ordinary empirical terms and statements have; their meaning is, in part, "descriptive". The second kind of meaning, Stevenson feared, is not so clearly and unmistakably identified by the working models. This kind of meaning was supposed to be rendered by the imperative clauses. But Stevenson thought that although moral judgements and imperatives are both used "more for encouraging, altering, or redirecting people's aims and conduct than for simply describing them" (EL, 21), to assume that the kind of meaning which moral terms and judgements partially have is *exactly* the same as that of imperatives, would distort the purposes and motives of persons using moral language and the effects it has on human minds. The second kind of meaning involved in moral terms and judgements is, as Stevenson explained, a "characteristic and subtle kind of *emotive meaning*" (EL, 33).

In virtue of this kind of meaning, ethical judgments alter attitudes, not by an appeal to self-conscious efforts (as in the case of imperatives), but by the more flexible mechanism of *suggestion*. Emotive terms present the subject of which they are predicted in a bright or dim light, so to speak, and thereby *lead* people, rather than command them, to alter their attitudes. (EL, 33.)

But also the declarative or descriptive parts of the working models, Stevenson had to admit, are not really quite adequate. He said that the kind of meaning which moral terms in part have is quite correctly identified by them, but that it is seldom that their descriptive meaning is so thin as to include reference only to the attitude of the speaker. Ethical terms as they are commonly used, he claimed, are "ambiguous", "vague", and "flexible" (EL, 34-35).

Thus both the imperative or emotive and the declarative or descriptive parts of the working models were in need of clarification. As they stood, the working models were far from being self-explanatory and convincing; they had to be interpreted and defended by further discussions. A moral judgement involves a combination of emotive and descriptive meaning. But what exactly is then the nature of these two types of meaning? And, first of all, we must ask Stevenson, what is meaning in general?

Stevenson developed a psychological theory of meaning.

According to this theory, meaning is the tendency or disposition of an expression to cause, or to be caused by, certain mental states or processes. From the hearer's point of view, it is

. . . a dispositional property of the sign, where the response, varying with varying attendant circumstances, consists of psychological processes in a hearer, and where the stimulus is his hearing the sign.

(*EL*, 54.)

From the speaker's point of view, the stimulus becomes the response and vice versa. On the basis of this generic notion of meaning Stevenson went on to define the two species: the emotive and the descriptive. Emotive meaning is a "meaning in which the response (from the hearer's point of view) or the stimulus (from the speaker's point of view) is a range of emotions" (*EL*, 59). Descriptive meaning, on the other hand, is the disposition of the term or expression "to produce *cognitive* mental processes" (*EL*, 62).

The descriptive meaning of a term, Stevenson went on to explain, is capable of great precision and fine discriminations: e.g. the two statements, 'There are 1065 parts in this apparatus' and 'There are 1063 parts in this apparatus' have different descriptive meanings. But how are we to describe this difference in terms of stimulus and response without circularity? What are the psychological processes that according to Stevenson must constitute the meanings of these two statements and how do they differ from one another? Would we not have to resort simply to saying that in the case of the first statement the psychological process or state is the belief that the apparatus has 1065 parts and in the case of the other the belief that the apparatus has 1063 parts? How does the disposition of '1065' differ from the disposition of '1063'? With, for example, 'horse' and 'cow' it is perhaps easier. The disposition of 'horse' is to cause or to be caused by beliefs connected with riding, ploughing, &c., whereas the disposition of 'cow' is to cause or to be caused by beliefs connected with, say, milking. But how are we to describe the difference between the beliefs that constitute the meanings of '1065' and '1063' respectively? It does not seem to be possible to do so without circularity, without mentioning '1065' and '1063' in our descriptions.

In order to explain the existence of great precision and fine distinctions in descriptive meaning Stevenson supplemented his theory by the notion of "*linguistic rules* which relate symbols *to each* other" (*EL*, 68). By virtue of such rules the exact place of a symbol is determined within the framework of a whole system of symbols and great precision becomes possible together with great complexity. In terms of such rules, he explained, we can also distinguish between what, in the strict sense, the meaning of a term is and what the term merely suggests. What is the nature of such rules? For Stevenson linguistic rules were "simply fixed procedures, established by rote memory or written tables of reference of going from one symbol to another in a mechanical way" (*EL*, 68). He claimed that "they are by no means sufficient to establish a meaning from the beginning, but they render more fixed any rough meanings that may have developed in other ways" (*EL*, 68–69). What are these other ways? They were said to be the processes of conditioning by which the disposition of expressions to cause or to be the effects of psychological events is created. The descriptive meaning of an expression was thus fully defined as:

. . . its disposition to affect cognition provided that the disposition is caused by an elaborate process of conditioning that has attended the sign's use in communication, and provided that the disposition is rendered fixed, at least to a considerable degree, by linguistic rules.

(*EL*, 70.)

In contrast to this type of meaning, Stevenson claimed that the emotive meaning of expressions "can be best understood by comparing and contrasting it with the expressiveness of laughs, sighs, groans, and all similar manifestations of the emotions, whether by voice or gesture" (*EL*, 37). Emotive expressions like 'hurrah', just as laughs and groans, "give vent to" emotions. However, Stevenson had to admit, in case the expression in question is a regular word, the analogy does not go any further because the expressiveness of emotive *words*, unlike that of laughs and groans, "depends on conventions that have grown up in the history of their usage" (*EL*, 39). The emotive meaning of words includes, just as their descriptive meaning does, an element of conditioning.

The emotive meaning of a word is the power that the word acquires, on account of its history in emotional situations, to evoke or directly express attitudes, as distinct from designating them.
(*EL*, 33.)

An emotive word makes use of an elaborate process of conditioning, of long duration, which has given it its emotive disposition. (*EL*, 61.)

Both emotive and descriptive meaning thus seem to be quite similar in their psychology, for they both involve an "elaborate process of conditioning". Nevertheless, we have seen that for Stevenson there is a difference *in kind* between emotive and descriptive meaning. First, there is the difference that emotive meanings are emotional dispositions, whereas cognitive meanings are cognitive ones. Second, descriptive meaning involves, besides the history of an expression, linguistic rules which determine its meaning and by virtue of which the distinction can be made between what it means and what it merely suggests. Emotive meaning involves no such linguistic rules and therefore no distinction can be made between what an expression emotively means and what it merely suggests. Emotive words, in as far as they are purely emotive, do not mean anything besides what they suggest; they operate solely by setting to work a "flexible mechanism of suggestion" (*EL*, 33).

2. *The Basic Inadequacy of Stevenson's Theory of Meaning*

What are we to say about these two ideas that are crucial to Stevenson's distinction between emotive and descriptive meaning? As to the first, of course doubts may be raised concerning the ultimate validity of the distinction between emotional and cognitive dispositions. What will interest us, however, is the question of how helpful it is to talk about psychological dispositions of any sort when investigating the nature of meaning in language. As to the second, both the concept of linguistic rules and the notion that emotive meaning is all a matter of suggestion will have to occupy our attention. Let us start with the idea that emotive meaning is the suggestiveness of words.

Stevenson's main point seems to have been that what an expression suggests has nothing to do with the rules or conventions but only with habit, association, and conditioning. This comes out in the following two passages:

It must be remembered, however, that no sentence can ever descriptively mean *exactly* what another (metaphorically) suggests. This is so, if for no other reason, because the descriptive meaning of a sentence is made definite by the operation of linguistic rules, which cause it systematically to be modified by the descriptive dispositions of many other terms in the language; whereas the suggestiveness of a sentence, going beyond any fixed rules, will be far more vague. (*EL*, 74.)

Again, consider the sentence, "John is a remarkable athlete." This might have a disposition to make people think that John is tall, simply because so many athletes are. But we should not ordinarily say that it "meant" anything about tallness, even though it "suggested" it. The reason for this is simply that linguistic rules do not connect "athlete" with "tall". Rather, we say, "An athlete may or may not be tall"; and this very remark emphasizes a rule. It *isolates* the disposition of the word "athlete" from that of "tall", and so isolates what "athlete" *means* from what it *suggests*. (*EL*, 69.)

Here there is a great deal of confusion. In the first of the above passages the point seems to be that the suggestiveness of a sentence cannot be governed by rules but only by psychological associations because the suggestiveness of a sentence is very vague. But why could not the suggestiveness of a sentence be very vague simply because the rules which determine it are very vague? Stevenson seems to have thought that a vague rule is not a rule at all, but this is simply due to a tendency on his part to think of all linguistic rules as being like the rules of formalized systems such as, say, arithmetic. We shall return to this point shortly. Furthermore, why should rules be more precise and fixed than associations? The mental associations of a pedantic person are in fact too precise and fixed. The truth of the whole matter is that for every learnt rule there must be an established association, a mental connexion, and thus the association is as vague or precise as the rule is and vice versa.

In the second passage it is maintained that what a sentence suggests has nothing to do with linguistic rules and is thus contrasted with what a sentence descriptively means which is said to be a matter governed by rules. All this can certainly be questioned. At least in one sense of the word, to suggest something is to perform a linguistic, that is, a conventional or rule-governed act. Further, there is normally no sharp line between what a sentence means and what it suggests. There is such a line only if we draw one for a particular purpose. 'She is very intelligent' may imply, mean in part, or suggest 'She does not have to work very hard' unless we explicitly deny that it does. Stevenson seems to be trading on the ambiguity of the word 'suggest'. One sense of that word is 'induce or arouse a thought, feeling, &c.' Thus by saying 'The red sky suggested to me blood' I probably mean that the red sky induced me to think of blood. It is this sense of the word 'suggest' which Stevenson had in mind when he denies the relevance of rules to what a sentence suggests and contrasts what a sentence suggests with what it descriptively means (cf. "subliminal suggestion"). But in this sense of 'suggests', what a sentence suggests cannot be said to be part of any meaning of a sentence, be it descriptive or emotive. 'He is an unspeakable tyrant' may induce me to think of and imagine all sorts of things none of which would be said to be part of the meaning of that utterance.

There is, however, another sense of the word 'suggest' in which to suggest something is to perform a conventional linguistic act governed by rules. What makes Stevenson's claim that we can separate the descriptive meaning of a term from what that term suggests whereas the emotive meaning of a term is wholly made up by what it suggests at all plausible is the fact that he slurs over the two senses of the word 'suggest'. While contrasting descriptive meaning with suggestiveness he uses that word in the sense of 'induce or make to think of', but while assimilating emotive meaning to suggestiveness he lets the second sense of that word carry the weight of the argument. Of course he never makes that second sense explicit. But if we do, it becomes evident that meaning must always be governed by linguistic rules.

What then is exactly this second sense of the word 'suggest'? Let us start by considering the fact that if I use that verb in the first person present tense, I am engaged in performing a speech-act of a kind quite different from the speech-act I would be engaged in were I to use that verb in other tenses and persons.[1] If I say 'I suggest...', I will be actually *making* a suggestion, I will not be saying *that* I am making it. In saying 'He suggests...', on the other hand, I would be saying *that* he is making a suggestion. In saying 'I suggest...' I am not describing my act of suggesting, but in saying 'He suggests...' I would be describing or reporting his act of suggesting. This asymmetry with regard to tenses and persons does not hold in the majority of other verbs. In saying, for example, 'I raise my arm' I am describing my action just as I would be describing or reporting his action in saying 'He raises his arm'. It seems then that 'suggest' is one of those verbs which, as Austin has pointed out, when used in the first person singular present tense, serves to isolate and make explicit a kind of speech-act or linguistic performance. To say 'I suggest...' is to engage explicitly in suggesting. But I may be engaged in performing the linguistic act of suggesting also when I am not using that special formula. Thus I may say 'I suggest that you report this to the authorities' or 'I think the authorities may want to hear about this' and in each case communicate the same thing. The difference is merely that in the first case my speech-act carries its own label and is thus what Austin called a 'performative utterance', whereas in the second case it does not.[2]

It is of course true that by performing that act of suggesting I am also setting in motion "a subtle mechanism" which may induce you to report the matter to the authorities. But to suggest something is not identical with bringing a psychological mechanism to bear on your future actions. By suggesting that you do X, I am also, *eo ipso*, inducing you to do X, but you may reject my suggestion

[1] Here again I am making use of Austin's ideas, particularly of those developed in his treatment of "performative" utterances and of the "illocutionary forces" of utterances. See Austin, *How to Do Things with Words*.

[2] There seems to be some confusion as to what exactly did Austin mean by 'a performative utterance' or 'a performative'. His earlier view seems to have been dominated by the idea that when I say, for example 'I promise...', and thus engage myself in the performance of the act of promising, I am not saying anything that is either true or false. Performatives were thus contrasted with 'statements'. His later view seems to have been centred around the thought that utterances like 'I promise ...', as opposed to, for example, 'I will...', make it explicit what kind of linguistic act I am engaged in performing and are for *that* reason performatives.

and not the inducement. If you reject my suggestion, the inducement will simply not have been strong enough. I will then have failed in inducing, but all I had to do in order to be successful in suggesting was to utter the appropriate words in appropriate circumstances, that is, to use language correctly. What would count here as misusing language, breaking a linguistic rule, as opposed to being unsuccessful in inducing? Well suppose that the authorities know it already, or that I wanted you to report it but knew also that you would not do it unless I ordered you to, or I knew that you could not report it since you were lying there with a broken leg.

It is one thing to talk of ethical terms in so far as they possess "emotive meaning" as being used for suggesting in this latter sense; it is quite another thing to talk of them as, owing to that meaning, setting to work a subtle psychological mechanism of suggestion. To say the former is not to deny that rules and conventions have relevance for emotive meaning. To say the latter, on the other hand, is to say that ethical terms may be used for inducing, that is causally bringing about, feelings and attitudes. It is misleading to call the inducing and arousing power, which ethical terms without doubt have, part of their meaning. We can induce by other than linguistic means. And the power to induce emotions and attitudes cannot be the differentia of moral language since all types of language, including purely descriptive language, may, on an occasion, possess this power.

Let us next take a closer look at Stevenson's conception of linguistic rules. Whatever else may be said concerning linguistic rules, the most important thing about them is that it is with reference to them that we can call particular uses of expressions correct or incorrect, appropriate or inappropriate. Linguistic rules relate expressions to one another as well as to the occasions of their utterance; and by reference to them we criticize people for misusing language. Stevenson thought of linguistic rules as merely relating expressions to one another. But surely this view is too narrow. Rules which relate expressions only to one another determine what expressions or concatenation of expressions are correct or incorrect regardless of the actual occasion on which they are used.

To think of linguistic rules as rules for combining signs with signs is to think of the syntactical rules of formalized systems.

The syntactical rules of such systems *are* "simply fixed procedures, established by rote memory or written tables of reference of going from one symbol to another in a mechanical way". But ordinary language is not such a system and it is very doubtful that it has any rules of this kind. In it a normally self-contradictory or tautologous expression can have a point and be capable of communicating a meaning when uttered in certain special circumstances. Furthermore, besides syntactical rules, ordinary language also possesses semantical rules—rules which connect expressions with things in the world—and pragmatic rules—rules which connect expressions with the actions, purposes, and intentions of their users. If we conceive of linguistic rules in Stevenson's narrow sense, then not only is emotive meaning not governed by linguistic rules, but the same applies to the descriptive meaning of ordinary words. It is just not the case that the emotive meaning of ordinary words is more vague and flexible than their descriptive meaning. As Stevenson himself pointed out, the descriptive meaning of ordinary moral terms also has these characteristics and depends to a very large extent on the occasions upon which they are used.

It is clear, on the other hand, that the use of ordinary words, both descriptive and emotive, is a matter governed by rules although these rules are not like the rules of formal systems. This is proved by the simple fact that we often say that a certain speaker or hearer on a given occasion got the meaning of a word wrong or was using it in an incorrect sense regardless of the "kind of meaning" involved. For example, we criticize a person for saying 'dusk' when he meant 'dawn', but we also criticize him for saying 'supreme' when he meant merely 'not too awful'. To speak of correct and incorrect use of ordinary terms requires reference to conventions. It is due to conventions that certain uses of words are considered orthodox and others unorthodox. The question of what, in the strict sense, is to be considered as the meaning of an ordinary word and what is merely suggested by it is a matter of how rigid the conventions of its use are. But unlike the only linguistic rules recognized by Stevenson, such conventional rules of language do not ever make it possible to determine once and for all the difference between what the word means and what it suggests. There is nothing besides usage, that is, success in communication, that establishes these conventional rules and there is always a margin of freedom or indeterminacy in their application. In ordinary language the line between correctness and incorrectness, between efficacy and failure in communication, is not sharp. A certain degree of unorthodoxy in a particular case, instead of leading to a breakdown of communication, might broaden the field of what can be said effectively, and therefore correctly. Novel uses of words, when successful and when adopted by the community of speakers, can lead to new conventions.

Stevenson held that the difference between the emotive and the descriptive meaning of words is that the latter is a matter of both linguistic rules and processes of conditioning, whereas the former is solely a matter of processes of conditioning. But clearly, the only reason that he had for this claim was his idea that linguistic rules only relate symbols to one another in fixed systematic ways. Now it is true that in ordinary moral language we find no such rules. But it does not follow from this that moral language lacks rules altogether. If, unlike Stevenson, we conceive of linguistic rules more broadly as the conventions that include the occasions or circumstances for the use of expressions, then it becomes clear that it is impossible to distinguish between two kinds of meaning on the ground that one of them is governed by both linguistic rules and processes of conditioning while the other is governed by processes of conditioning alone.

Rules and processes of conditioning cannot be constitutive of one and the same thing—meaning. To talk about rules is to choose one way of talking about language, to talk about processes of conditioning and dispositions is to choose another. And it is only when we talk about rules that we talk about meaning in the proper sense. Meaning can be learnt or forgotten, we can get it right or be mistaken about it and the same things can be said about rules. But we cannot say that someone has learnt a disposition or forgotten it or that he has got a disposition right or is mistaken about it. A disposition is not the object of learning, it is not something one tries to learn, although to learn is to acquire a disposition. And similarly in making a mistake I am not mistaken about a disposition although if I make a mistake, I do not have the right disposition. It can never be the case then that the meaning of an expression is either wholly or partially made up of the psychological dispositions connected with that expression.

Stevenson's theory of the two types of meaning is thus in many ways quite inadequate. Nevertheless, the basic idea of a distinction between two kinds or aspects of meaning of moral terms, an idea which has dominated ethical writings since Stevenson, seems to contain an undeniable element of truth. The function of some words, including ethical words like 'good', 'right', and 'ought', is, at least on some occasions of their use, primarily to influence our attitudes and actions and not just to describe things and events and to impart information. The fault of Stevenson's theory does not lie in the emphasis on this fact but rather in the explanation which he offers for it. The roots of Stevenson's difficulties lie in his psychological theory of meaning which made him conceive of the connexion of moral discourse with actions and attitudes as a merely psychological one. What he failed to see, owing to his inadequate notion of what constitutes a linguistic rule, is that this connexion is not just a matter of conditioning, but more importantly for moral philosophy, of conventions and rules. This psychologism on the part of Stevenson, resulting from his misunderstanding the nature of linguistic rules and their role in ordinary language, affects his whole theory concerning the meanings of ethical terms and eventually, as we shall see, also his views on the nature of moral reasoning.

3. *Dependent Emotive Meaning*

It is not enough to say that moral terms have two kinds of meaning, whatever that is shown to mean in detail; eventually we must ask, 'How are these two kinds of meaning related to each other?' If a moral theorist claims that moral terms and judgements have two kinds of meaning, it becomes one of his major tasks to show the connexion between them. Only if there is such a connexion can moral judgements be defended by reasons; and what we take this connexion to be, will determine our views concerning the nature of moral argument and justification.

This point was behind Moore's insistence that goodness is a supervenient or dependent property. Only if there is a connexion between goodness and good-making characteristics, can we speak of value-judgements as being capable of being supported by reasons. For Moore the search for the nature of this connexion of dependence was thus the search for the nature of reason in ethics. But we saw that his search did not bear fruit. The relation between goodness and good-making characteristics remained an unsolved problem and the evidence on which moral judgements rest turned out to be, paradoxically, a peculiar form of self-evidence. Moore's efforts did make it plain, however, that whatever this all-important but puzzling connexion of supervenience is, it cannot be, as the naturalists wanted it to be, an analytic one. One of the conclusions which we drew from all this was that the "supervenience" of value is not the sort of thing that fits the usual notion of evidence at all. Evidence is a concept that belongs to purely descriptive discourse, supervenience belongs to the realm of value. But once we have drawn this conclusion, it becomes incumbent upon us to explain in what sense we can then still talk of moral judgements as being capable of being supported by reasons. If we are not willing bluntly to banish reason from ethics altogether, our search must continue.

Stevenson was persuaded by Moore's arguments, and by similar ones which he himself developed in terms of the distinction between descriptive and emotive meaning, that classical naturalism, since it involves definitions of ethical terms in descriptive terms, would not do. And he saw furthermore what Moore did not see—namely, that naturalism is untenable basically because giving reasons in ethics is not the same as giving evidence in the usual and relatively clear sense of that word which we discussed above.[1] The task which he set to himself was therefore to explain in what sense we can then speak of supporting moral judgements by reasons at all.

The way in which the problem of moral reasoning presented itself to Stevenson was, at bottom, very similar to how it presented itself to Moore. For Moore the question was: Since 'good' is not

[1] See pp. 23–24 above.

definable in terms of any natural properties, how then is goodness connected with them, how does it supervene or depend on them? For Stevenson the question became: Since 'good' and other ethical terms are only in part descriptive, what is the connexion between the part of their meaning which is descriptive and the part which is emotive? The answer that Stevenson gave to that question determined his views on the nature of moral reasoning.

In discussing the relation between the emotive and the descriptive meanings of ethical terms Stevenson claimed that the former is in part dependent and in part independent of the latter. His general and initial statement concerning this dependence and independence ran as follows:

> To whatever extent emotive meaning is *not* a function of descriptive meaning, but either persists without the latter or survives changes in it, let us say that it is "independent" .... On the other hand, to whatever extent emotive meaning is a function of descriptive meaning, changing with it after only a brief "lag", let us say that it is "dependent". (*EL*, 72–73.)

What Stevenson meant by dependent emotive meaning is relatively clear. As we saw in the preceding section, he defended a psychological theory of meaning according to which the meaning of a term is its disposition to cause or to be caused by psychological states which are either emotive or cognitive. Therefore, when only dependent emotive meaning is concerned, we can picture the relation between the two types of meaning as follows: the dependent emotive meaning of a term is the pattern of emotive responses which is caused by the cognitive psychological states attending the use of that term. When these cognitive states, as stimuli, change, the emotive states attending the use of the term will therefore correspondingly change. If the emotive meaning in question is dependent, the relation between the two types of meaning is thus factual and psychological. Which emotive and cognitive meanings go together is a matter discoverable through observation and experiment.

Once again the basic inadequacy of thinking of meaning in psychological terms becomes evident. If dependent emotive meaning is merely the pattern of emotive responses caused by a belief as a mental state, we could never say that someone has made a mistake regarding it. It is just that someone's stimulus—response pattern will have been abnormal or unusual. But we do make mistakes with regard to meaning, of whatever "kind", and that is not at all the same thing as merely responding in abnormal or unusual ways. It is true that when a person makes a mistake with regard to meaning, his stimulus—response pattern shows irregularities, but it is not those irregularities that constitute the mistake. Whenever I make a linguistic mistake—get the meaning of an expression wrong, use the term incorrectly—I sin against the rules of language. To make a mistake is different from a mere slip. If I make a mistake in using a word, I may be blamed and held accountable. I may have broken the rule outright, simply because I decided to out of caprice or from a desire to modify the rule since I found it too restrictive. But even if I did not break the rule outright and for these reasons but did so because I did not know the meaning of the term, that is, the rules governing its use, the situation is essentially the same. I am to be blamed because I had then no business using the term or acting as if I was using it. In what I was doing the rule was already involved; I cannot beg off without admitting ignorance.

On the other hand, the emotional reactions that I may have on hearing an expression on an occasion may be beyond my control and hence not part of my understanding or misunderstanding that term. No matter what these reactions are, I can then still claim that I fully understood what was said by the use of that expression. I can explain the incongruity between the words heard and my reactions by pointing out that I simply could not help myself. The mere mention of oysters may make me sick, but my sickness would not be a linguistic mistake. Similarly, owing to emotional strain I may say something that makes no sense. But this need not be a linguistic mistake on my part. To make a linguistic mistake is not to manage to say what one means. But I may be in an emotional state in which I would not be able to mean anything although I may still be able to utter words. And no matter how bizarre my utterance may be, I could still maintain that, although I spoke as a parrot, I understood what I said. It is just that I did not say those words *because* I understood them. If my stimuli and responses, although involving certain vocables, are not governed by conventions or rules, I would not be using language for communication at all. Therefore, we must conclude, if "dependent emotive meaning" is not governed by rules but only by *de facto* psychological regularities, it would not be of any interest in the analysis of ethical discourse.

But quite apart from the general wrong-headedness of speaking of meanings and their interrelations in psychological terms, if moral terms possessed emotive meaning only in the sense of "dependent emotive meaning" they could not be successfully used for what Stevenson says they are used—namely, for influencing people's attitudes and conduct. If moral terms possessed only dependent emotive meaning, they would be redundant and, in principle, eliminable from language. Suppose that I wish someone to have a favourable attitude toward a certain object, A. I therefore utter the words 'A is good'. If the emotive meaning of 'good' is completely dependent on its descriptive meaning, I would have chosen my words intelligently if I knew (*a*) that the hearing of the words 'A is good' was likely to elicit certain cognitive responses (say, the belief that A has the characteristics X, Y, and Z) in the person concerned, and (*b*) that these cognitive responses were in turn likely to cause the desired emotive result (that is, a favourable attitude towards A). And in that case instead of 'A is good' I could equally well just have said 'A is X, Y, and Z'.

By the use of "dependent emotive meaning" I could never *influence* someone's attitudes, I could only *cater* to them. In calling A good I could only be pointing out to the hearer that A is the proper object of an attitude which he already has. The whole matter would hinge on my cleverness in guessing what beliefs concerning the characteristics of the object in question would dispose the hearer in the desired way toward it. Thus the point could only be to make him believe what he likes, to fit his beliefs to his existing attitudes. But in order to attempt to influence someone's attitudes I must attempt to change them, not merely try to bring them out into the open. I must try to make him like or dislike what he believes, fit his attitudes to his beliefs. It is obvious then that if moral terms possessed emotive meaning only in the sense of "dependent emotive meaning", they could not perform the function which, according to Stevenson, they in fact do perform.

The same point can be brought out also in the following way. If the term 'good' had only dependent emotive meaning, then by saying 'A is good' I would have succeeded in communicating, in saying what I wanted to say, only if the hearer is conditioned to respond to the same beliefs with the same attitudes as I am. In other words, he would have to be conditioned to approve exactly of the same characteristics of A as I am. Let us assume that from my, the speaker's, point of view, the dependent emotive meaning of 'A is good' is the disposition of that expression to have its utterance caused by my approval of A which results from my belief that A is X, Y, and Z. For the hearer, if he is to understand me, if I am to be successful in communicating with him, the dependent emotive meaning of the expression 'A is good' would have to be the disposition of that expression to cause, when heard, the belief that A is X, Y, and Z and to have that belief in turn cause the approval of A. Under any other conditions, I would simply not have managed to say what I wished to say to him. All this has the absurd consequence that I would have made myself understood to my hearer only if he approves of the same things as I do. If he does not, I would simply not have communicated with him.

The corollary of this absurd consequence is that if there is only dependent emotive meaning, we could never, in terms of moral language, express and communicate our disagreements in attitude unless there is also disagreement in belief. If I agree with the other party in belief, I could communicate my attitudes to him only if they are the same as the attitudes he has. If our beliefs agree and our attitudes disagree, I must either keep silent or change my attitudes and bring them in line with those of my hearer before I say anything. And in that latter case there would no longer be any point in my saying anything anyhow. But surely, when I say 'A is good' and the hearer answers 'No, A is not good', our disagreement may go beyond disagreement concerning A's factual characteristics. If the hearer does not approve of A and I do, I may still have communicated my meaning perfectly well, said what I wanted to say, even though all possible disagreement in belief has been dispelled. To say that there is only "dependent emotive meaning" would make nonsense of the fact that we can understand expressions like 'A is good' and use them to some purpose even though disagreement in attitude persists beyond disagreement in belief.

4. *Independent Emotive Meaning—Meaning as Impact*

If the point of moral judgements is ever to be to influence attitudes and conduct, emotive meaning cannot be wholly dependent on descriptive meaning. But Stevenson himself, as we have already said, did not think that it was; he thought that emotive meaning was in "a great part" (*EL*, 87), but not entirely, dependent on descriptive meaning. The contention that some emotive meaning is independent of descriptive meaning is a very important part of Stevenson's theory and we must therefore look at it closely.

He explained that part of the emotive meaning of a word may be independent of its descriptive meaning since although that word might initially have acquired its emotive meaning through its descriptive meaning, the influence may be reversed: once the emotive meaning of that word is established, it can become capable of having an effect on its descriptive meaning.

Suppose, for example, that a group of people should come to disapprove of certain aspects of democracy, but continue to approve of other aspects of it. They might leave the descriptive meaning of 'democracy' unchanged, and gradually let it acquire, for their usage, a much less laudatory meaning. On the other hand, they might keep the strong laudatory meaning unchanged, and let 'democracy' acquire a descriptive sense which made reference only to those aspects of democracy (in the older sense) which they favoured. (*EL*, 72.)

It must be granted that the sort of thing described in the above passage does as a matter of fact occur; there certainly are shifts in the meanings of words. But let us follow Stevenson's ideas a little more closely. The difference between "dependent" and "independent" emotive meaning seems to be then that while the former is influenced by descriptive meaning, the latter may itself influence descriptive meaning. What we would have in the second case could be also appropriately called dependent descriptive meaning. As Stevenson himself sometimes says, descriptive and emotive meaning are often interdependent. For example:

The growth of emotive and descriptive dispositions in language does not represent two isolated processes. There is a continual interplay. (*EL*, 71.)

Emotive and descriptive meaning, both in their origin and practical operation, stand in extremely close relationship. They are distinguishable *aspects* of a total situation, not "parts" of it that can be studied in isolation. (*EL*, 76.)

The total situation concerning the relation between descriptive and emotive meaning can perhaps be summed up as follows. The two types of meaning are always interdependent; sometimes, however, one or the other possesses a degree of greater stability than the other. In that case we say that the type of meaning with greater stability is independent whereas the other is dependent. What lends this degree of greater stability? With regard to descriptive meaning Stevenson seems to have thought that stability is due to linguistic rules. This comes out in his interesting discussion of metaphor which he said throws light also on the whole question of the relation between descriptive and emotive meaning. He wrote:

A statement such as "All the World's a stage" has a verbal similarity to "All the third floor is a laboratory", "All the eastern district is an army camp", etc., and so suggests that application of the linguistic rules *by which the cognitive dispositions of language are usually preserved.* To say that the metaphorical statement "has a literal meaning" is a way of saying that, *in accordance with these rules, including the rules that govern the individual words in other contexts, it has an ordinary descriptive meaning.* (*EL*, 73, my italics.)

The very distinction between a sentence's metaphorical and literal import cannot adequately be made clear without reference to the linguistic rules (syntax) that govern its component words throughout a linguistic system, and thereby preserve descriptive dispositions that are *usually* realized in a nonmetaphorical way. (*EL*, 73–74.)

. . . the descriptive meaning of a sentence is made definite by the operation of linguistic rules, which cause it systematically to be modified by the descriptive dispositions of many other terms in the language . . . . (*EL*, 74.)

It seems then that, according to Stevenson, when descriptive meaning has the upper hand and forces emotive meaning to depend on it, this is due to the fact that the descriptive meaning of the expression in question is too firmly anchored by linguistic rules to be dislocated. If change there be, it would have to be in the emotive meaning.

What is there in emotive meaning that may, on occasion, make the reverse process possible? How can emotive meaning possess a degree of independence? It would seem natural to explain this too by reference to linguistic rules. The linguistic rules, that is, the conventions, governing the emotive meaning of a term may be just firm enough so that when a shift in meaning takes place, it will have to be in the descriptive dimension. For Stevenson, however, emotive meaning, as we have seen, is not governed by any rules at all. Therefore he would have to reject the explanation in terms of a special kind of meaning-rules which naturally seems to offer itself for the phenomenon of "independent emotive meaning". For him, the explanation has to be in purely psychological terms. We have already repeatedly pointed out the inadequacy of psychological discussions of meanings. This inadequacy becomes once again, and in a particularly poignant form, evident in Stevenson's account of independent emotive meaning.

We recall that Stevenson postulated the existence of independent emotive meaning in order to account for the fact that moral terms, such as 'good', may be used for influencing attitudes. If moral terms only had dependent emotive meaning, they could not serve this purpose. They could be used only for catering to attitudes that people already have. So far we have not mentioned anything that Stevenson says that would explain how independent emotive meaning would be used for genuinely influencing men's attitudes either. The passage which we cited above in which he discusses the term 'democracy' mentions only what may happen to that term if there already is a change in men's attitudes toward democracy.

He said there, as we recall, that when people's attitudes change toward certain aspects of democracy, then, if the emotive meaning of the term 'democracy' remains unchanged, there will be a change in what the term 'democracy' descriptively means. In general, it would thus seem that the use of the emotive meaning of a term to change its descriptive meaning depends largely on what certain people as a matter of fact are coming to favour or disfavour at a given time. Often we cannot change the descriptive meaning of an emotive word in just any direction we wish, but only in accordance with the shift and flux of human attitudes and desires. We can effectively propose new descriptive meanings to emotive words only if we bide our time and watch the drift of opinion. If we do not do so, we might easily undermine our own purpose. The proposed descriptive meaning of an emotive word may be adopted, but its emotive meaning might also undergo its own changes. Stevenson himself offered a wealth of material concerning how the emotive meanings of words may be advertently or inadvertently neutralized or changed through descriptive meaning (*EL*, chapters xi and xiii, *passim*). It could thus be that the descriptive meanings of words change and their emotive meanings remain constant only when emotional climate changes and not vice versa.

It would seem then that the emotive meaning of moral terms may be "independent" without those terms possessing any genuine prescriptive force. We would not be able to use them as persuasive tools for influencing the attitudes of people, we could use them only for expressing and echoing these attitudes. Independent emotive meaning of moral terms, if conceived in this way, would merely keep a check on what in a community is called morally 'good', or 'right'; it would merely account for the fact that the morality of a given society must be, at least to a certain extent, in keeping with the preponderant wishes and desires of its members.

But this is certainly not the whole function of moral terms. In passing moral judgements, we are not merely echoing the desires and wishes prevalent in our society and reminding others of their existence. The point of using moral language is to influence people's actions and attitudes, and not just to reflect them. How, according to Stevenson, is this possible? In order to explain this, he carried his theory a step further and stated flatly that moral terms may have independent emotive meaning in the sense of exerting a "sheer, direct emotional impact" (*EL*, 139). The emotional response which initially might have supervened on the cognitive response caused by a word, Stevenson explained, can become conditioned to the sheer sound of that word so that it will occur without the mediation of cognition and descriptive meaning. This idea is described more fully in the following passage:

A particularly interesting phenomenon depends upon the "inertia", so to speak, of meaning. Suppose, though quite artificially, that a term's laudatory emotive meaning has arisen *solely* because its descriptive meaning refers to something which people favour. And suppose that a given speaker succeeds in changing the descriptive meaning of the term in a way which his audience temporarily sanctions. One might expect that the emotive meaning will undergo a parallel change, automatically. But in fact it often will not. Through inertia, it will survive a change in the descriptive meaning on which it originally depended. And if we remember, dropping the artificial assumption above, that emotive meaning seldom depends on descriptive reference alone, but likewise on the gestures, intonations, and emotionally vigorous contents with which the term has previously been associated, it is easy to see why emotive meaning can often survive quite sharp changes in descriptive meaning. (*EL*, 72.)

A speaker may be actively engaged in changing the descriptive meaning of an emotive term and thus in changing people's attitudes, that is, what they approve or disapprove, because independent emotive words possess a kind of "inertia", since they have a "sheer, direct emotional impact". This brings the absurdity of conceiving of meaning in purely psychological terms into focus. The question is, can something like the sheer, direct emotional impact of a word be called a part of its meaning at all? Stevenson claimed that emotive meaning partially depends on "gestures" and "intonations", and that "non-metaphorical interjections will have a wholly independent emotive meaning" (*EL*, 72–73). But interjections, gestures, and intonations either mean nothing at all and function merely as natural signs or symptoms of mental states or they are used in accordance with certain rules or conventions. It is true that we usually do not speak in a monotone similar to that of the Morse code, but from this it does not follow that the variety in the sheer amount of breath or nervous energy that we put into our speech is by itself capable of serving as a vehicle of communication. Other things are also relevant. Rhetoric and oratory are arts only because what we communicate by tone and gesture depends on rules and conventions.

When someone laughs, shouts, groans, or weeps, this may affect us emotionally in the same way in which a piercing factory whistle may shock or frighten us. But in such a case the fact that certain sounds or noises are made does not *say* anything. Whenever certain sounds communicate a meaning, they do so because certain rules or conventions combine the utterances of these noises with certain situations and contexts. In so far as our attitudes and emotions are mere conditioned reflexes to the sound of moral terms, we are not reacting to those terms as words. Meaning, whether descriptive or emotive, does not then enter upon the scene at all. Meaning is always a matter of conventions and rules. Clearly, to speak of the inertia, or of the sheer direct emotional impact of words cannot therefore be in the least illuminating concerning the nature of moral terms as parts of language. If emotive meaning is merely the direct emotional impact of moral words, it would not be of any interest to ethical theory. As Hare was to point out, even if people were much less emotional than they in fact are and moral discourse much more cool and considered than it often is, moral terms could still fulfil their linguistic functions.

The function of moral language, as language, is not to produce, that is, cause, emotional effects. When I say that I accept a moral judgement, I cannot deny in the same breath that I have an attitude or intention. But to accept a moral judgement is not to confess a feeling that the hearing of that moral judgement might have produced in me. In accepting a moral judgement I have committed myself in some way, therefore it may be that I cannot at the same time denounce the having of a certain feeling. When I am told that the doing of a certain action would be morally wrong, I cannot both say that I agree and that I feel absolutely no aversion against doing it. If I did say both of these things, I would be flouting morality.

But this does not mean that to say that I accept a moral judgement is the same thing as to report the emotional impact that hearing a sentence might have made on me. To accept a moral judgement is not at all the same thing as to yield to an emotional impact or to say that I have yielded to it. An emotional impact is not the sort of thing with respect to which it makes sense to talk of accepting or not accepting it; I can only resist or give way to it. A moral judgement, on the other hand, is exactly the sort of thing I am free either to accept or to reject.

5. *General Principles and "Persuasive Definitions"*

Until now we have been concerned with problems connected with what Stevenson called the "working models", or the "first pattern of analysis". But, as we have pointed out, Stevenson himself recognized that the first pattern is inadequate in several ways; in particular, he thought that the descriptive meaning of ethical terms could not be treated adequately through the working models. He therefore believed that the working models must be supplemented by a "second pattern of analysis".

Stevenson's discussion of the "second pattern" was in effect a discussion of the role of general principles in ethics. What he had to say is extremely complicated; it is often illuminating but also full of puzzles. The first of these puzzles is connected with his claim that the entire role of general principles in ethics is itself really an ethically normative issue. He urged that since this is so, reference to general principles should not be made part of the "working models" which were presumably ethically neutral.

Now it is true that putting forth a specific general standard, norm, or principle constitutes a normative claim. Anyone who is enunciating a general standard or a principle, is, just as Stevenson points out, "pleading a cause" (*EL*, 210) and "taking sides with respect to a normative issue" (*EL*, 210). But he also seemed to believe that the whole question of the generality, or what is now often called the universalizability, of moral judgements is also a normative issue. Whether this is the case is not so clear. Stevenson argued that it was unnecessary to include reference to general principles in the first pattern *definitions* of ethical terms since we can always make such generality the subject of our first-pattern *judgements.*

But clearly, one can urge that it is good to act on principle (that it is good to make and heed general judgments about what is good) without departing from the first pattern. Such a normative contention does not *follow* from the *definition* of "good" by this pattern, but anyone who approves of acting on principle, and wishes to induce others to do so, can still make *use* of "good", in the first pattern sense, without abandoning his moral aim. If controversy should arise about *what* principle is to be acted on, one can readily use the same sense of "good" in stating the principle. 'It is good to act altruistically," for instance, states a principle which the speaker is recommending; and it can be recommended without being made true by definition.

(*EL,* 94–95.)

This passage is puzzling. To say 'It is good to act altruistically' is, no doubt, to pass one sort of normative moral judgement. But if someone were to say, as Stevenson suggests he may, 'It is good to make and heed general judgements about what is good' the situation is not so clearly the same. In making a remark like this a person may be passing a moral judgement of a sort, he may be urging someone to take a certain attitude towards life, to be more steadfast and not so fickle, to be a man of principles. But he may also, in making a remark of this sort, be pointing out that without reference to general norms and principles our actions and attitudes would be rather arbitrary. In other words he would be urging us to be more rational; to care about having some reason or other for what we do. In that case his point would not be a moral one. It would indeed be odd to claim that it is morally good or right or our duty to make and heed (just any) general standards and principles.

Before we attempt to go to the root of the difficulties involved in Stevenson's treatment of the generality of moral judgements and the role of principles in ethics, let us consider another confusing passage.

It is indubitable that principles have a conspicuous place in normative ethics. Even when a man makes a specific judgment about X, his influence on the hearer's attitudes will usually extend more widely, over some class of objects into which X falls; for the hearer, like the speaker, will instinctively avail himself of the psychological economy that comes from ordering the objects of his attitudes in some rough sort of classification. (*EL*, 95.)

There is nothing in this passage that justifies the contention that reference to principles as such is a normative issue. To the contrary, it suggests that it is not. If it is the case that the judgement 'X is good' has a disposition to influence the hearer's attitudes not just with regard to X but with regard to a whole class to which X belongs, generality seems to be part of the meanings of ethical terms. Why is this not taken into account in the working models? The formula 'I approve of this, do so also' presumably aims to take into account the whole psychological disposition of 'This is good'. But that formula ignores the more extensive disposition described in the passage quoted above as part of the meaning of 'This is good'. Should not the working model for 'This is good' instead read: 'This is good' means 'I approve of this and all similar things, do so also'?

Why then did Stevenson insist that reference to general principles should be excluded from the "working models" or the "definitions" of ethical terms? The reason is not far to seek. It lies again, basically, in his psychological theory of meaning. If we take, as Stevenson does, moral judgement to be in part statements or reports about the speaker's attitudes, we will miss the implicit generality of these judgements. As we saw in our discussion of Moore, it does not make sense to say that two things A and B are exactly alike in all other respects, but A is good whereas B is not. If A is good, then all things exactly similar to it must also be good. Thus in claiming that A is good, I am claiming that a whole class of objects are good. My claim involves reference to a general standard. On the other hand, when I merely report my feeling or attitude with respect to something, that is, describe my psychological reaction to it, I do not commit myself to having the same feeling or attitude towards every exactly similar object. I may agree that I like A, and that B is exactly like A, but nevertheless, without contradicting myself, claim that I dislike B. In such a case I would be fickle but I would not be contradicting myself in the way in which I would be doing so were I to say that A is good but B is not although they are exactly similar.

I may dislike B simply because by the time they showed me B, I may have got tired of looking at things of that kind.

Now it is true that there is a "psychological economy that comes from ordering the objects of . . . [our] attitudes in some rough sort of classification" as Stevenson points out in the last passage we quoted from him. But such psychological economy is a quite different matter from the logical generality of moral judgements and to mention it is really beside the point. If someone is fickle and keeps changing his mind it makes sense to urge him to avail himself of such economy and it is sometimes perhaps just this that we would be doing were we to say, à la Stevenson, "It is good to make and heed general judgements about what is good." On the other hand, we cannot urge someone to make it the case that moral judgements involve implicit reference to general standards and principles. That this is the case is part of the nature of moral language. What exactly is this logical generality and how it operates is a question which we shall postpone until we come to discuss the theories of R. M. Hare, who has a great deal to say on the subject. At the moment we must be content with the negative conclusion that Stevenson's claim that generality is not a part of the meanings of moral terms and is therefore to be excluded from the "working models" is based on a confusion between the "psychological economy" that comes from classifying and ordering the objects of our mental attitudes and the logical generality of moral judgements. We have of course not argued against that part of Stevenson's doctrine which says that which *specific* general standards and principles moral terms are taken to make reference to is a normative matter and hence cannot be incorporated into the morally neutral definitions of those terms. We have been concerned only with the ethically neutral point that in using moral terms we are implicitly making reference to some general principle or standard. At this point it could also be argued that the second parts of Stevenson's working models—the imperatives—do not do justice to the generality or universality of moral judgements either. But we shall postpone the consideration of this matter as well. For our present purposes there are more pressing issues to consider in connexion with Stevenson's discussion of his second pattern of analysis.

According to Stevenson, the difference between the two patterns of analysis was the following: while the first pattern (working models) restricts the descriptive meaning of moral terms to the speaker's own attitudes, the second pattern allows "the descriptive references of the ethical terms to become as complicated as any occasion or context may require" (*EL*, 89). What is classified in the first pattern as only "*suggested*" by statements like "This is good" becomes in the second pattern part of their *meaning*. The second pattern typically has the following form:

"This is good" has the meaning of "This has qualities or relations X, Y, Z . . .," except that "good" has as well a laudatory emotive meaning which permits it to express the speaker's approval, and tends to evoke the approval of the hearer. (*EL*, 207.)

Stevenson held that if we follow the "dictates of common usage", some definitions which can be offered according to this pattern are very general, while others are much more restricted and specific. Thus, when we talk about a college president, 'good' might mean "industrious executive, honest and tactful in dealing with his faculty, and capable of commanding universal respect for his intelligence and longsighted aims" (*EL*, 208). Such a definition, Stevenson explained, would specify only a "local" and "temporary" sense of 'good'. But 'good' can also be taken to mean, for example, "conducive to the greatest happiness of the greatest number". He claimed that when certain standards or principles become generally accepted, "It is by no means unnatural" to define 'good' "with explicit reference" to such standards and principles (*EL*, 209). Within the bounds of "linguistic propriety" there are, because of the vagueness of terms like 'good', a great many different definitions possible in the second pattern (*EL*, 209). The "linguistic rules" which govern the descriptive meaning of terms like 'good' are not precise and rigorous. There are only some very general rules which can be "discovered" from usage, but very often when we try to analyse terms like 'good' the rules must be "provided", that is, what we take these rules to be in a given case is often a matter of "decision" (*EL*, 86).

This freedom has its consequences. Stevenson claimed that the important point about analyses according to the second pattern is that they function as persuasive definition. They "involve a wedding of descriptive and emotive meaning" and therefore have a "frequent use in redirecting and intensifying attitudes" (*EL*, 210). "To choose a definition" in the second pattern, Stevenson claimed, "is to plead a cause, as long as the word defined is strongly emotive" (*EL*, 210). We have seen that Stevenson viewed the connexion between the emotive and descriptive meanings of moral terms as being psychological and factual. Which emotive and descriptive meanings go together was thus for him a question answerable by empirical investigation. Through his theory of persuasive definitions, however, Stevenson was saying that the relation between the two types of meaning of moral terms is also a normative issue. Such a relation is specified by a persuasive definition, but to choose such a definition amounts to "pleading a cause" and "redirecting and intensifying attitudes".

How are these two views compatible? Perhaps Stevenson viewed the matter as follows. When we ask a person for an analysis of an ethical term in the second pattern then, if we knew enough about his psychology we could, in principle, predict with greater or less probability what answer he will give. The answer that he in fact does give will be revelatory of his mind and it will serve as a confirmation or refutation of our hypothesis. But, strictly speaking, we could never say that his answer was incorrect or false. If, for one reason or another, we are dissatisfied with his answer we might try (causally) to make him change it, but we could not (logically) show that he was mistaken. To say that analyses in the second pattern or persuasive definitions are normative must thus, at bottom, mean this: such analyses and definitions are the expressions of the speaker's attitudes. There is no other point of reference or standard to which one could refer in trying to decide which such analysis or definition to accept. For analyses in the first pattern, or the working models, there is such a standard—namely, linguistic rules. But, Stevenson claimed, the linguistic rules of ordinary usage fix the reference of terms like 'good' only to the speaker's approval or disapproval (*EL*, 96). Any other descriptive meanings that moral terms might have were looked upon by him as something determined not by linguistic rules but solely by the attitudes of a given speaker. The only justification for persuasive definitions, for attempts to specify the descriptive meaning of moral terms in a particular way, is the speaker's attitude. They are themselves normative judgements which are wholly analysable in the first pattern and as such shown merely to express the approval or disapproval of the speaker and to aim to evoke similar states of mind in the hearer.

To digress for a moment, it is here that the strong motivation that Stevenson and writers who hold similar views have for developing what they call "meta-ethics" becomes evident. Meta-ethics is conceived to be a purely theoretical and ethically neutral enterprise very sharply distinguished from ethics proper or morality. To be engaged in writing on ethics proper would be, as Moore put it, to try to say in a general way what things are good and what are the sorts of action we ought to perform. Now in Stevenson's terms it would be to set up and defend analyses of ethical terms in the second pattern, in other words, persuasive definitions. But such definitions are themselves moral judgements and as such, in Stevenson's view, voicings of the writer's own attitudes. They can themselves be analysed in the first pattern as statements concerning what the writer himself happens to approve or disapprove and as attempts, through the "independent emotive meaning", that is, through the "sheer, direct emotional impact" of ethical terms, to make others approve or disapprove of these things also. And surely voicing one's approvals or disapprovals and goading others to approve or disapprove likewise do not seem to be a proper part of philosophy.

Stevenson did not think that the whole meaning of moral terms was brought out by the "working models". The working models, or the first pattern of analysis, were designed primarily to clarify the emotive meaning of moral terms and judgements and had to be supplemented by the second pattern of analysis through which the descriptive meaning of these terms and judgements, that is the whole question of moral standards and principles, was to be studied. But the second pattern was not just an alternative method for clarifying the meanings of moral terms. The working models were confined to purely "linguistic questions" and were therefore morally neutral. Analyses in the second pattern, on the other hand, consisted of persuasive definitions and were therefore not morally neutral. To give an actual analysis in the second pattern is, according to Stevenson, tantamount to making a moral judgement. As far as neutral analysis is concerned, the working models are therefore final, and cannot be supplemented by any definitions in the second pattern. The ethical theorist cannot himself *give* an analysis in the second pattern. To give such an analysis would be to make a moral judgement which is itself analysable in terms of the working models, and therefore a matter decided sheerly by our attitudes.

It is Stevenson's theory of persuasive definitions which is directly responsible for the inadequacies in his views on moral reasoning, to which we shall turn in the next section. The second pattern of analysis does not really go any further than the working models in explaining how moral judgements can be supported by reasons. In Stevenson's theory any appeal to the descriptive meaning of moral terms that we make in the course of a moral argument cannot go beyond the attitudes that we and our opponents happen to have. Suppose someone passes a moral judgement J_1—namely, that a particular action A is good; and suppose that the descriptive meaning of the term 'good' as used in J_1 is D_1—namely, 'is in accordance with the mores of society'. Now according to Stevenson's line of thought we can imagine someone else, or the same person, when pressed, passing another moral judgement (or giving a persuasive definition) J_2—namely, that calling action A good in sense D_1 is itself good. J_2 can now be analysed according to the working model as meaning 'I (the speaker) approve of calling action A "good" in sense D_1; do so as well'.

This *might* not be the end of the matter. What the person in question might have meant when he passed judgement J_2 is that to call A 'good' in sense D_1 is a good social practice. And in that case the descriptive meaning of the predicate 'good' in judgement J_2 might have involved more than the reference to the first personal approval of the speaker. In other words, D_2 might have been not 'is approved by me' but 'is conducive to the happiness of the greatest number'. If this were the case, then according to Stevenson's analysis there would have to be a further judgement (or another persuasive definition) J_3 possible, which says that to call, in sense D_2, the calling of act A 'good' in sense D_1 is itself good. And J_3 in its turn, can be analysed according to either the first or the second pattern of analysis. Theoretically, there is no reason why we should ever stop and analyse a moral judgement of the series $J_1 \ldots J_n$ according to the working models, that is, as involving descriptively just the speaker's attitude. Theoretically, there could always be further J's and further D's.

Stevenson's point seems to have been that a person *can* always, at any point, *make* an end to this series by considering an analysis according to the second pattern as final and refusing to give or accept any further reasons. These analyses rest simply on our attitudes. But, and this is the crucial question, on what attitudes? If moral principles depend on just any attitudes that people happen to have, moral criticism would be impossible. If someone tried to criticize the attitudes we have as morally wrong, we may just answer that we like what we like and that this is the end of the matter. If the descriptive meanings of moral terms were not merely a matter depending on our attitudes, then it would be possible to understand how moral judgements can be supported by logical reasons. If analyses in the second pattern did not just reflect the facts of our psychology, they could serve as major premises or rules of inference in a moral argument. In that case, given the premise that a certain object has the characteristics or relations X, Y, and Z, and an appropriate analysis of the meaning of the term 'good' in the second pattern, we could legitimately conclude that that object is good. If, however, the only backing available for analyses in the second pattern is attitudes, then the validity of our inference would itself have to depend on the attitudes that we happen to have. We might accept the premise, but we need to accept the conclusion only if we find ourselves having the "right" attitude. Stevenson's theory of the two types of meaning of moral terms and the relation between them thus paved the way for his paradoxical views on the nature of moral reasoning. To these views we shall now turn in detail.

6. *The Paradoxical Character of Stevenson's Theory of Moral Reasoning*

For Stevenson, moral reasoning or argument springs from the disagreement between two or more people concerning a moral issue. He admitted that there is such a thing as personal moral deliberation, but claimed that the methods of all moral reasoning can be best studied through cases between persons. He contended further that moral disagreements involve an element which makes them very different from the kind of disagreements which "occur in science, history, biography, and their counterparts in everyday life" (*EL*, 2). In the latter

cases one man believes that P is the answer, and another that not-P, or some proposition incompatible with P, is the answer; and in the course of discussion each tries to give some manner of proof for his view, or revise it in the light of further information. Let us call this "disagreement in belief". (*EL*, 2.)

Besides disagreements of this kind there occur, according to Stevenson, disagreements of a different kind.

They involve an opposition, sometimes tentative and gentle, sometimes strong, which is not of beliefs, but rather of attitudes— that is to say, an opposition of purposes, aspirations, wants, preferences, desires, and so on. (*EL*, 3.)

Such disagreements Stevenson called "disagreements in attitude":

Two men will be said to disagree in attitude when they have opposed attitudes to the same object—one approving of it, for instance, and the other disapproving of it—and when at least one of them has a motive for altering or calling into question the attitude of the other. (*EL*, 3.)

Stevenson argued that ethical or moral controversies involve disagreements of both sorts.

There is almost inevitably disagreement in belief, which requires detailed, sensitive attention; but there is also disagreement in attitude. (*EL*, 11.)

Moral questions involve disagreement in attitude because:

> Moral judgments are concerned with *recommending* something for approval or disapproval; and this involves something more than disinterested description, or a cold debate about whether it is already approved, or when it spontaneously will be. That a moralist is so often a reformer is scarcely an accident. His judgments plead and advise, and open the way to counteradvice. In this way moral judgments go beyond cognition, speaking to the conative-affective natures of men. (*EL*, 13.)

It is therefore disagreement in attitude which distinguishes moral discourse from discourse of other kinds such as science:

> It is disagreement in attitude, which imposes a characteristic type or organization on the beliefs that may serve indirectly to resolve it, that chiefly distinguishes ethical issues from those of pure science. (*EL*, 13.)

And the task of the moral philosopher is to study the relation between these two kinds of disagreement:

> The central problem of ethical analysis—one might almost say "the" problem—is one of showing in detail how beliefs and attitudes are related. (*EL*, 11.)

Finally, the answer to the question of how the two types of disagreement are related—the answer to the "central problem of ethical analysis"—that Stevenson himself gave is the following:

> The relationship between the two sorts of disagreement, whenever it occurs, is always factual, never logical. So far as the logical possibilities are concerned, there may be disagreement in belief without disagreement in attitude; for even if an argument must always be motivated, and to that extent involve attitudes, it does not follow that the attitudes which attend opposed beliefs must themselves be opposed. (*EL*, 6.)

This is the essence of Stevenson's theory about the nature of moral reasoning. All else that he had to say on this topic consisted, more or less, of further elaborations of these points.

Stevenson claimed that the theory just outlined is "based upon observations of ethical discussions in daily life, and can be clarified and tested only by turning to that source". Is this claim justified? It must be admitted that in daily life we often observe a distinction between beliefs and attitudes. It must also be admitted that we ordinarily show a concern for the connexion between beliefs and attitudes and how they should influence one another. But Stevenson's theory is really paradoxical as an account of "ethical discussions in daily life". The connexion between beliefs and attitudes, he says, is causal and factual, never logical. You therefore like, wish, and favour what you like, wish, and favour, and this, although you ordinarily might not think so, is the end of the matter. In following Stevenson, we would have to hold that people are constantly misled about the language they use in discussing moral matters. In ethical discussions of daily life it becomes evident that there is a logical connexion between beliefs and attitudes since we try to appraise and evaluate the influence that someone's beliefs may have on his attitudes. We try to correct not just our beliefs but also the attitudes that may go with those beliefs. We believe that if a person has certain beliefs then he ought to have certain attitudes, that from certain beliefs certain attitudes follow as proper and correct. When a person refuses to let his attitudes be influenced by his beliefs, we at least sometimes blame him for having made a mistake and not merely for having been perverse. According to common sense our moral deliberations can be either rational or irrational, and this according to whether or not we observe the logical connexions which we believe exist between beliefs and attitudes.

Therefore, if according to a philosophical theory of moral reasoning it turns out that it is neither logical nor illogical ever to let our attitudes be guided by our beliefs, that theory is open to the criticism that it does not square with what ordinarily happens in our ethical discussions in daily life. Such a criticism, we recall, was in order with respect to Moore's theory. Beliefs about intrinsic value and moral obligation were construed by him in such a manner that they could have no logical relevance to our actions and attitudes. Moore had introduced the notion of beliefs about non-natural properties with the explicit purpose of establishing reason in ethics, but since those beliefs turned out to have no logical connexion with our attitudes, the result was a failure. If in a moral theory beliefs and attitudes turn out to be logically disconnected, the paradoxical conclusion follows that our actions can have no reasoned support. Stevenson's theory, unlike Moore's, displays its air of paradox quite openly. The connexion between beliefs and attitudes is causal and factual, never logical. We believe that there is a logical connexion between beliefs and attitudes and that therefore some statements of fact are good reasons for a moral conclusion whereas others are not. But, Stevenson would have to say, in reality we are in those cases always wrong and suffering under an illusion. According to him, all that we ever say in moral discourse consists in bringing to bear on those who disagree with us causal or psychological influence of one sort or another, and never in presenting an argument in the ordinary sense of the word. To appraise a particular instance of moral reasoning is therefore, according to him, not to call it valid or invalid, correct or incorrect in the logical sense, but rather, as we shall see, to call it either efficient or inefficient, fair or unfair, blunt or subtle, moral or immoral, and the like. In Stevenson's theory, an instance of moral reasoning can be called 'good' or 'bad', not according to the validity of its logic, but merely according to its efficacy or its moral or quasi-moral worth.

7. *Stevenson on Validity*

According to Stevenson there are three types of arguments used in moral reasoning. The first consists in employing inductive and deductive methods for establishing the beliefs which are relevant for supporting the moral conclusion. This is the factual or descriptive element in moral reasoning and no problems peculiar to moral reasoning arise in connexion with it. We saw that Moore, at least in *Principia*, identified all moral reasoning with reasoning about beliefs concerning cause–effect relations. We pointed out then that reasoning about beliefs is really a mere preliminary to moral argument proper. It is only concerned with establishing the premises, the essential step is the drawing of a moral conclusion. The same point is relevant here. Of course we may have occasion to use inductive and deductive methods in establishing the premises of a moral argument. But the question is, once we have the premises, are there any valid inferences that can be drawn from them that lead to a normative conclusion? And just as with Moore, we are in for a disappointment since Stevenson's answer will, in the end, be a negative one.

The second type of argument in moral discourse Stevenson called "persuasion"; it consists in the use of emotively charged words which causally or psychologically force the hearer to alter his attitudes in the desired direction. Finally, there is a third type of argument called "giving reasons", that is, bringing forth statements or beliefs with the aim of, again psychologically or causally, making the hearer change his attitudes and accept the moral judgement in question.

How do we evaluate the soundness of arguments of these three types? How do we distinguish the valid from the invalid arguments in each of these three groups? The question of validity is easily answered, Stevenson claimed, with respect to the first two types of argument:

If an ethical argument applies formal logic . . . it will be valid or invalid in whatever sense the logic is valid or invalid. If it uses empirical reasons, the inductive support given to *them* in their turn (as distinct from the support given *by* the reasons *to* the ethical judgment) may be called valid or invalid in whatever sense the empirical methods used are valid or invalid . . . . On the other hand, validity has *nothing* to do with persuasive methods. It is cognitively nonsensical to speak either of "valid" or of "invalid" persuasion. If one is led by the excitement of persuasion into making logical errors, it is the logic, and not the persuasion, that is invalid. One may, of course, call a certain kind of persuasion "invalid" in order to reject it —to indicate that it is objectionable or ineffective; but the emotional impact of a military band could be "invalid" in the same way. (*EL*, 152-3.)

With respect to the third type of argument used in moral reasoning the question is more complicated. Here, according to Stevenson, though we do not speak of deduction or induction, we nevertheless speak of inference. "One of the peculiarities of ethical argument lies in the inference from a factual reason to an ethical conclusion." The question therefore arises, "Is there not some *other kind* of validity, peculiar to normative argument?" (*EL*, 153.) After some reflection and hesitation, Stevenson decided to answer in the negative. For Stevenson, the term 'valid' was intimately connected with the term 'true'; to call an argument 'valid' is to say that it "is more conducive to establishing truths, or probable truths, than any 'invalid' one" (*EL*, 154). But, he continued, in so far as ethical arguments are designed to *affect* attitudes, and are not concerned merely with the facts of the case, they are not concerned with establishing the truth of a moral judgement. In his view, a moral judgement is only partially capable of being true and false. Its descriptive part can be true or false, but its emotive part—that is, the really interesting part for ethics—cannot. That part, as we saw, is like an imperative. Therefore, he concluded, moral arguments, in so far as they consist of "giving reasons", since they consist in passing from factual premises to normative, that is, quasi-imperative, conclusions, are neither valid nor invalid: with respect to them "questions about validity, in any helpful sense of the term, are irrelevant" (*EL*, 155–6).

This is clearly an unsatisfactory conclusion. If we cannot call an ethical argument either valid or invalid, how can we call it an argument at all? Stevenson tried to soften this paradox as follows. The lack of validity does not mean that there are no grounds whatever on the basis of which one can discriminate between different "methods" in moral discourse.

There are any number of grounds for choice between methods; and if in certain cases these do not depend upon validity, it does not follow that they depend on oratorical strategy. We have seen that whenever validity has any relevant application, it is wholly available for the moralist's purposes. Whenever it does not have application, there are other considerations, equally available to the moralist, that free his choice of methods from any necessity of callousness or caprice.

(*EL*, 156.)

What are these other considerations? Well, they seem to be considerations of a moral or quasi-moral sort. From the passages in which these matters are discussed (primarily *EL*, 156–60) one gathers that among the sorts of question one ought to raise here are the following: 'Does this method show callousness or caprice?', 'Is this method "rational" (does it make use of "cognitive" issues) or is it purely persuasive?', 'Is it blunt or subtle?', 'Does it contribute to neutral enlightenment?', 'Is it forensically effective?' The question of which "methods" one is to use is "itself a normative ethical matter" (*EL*, 158).

To evaluate or recommend an ethical method (whenever validity can have no bearing on the case) is to moralize about the ways of moralists. Ethical judgments may be made about innumerable actions, and the procedure of supporting a judgment, being itself an action, is open to judgment in its turn. When a man makes a judgment E_1, which is about X, we make a judgment E_2, which is about his way of supporting E_1. Our way of supporting E_2 will then be open to the judgment E_3; and so on.

There is nothing vicious about this series of judgments. It would be vicious only if we had to begin at "the other end" of it, the series by its very nature having no "other end". In point of fact, we usually and quite feasibly begin right at "this" end. We do not withhold all expression of approval until having first decided whether we approve of approving of approving . . . of this kind of expression of approval. We simply *find* ourselves approving, and using certain methods to defend what we approve; and we call our procedure into question only when there is a practical likelihood of conflict or disagreement.
(*EL*, 158–9.)

It seems, however, that there *is* something vicious about such a series of judgements. The viciousness of it is not that we have to begin at "the other end". We do begin at "this" end. But the viciousness lies in the fact that we never get beyond the beginning. What we would have in Stevenson's theory is not a series but a circle. I "find myself" approving of X. Ought I to approve of X? This may lead me to ask: How ought I to support my approving of X? The answer may be given by the fact that I "find myself" approving of supporting my approval of X in a certain way. Of course, it may be that I continue my quest for reasons: Ought I to approve of supporting my approval of X in this way? But what point would there be in my continuing the quest? Or in having ever started it? The answer will always be given by my simply finding myself approving of something with no support or reason.[1]

There is something even more seriously wrong with Stevenson's attempt to soften the paradox that we cannot make use of validity in appraising moral arguments. The attempt is based on a confusion. On the one hand we may raise the question of the validity of a whole method of reasoning or a mode of discourse. In this sense philosophers have asked 'Is induction valid?', 'Is scientific method valid?', or even 'Is reason itself valid?' And in this sense one may also ask 'Is moral reasoning valid?' I am not concerned to argue what is the *exact* sense of these questions, if they have any exact sense. The gist of all of them seems to be whether we should think a certain mental activity important and worth while, whether we should put our faith and time into it. In short, whether or not a certain kind of activity is worthy to be engaged in. In a quite different sense the question of validity is raised with regard to what constitutes the soundness of particular moves, that is, arguments, within a given method of reasoning or mode of discourse.

Now the first kind of validity questions which we described are similar to questions concerning the callousness, rationality, enlightenment, subtlety, effectiveness of what Stevenson calls "methods". In both cases what is at issue is the acceptability of a whole practice or procedure. Questions of a quasi-moral sort concerning a method are on a par with and constitute alternatives to questions of validity of the first kind that we mentioned. But questions which are concerned with the validity of particular arguments within a given mode of reasoning or method operate on a different plane. They are internal questions, whereas questions of quasi-moral worth, rationality, &c., are external questions. The latter could never be substitutes for the former. Stevenson's paradox thus remains unmitigated: there are no grounds for choosing between particular moral arguments which are *internal* to moral discourse.

We may see the same point also in the following way. On the one hand there is the problem of what *kind* of method one should use in order to sway one's opponent in a debate concerning a moral issue; on the other, there is the question whether a given argument, a given piece of moral reasoning, should be accepted or rejected. To ask 'What kind of reasoning ought we to use in moral discourse?'

is different from asking 'Ought we to accept this given moral argument?' There may be arguments which are good arguments or arguments which are, to use Stevenson's phrase, "rational, co-operative and modest", but which nevertheless must be rejected because they are not valid, that is, because their premises do not establish the conclusion. It is one thing to reject an argument because it is irrational (in the sense of not being concerned with "cognitive issues") or non-co-operative or immodest; it is another to reject it because it is a *non sequitur*.

It is true that which methods of argument we decide to use is in some sense a matter of choice, but once we have made our choice, whether or not we can be said to be using that method correctly depends on the rules of that method. I can decide whether or not to adopt a rule of inference, or better, a system or body of such rules, but once I have made that decision it is no longer up to me which of the inferences that I actually draw are in accordance with those rules, or which violate them. Similarly, if I decide to use persuasion, I may have committed myself to certain rules by reference to which some particular thing I say or do might be rejected as improper. A good persuasion need not be just one which as a matter of fact succeeds in redirecting people's attitudes no matter how; there is even a sense in which a good boxer is not necessarily he who always manages to knock out his opponents. A good performer does not achieve his end by just any means. If persuading is a "method", it will have its rules and canons, perhaps even different schools; factual success will not be the only criterion for judging a particular piece of persuasion.

Now the sort of thing that Stevenson calls persuasion is probably not a very well-developed method and does not have any canons in the proper sense of that word. The rules that govern it are at best rules of thumb which one has found useful in practice and factual success will easily create new such rules. But even so, some matters will be irrelevant in judging persuasion. It is true that one of two cases of persuasion, just as one of two proofs, can be better than another in the sense of being, say, more elegant. But the degree of elegance is irrelevant to the question whether a proof is conclusive and it may also be irrelevant to the question

whether a case of persuasion will be effective. As far as the conclusiveness of proofs and the effectiveness of persuasions go, it may be
immaterial whether we accomplish our purpose in two or twenty
steps, whether we tell truth or falsehoods, or whether we corrupt
or edify the minds of our opponents.

The same can be said about what Stevenson calls the method of
"using reasons". Once we have decided to use this method instead
of some other, in order to give good reasons, we must only make
statements which are more likely to lead to the desired result—that
is, to the change of attitude desired. And there are again rules of
thumb to which the method should conform. It is true that we
usually have a great latitude of choice as to exactly which statements to make, since for changing attitudes through this method
almost everything in heaven and on earth might be relevant. But
at least we cannot say those things or recite those beliefs which
actually would undermine our purpose. Among the things that can
be said we can choose. We might concentrate on biology, but we
can also bring in psychology; we may speak in prose or in penta-
meter; as far as the gullibility of our hearer stretches we can use
lies, or if he is not versed in logic, we can affirm the consequent, &c.
But nevertheless, if we have made up our minds to use "reasons",
then, in order to "reason" properly, we can say only those things
which are found on the whole and sooner or later to get the hearer
to agree with us.

Thus even persuasion and "giving reasons" have their own
logic and instances of the use of these methods could be called
either valid or invalid, proper or improper. There are good
and bad instances of persuasion and good and bad instances of
"giving reasons" according to how closely they conform to the
rules which are helpful in assuring the effectiveness of these methods.
What is very doubtful, however, is whether the rules according to
which we judge the validity of moral reasoning are the same as
those pertinent to persuasion and "giving reasons".

To say that a particular moral argument is in accordance with the
rules and thus valid is to say that if one accepts its premises, one
must accept its conclusion. What is the exact meaning of the term
'must' in the previous sentence is indeed far from clear. It *is* clear,

however, that it is not the kind of 'must' which we use when we say that when a man has been listening to his nagging wife for a whole week, he must go to the pub on Saturday. But it is this psychological kind of 'must' that is relevant to persuasion and "giving reasons". An instance of persuasion or of "giving reasons" will have been successful if the person addressed is psychologically constrained to change his attitude as a result. We have to conclude then that moral reasoning, although it is practical, is, if it exists at all, quite different from persuasion and "giving reasons" in Stevenson's sense. This conclusion will be reinforced by a closer examination of Stevenson's views.

8. *The Insufficiency of "Giving Reasons"*

Suppose that two people, A and B, disagree concerning the moral goodness of an object, X: A says that X is good, whereas B asserts the opposite. Suppose further that A tries to bring B to agree with him. Since, according to Stevenson, the disagreement in question involves both attitudes and beliefs, A would have to produce an argument designed to change both the beliefs and attitudes of B. If, in other words, by following the working model, for the term 'good', we view A's position as expressed by him in the assertion:

(1) (*a*) I approve of X;
  (*b*) do so as well,

his argument, in order to convince B, would have to bring B to consent to both (*a*) and (*b*). It is easy enough to understand the kind of argument which would convince B with respect to (*a*). A would have to bring evidence relevant to the truth or falsity of (*a*)—that is, make other statements which B agrees to be true and from which (*a*) logically follows. But the second part of A's assertion, Stevenson claimed, presents a difficulty

Since it is an imperative, it is not open to proof at all. What is it like to prove a command? If we told a person to close the door, and received the reply, "Prove it!" should we not, to speak mildly, grow somewhat impatient? (*EL*, 26.)

This consideration led Stevenson to the conclusion that

> it would seem that ethical judgments are amenable only to a partial proof. So far as "This is good" includes the meaning of (*a*) a proof is possible, but so far as it includes the meaning of (*b*) the very request for proof is nonsensical. We seem forced to a distressingly meager conclusion: If a man says "X is good", and if he can prove that he really approves of X, then he has all the proof that can be demanded of him. (*EL*, 26.)

But, Stevenson went on to say, we must not assume that "a proof in ethics must be exactly like a proof in science'. Ethical judgements "may have a *different sort* of proof", or a "substitute for a proof"; there may be some "reasons or arguments which may at least support ethical judgements" (*EL*, 27).

Thus, he claimed, we often give reasons also for imperatives. When someone is told to close the door and asks 'Why?' we can give as reasons such statements as 'It is too draughty', or 'The noise is distracting' (*EL*, 27). And these statements are reasons or arguments, Stevenson explained, because they, as a matter of fact, make the person in question comply with the imperative. But to what do such reasons owe their efficacy?

> The supporting reason . . . describes the situation which the imperative seeks to alter, or the new situation which the imperative seeks to bring about; and if these facts disclose that the new situation will satisfy a preponderance of the hearer's desires, he will hesitate to obey no longer. (*EL*, 27–28.)

It seems, then, that "reasons" can be given for an imperative only if the person in question would have done anyhow what the imperative told him to do, had he known or thought more about the relevant facts, paid more attention to the relevant laws of nature, &c.

Now this may be a true psychological account of how people in fact come to follow imperatives if they are prudent and "rational". As a piece of psychology, this account seems to hold for at least some cases where we come to do what we are told not merely on the authority of the speaker. To follow an imperative just on the authority of the speaker requires a higher degree of sophistication; our natural inclination is to ask first whether following the imperative in question would or would not contribute to the satisfaction of the desires that we happen to have. We may also realize that the speaker himself is a potential source of rewards and punishments. His will and what is in his power must be reckoned with by the hearer if he is to come to a prudent conclusion concerning what is and what is not conducive to the satisfaction of "a preponderance of his desires".

Whenever psychological reasons of the kind that Stevenson describes are appropriate, the imperative in question is, from a logical point of view, a hypothetical imperative of the kind that Kant called "counsels of prudence". But such imperatives, as all hypothetical imperatives, are clearly capable of being supported by reasons in a straightforward logical, and not just in Stevenson's psychological, sense. It is the mark of a hypothetical imperative of prudence that the content of the imperative—what one is told or asked to do—is conditional on the usually warranted assumption that the person addressed wants to satisfy his desires. Such an imperative thus implies that doing what one is asked or told *is* a means to the realization of that end. The reasons that one can give for an imperative of this sort are therefore statements which elaborate on why doing what one is asked or told is a means to that end. From a logical point of view, good reasons for such imperatives are statements which allow us to predict that if the person addressed does follow the imperative, he will succeed in satisfying a preponderance of his desires. Now as Kant also pointed out, since happiness—the satisfaction of one's desires—is a very vague and indeterminable concept, we can never be certain that we have discovered an imperative or counsel of prudence. Searching for happiness can only be a piecemeal and hit-or-miss process. In practice what one must use are thus "problematic" imperatives of skill. An example of these would be Stevenson's 'Close the door'. Since it is only problematic that closing the door will be conducive to the happiness of the person in question, the speaker may want to avoid the implication that it is. Therefore he may be more tentative and say 'If you want to eliminate the draught, close the door' or 'If you are distracted by the noise, close the door'. Or perhaps, since the effective concern with another's happiness is not only difficult, but also presumptuous, such 'if'—clauses need not be spelled out, but may be left implicit or to the hearer to be filled in. At any rate, there will be again reasons by which such piecemeal and tentative prudential imperatives may be supported: 'The draught is caused by the open door' or 'The noise comes from the hall', &c. These reasons are again, from a logical point of view, good reasons if they permit us to predict that if the addressee does do what he is asked to do he will have satisfied one of his desires, if he has such a desire. The proviso 'if he has such a desire' may be necessary since imperatives of skill are "problematic". The implication that the person addressed has the relevant desire may be very weak indeed. Some writers (e.g. Kant himself and Hare) have gone so far as to assume that the implication is not there at all. Thus Hare writes that " 'If you want to go to the largest grocer in Oxford, go to Grimbly Hughes' seems to follow from and to say no more than 'Grimbly Hughes is the largest grocer in Oxford' " (*LM*, 34). And Kant said that in a hypothetical imperative the imperative content is "analytic".

What Stevenson has done is to take these facts concerning the logic of giving reasons for hypothetical imperatives and give them a psychological interpretation. Instead of asking how hypothetical imperatives can be supported by reasons in the logical sense he has asked what is the psychological process through which people come to accept, that is, follow, such imperatives if they are "rational", that is, try to do always what is to their best advantage. Stevenson's method of "giving reasons" is thus applicable to imperatives only in so far as they are hypothetical imperatives. We will have been successful in using this method when the person addressed comes to believe that if he does as asked, he will be happy.

Since Stevenson, as we saw, holds that moral judgements are in part like imperatives, it follows that they too can be supported by reasons only if the imperatives which they in part resemble are hypothetical imperatives. Thus, in so far as the process of giving reasons is concerned, the working models must be modified so that, instead of (1) above, what A is saying is really represented by

(2) (*a*) I approve of X;
    (*b*) if you want Y, do so as well.

or, ultimately, if A wants to go that far and risk making a guess concerning what constitutes B's happiness, by

(3) (*a*) I approve of X;
    (*b*) since you want to satisfy a preponderance of your desires, do so as well.

In order to win the argument, A would then have to show to B that approving of X will, in fact, satisfy a desire that B has or even a preponderance of B's desires. And by searching into the mind of B, and by exhibiting the relevant causal relations, he might be able to do this. In that case he would have perhaps managed to show that deep down B himself had really wanted to approve of X all along. If B was not initially willing to approve of X then it was only because he did not realize that approving of X was for him a way of satisfying a desire of his own or even a whole preponderance of his desires.

We have argued that what Stevenson has done in his theory of "giving reasons" is to psychologize the logic of supporting hypothetical imperatives by (logical) reasons. We have seen that in so far as "giving reasons" is relevant to moral judgements, those judgements must be looked upon as being in part not (like) categorical imperatives but (like) hypothetical imperatives which include the clause 'if you want Y' or 'since you want to satisfy a preponderance of your desires'. It follows that *if* moral judgements are in part hypothetical imperatives, as Stevenson's theory of "giving reasons" forces us to assume, then they can be supported by reasons in a straightforward logical sense and not only in a causal or psychological sense as Stevenson claims. If, in our example, A manages to get B to accept the statement 'Approving of X will satisfy a preponderance of your desires', he has provided a logical premise and not just a psychological incentive for 'If you want to satisfy a preponderance of your desires, approve of X'. What Stevenson claimed was that there are factual considerations or beliefs which may only psychologically and causally induce a person to accept a moral judgement in so far as it includes an imperative element. But if the imperative element in moral judgements is hypothetical, as Stevenson's theory of "giving reasons" demands, moral judgements would be capable of being given a straightforward logical proof. *If* to say 'X is good' is to say 'I approve of X, since you want to satisfy a preponderance of your desires, do so as well', then, if I can demonstrate to you that approving X will satisfy the preponderance of your desires, you *must* accept the imperative element of that moral judgement not in the psychological or causal but in the logical sense of 'must'.

It has been argued (by Kant and others) that the normativeness of moral judgements is not hypothetical but categorical. And it seems that with this Stevenson agreed. According to him moral judgements are used for influencing and redirecting attitudes; he does not say that moral judgements are merely, as it were, a form of psychotherapy by which we make people aware of the deep-seated and unconscious attitudes which they already have. In so far as moral judgements are capable of being supported by what Stevenson calls "reasons", they would have to be purely subjective in nature. In uttering a moral judgement, I express an attitude of mine, but I can give to you "reasons" for accepting that judgement only if it happens to reflect a similar attitude in you. The search for "reasons" is thus merely a search for the attitudes we happen to share. Moral argument would be *based* on existing agreements in attitude, rather than a means for dissolving or overcoming existing disagreements in attitude. It seems clear that Stevenson believed therefore that there is a categorical and irreducible element in moral judgements. This is reflected, for example, in his insistence that moral terms have "independent emotive meaning" and that the assumption that "all disagreement in attitude is rooted in disagreement in belief", is untenable (*EL*, 136). All this led him to the conclusion that moral discourse sometimes consists of even less "rational" methods than the one we have examined in detail so far.

9. *The Extravagance of "Persuasion"*

Besides using "reasons", that is, beliefs of various sorts which causally affect the attitudes of people, there are also what Stevenson called "nonrational methods" for gaining consent to our moral judgements, the most important of these being persuasion:

The most important of the nonrational methods will be called "persuasive", in a somewhat broadened sense. It depends on the sheer, direct emotional impact of words—on emotive meaning, rhetorical cadence, apt metaphor, stentorian, stimulating, or pleading tones of voice, dramatic gestures, care in establishing *rapport* with the hearer or audience, and so on. (*EL*, 139.)

Persuasive method thus consists largely in the use of the "sheer, direct emotional impact of words"—in other words, of their independent emotive meaning. Our criticisms of Stevenson's account of persuasion will therefore largely coincide with the remarks we have already made about the notion of independent emotive meaning. We concluded that independent emotive meaning in so far as it consists in the sheer emotional impact of words cannot be said to be part of language at all. Similarly, I shall argue, persuasion cannot be said to be in any useful sense part of reasoning.

In discussing persuasion, Stevenson used the following example:

Let us suppose, then, that A and B are discussing a mutual friend, and that their remarks take this form:

A. He has had but little formal education, as is plainly evident from his conversation. His sentences are often roughly cast, his historical and literary references rather obvious, and his thinking is wanting in that subtlety and sophistication which mark a trained intellect. He is definitely lacking in culture.

B. Much of what you say is true, but I should call him a man of culture, notwithstanding.

A. Aren't the characteristics I mention the antithesis of culture, contrary to the very meaning of the term?

B. By no means. You are stressing the outward forms, simply the empty shell of culture. In the true and full sense of the term, "culture" means *imaginative sensitivity* and *originality*. These qualities he has; and so I say, and indeed with no little humility, that he is a man of far deeper culture than many of us who have had superior advantages in education. (*EL*, 211.)

Stevenson pointed out that the issue between A and B involves more than the application of a word and the question of what characteristics their friend does, as a matter of fact, possess; since 'culture' is a word which has "laudatory emotive meaning", it involves A's and B's attitudes towards him. B is offering a *persuasive* redefinition of the word 'culture' and thereby attempting to re-direct A's attitudes towards the person in question. Now Stevenson claimed that B can use the word 'culture' for the purpose of re-directing A's attitudes only because the emotive meaning of that word is, at least in part, independent of its descriptive meaning. The word 'culture' could not be used for that purpose if, for A, its laudatory emotive meaning depended solely on the descriptive meaning which A himself initially attributes to that term—namely, 'subtlety and sophistication'. For then, if he accepted B's re-definition of the term 'culture' as 'imaginative sensitivity and origin-ality' that term would not retain for him its laudatory emotive meaning, and therefore his acceptance of B's redefinition together with the belief that their friend does possess imaginative sensitivity and originality would not entail his changing his attitude towards that person. Consequently, B can use the word 'culture' for redirecting A's attitudes only if the laudatory force of that word did not depend on its descriptive meaning. It is thus the "sheer emotional impact of words" on which persuasion as a method for dispelling normative disagreements must rest together with such things as "rhetorical cadence", "tone of voice", and "dramatic gestures".

But then it becomes impossible to hold that Stevenson's example represents a case of reasoning in any sense at all. If everything depended ultimately on the causal effects of the sheer sound of the word 'culture', A and B could not be said to have been engaged in an argument with one another. The absurdity of regarding per-suasion as a "method" for "the resolution of an ethical argument" (*EL*, 139) is easily seen by citing another of the several examples Stevenson discusses:

A: It is morally wrong for you to disobey him.
B: That is precisely what I have been denying.
A: But it is your simple *duty* to obey. You ought to obey him in the sheer interest of moral obligation. (*EL*, 141.)

Stevenson claims that A's second statement "supports" his initial judgement since the reiteration of ethical terms although it "does not provide any additional information" may nevertheless "have a strong cumulative effect on B's attitudes". But A could have "supported" his initial judgement in this sense also by swinging a big stick. He was not in any sense presenting an *argument* in favour of his initial judgement.

10. *Stevenson's Dilemma and Subsequent Developments*

Stevenson's theory of moral reasoning confronts us with a dilemma. If we conceive of moral reasoning as resting on the independent emotive meaning of moral terms, it would have a mere psychological impact which cannot be distinguished from the kind of impact sometimes produced by non-linguistic and non-conventional acts or even by such things as piercing factory whistles, detonations, and wind in the trees. If, on the other hand, we conceive of moral reasoning as ultimately dependent on the descriptive meaning of moral words and judgements, then moral reasoning, instead of being capable of influencing people's emotions and attitudes, could only cater to them. Moral judgements would then have only the force of hypothetical imperatives. Nevertheless, for all its inadequacies, Stevenson's theory of moral reasoning was provocative and did constitute an advance in twentieth-century ethical theory. In contrast to Moore's theory it constituted a serious effort to make sense of the fact that moral arguments are practical and are designed to influence our actions and attitudes. Subsequent writers, while trying to do justice to the practical character of moral language and reasoning, sought ways to escape the predicament into which Stevenson's views had led.

It might seem that the second horn of Stevenson's dilemma is the less vicious one and that rescue efforts in this direction might more easily meet with success. Surely, in order to talk about moral discourse in any philosophically illuminating way, the notion of independent emotive meaning would need to be abandoned. The problem of moral discourse is a problem of language, and we must therefore draw a distinction between the sheer psychological effects of words and their meanings as fixed by the rules that govern their use in communication. Persuasion is no topic for moral philosophy proper. Stevenson's theory of "giving reasons", on the other hand, merely appears to be in need of modification. Once we free it from its psychological disguise, it seems to make perfectly good sense. Any argument or process of reasoning is based on *antecedently* accepted premises. There is some degree of circularity present in any argument. Apart from its psychological formulation the inadequacy of the theory of "giving reasons" seems to consist merely in the fact that according to it, the circle appears too small. If we modified this theory by saying that it is not the immediate attitudes and interests of the persons concerned, but the attitudes and interests of a whole society as they are crystallized in a long process of social interaction which form the backing of moral arguments and reasoning, its air of paradox might disappear. It was Toulmin who developed a theory which was, in effect, a transformation of Stevenson's theory of "giving reasons" in this direction. For him, as we shall see in the next chapter, to support a moral judgement by reasons is to show that it is backed by the communal attitudes of a society as reflected in its moral code and ultimately, that it is conducive to the harmonization of the interests of a whole community.

Stevenson's notion of the independent emotive meaning of moral terms nevertheless also contains a grain of truth which cannot be ignored. To pass a moral judgement is clearly not just to say that a given object, person, or action does or does not measure up to an accepted standard or that it has or has not characteristics which make it valuable from the point of view of social harmony. A theory which does not pay enough attention to the "emotive" aspects of moral language would remain inadequate. Hare, in particular, was impressed by the irreducible normative force of moral judgements; we shall therefore reserve a detailed discussion of this point until we come to examine his views. A few remarks about the possibility of rendering a more satisfactory account of the evaluative feature of moral language emphasized by Stevenson could, however, be profitably made at this point. A more plausible case might be made for something like independent emotive meaning if, instead of the direct emotional impact of words, we would talk of their linguistic roles, functions, or uses. Rather than saying that moral terms have emotive meaning in Stevenson's sense, we could say that moral terms are used for performing such functions as commending and prescribing. And, we could claim, such functions have little or nothing to do with giving a description of some object or event or imparting information about it. It could be admitted that the capacity of moral terms to serve such functions may have had its origin in the fact that these terms, in virtue of their descriptive meaning, refer to things and situations towards which people had or have certain attitudes. But, in the course of history, we could claim, their commendatory and prescriptive force became independent of their descriptive role and acquired a life of its own. We can hold that moral language has an irreducible normative force without having to say that it is merely a vehicle for giving vent to personal wishes and desires, or for stimulating the nerve endings of others.

At the same time, we must note that descriptive meaning nevertheless remains relevant. Sometimes we are critical of the speech-rituals of our fellow men. And the more critical we are, the less independent force do these rituals exert over us and the more shall we become interested in the descriptive meanings of the terms used.[1] If we lose confidence in the judgements of our friends or if we come into an environment where different standards prevail, then, if we do not want to act blindly, we must start asking for reasons and depend more and more on the descriptive aspect of moral language.

A satisfactory ethical theory must therefore explain how the normative and descriptive aspects of moral judgements act together. In so far as moral judgements contain normative force, they serve as guides for action. But to the same extent it does not seem that they can be supported by argument. Reasons, it would seem, can be given for these judgements only in so far as they contain descriptive meaning. But in that case, the normative force of these judgements would depend on whether or not we happen to consider those reasons as motives for our actions. Stevenson's distinction between

[1] Cf. Henry D. Aiken, 'The Authority of Moral Judgments', in *Philosophy and Phenomenological Research*, June, 1952.

the two types of meaning in moral judgements thus presented twentieth-century ethical theory with a dilemma.

The roots of this dilemma go actually even deeper. Naturalism, if it were acceptable, would provide an explanation of how moral judgements can be supported by arguments. According to that view there is no fundamental difference between judgements of value and judgements of fact. Naturalism in this broad sense goes back to Plato and Aristotle. But that golden age of philosophy was destroyed and lost with the advent of modern science and the philosophies that gave expression to and reinforced the new world view in which facts and value were sharply separated. Many philosophers came to feel that the domain of reason could be firmly established only by limiting its boundaries to include only matters of fact.

This situation was expressed once more and brought into focus by Moore in his arguments against naturalism. Through these arguments it became evident that naturalism, at least when formulated in terms of the current epistemological categories, was impossible. But from this it followed that reason can reach beyond the boundaries of the purely factual only by a sort of leap, the nature of which remained hopelessly obscure. Pragmatism, particularly as represented by Dewey, was an attempt to break down the barrier that kept reason confined within the realm of pure facts. The expansion of the realm of reason to cover the domain of values meant for Dewey largely the imposing of the standard procedures of science for ascertaining factual knowledge on the human concern with the aims and goals of conduct. Pragmatism was thus too reductivistic. When formulated clearly, it was open to the Moorean charge that it committed the Naturalistic Fallacy. For Dewey, a moral judgement was just another empirical hypothesis to be validated by the usual methods of science. To say that something possesses value is simply to say that it serves and continues to serve as a source of human satisfactions. But it may be meaningfully questioned whether an object is really good even though it has fulfilled those conditions. Dewey was not able to account, to use his own terminology, for the "*de jure*" nature of moral judgements.[1]

[1] Cf. Morton White, 'Value and Obligation in Dewey and Lewis' in Sellars and Hospers, *Readings in Ethical Theory*.

Stevenson's work is very much in the Pragmatist tradition. He himself freely acknowledges his indebtedness to Dewey (*EL*, 253). But there are also fundamental disagreements. The predictive dimension of value-judgements, which Dewey emphasized, is not, Stevenson claims, "sufficient to mark off its *de jure* quality" (*EL*, 254). It is rather the imperative or quasi-imperative element in value-judgements, Stevenson insisted, that alone can account for this quality (*EL*, 257). The consequence of this was that while Dewey could claim that moral judgements rest on evidence of an ordinary scientific sort, Stevenson had to maintain that since moral judgements possess an imperative force, they are in the end neither true nor false and hence cannot rest on empirical evidence alone. What we have for moral judgements and imperatives, is, in the end, not evidence but merely "reasons" and persuasion.

Thus, although Stevenson appreciated the difference between empirical and moral discourse, his account of the latter was wholly inadequate. Factual beliefs are reasons in that they can be used to affect attitudes. By selecting such beliefs wisely, we may be able to sway the attitudes of our opponents. But our success or failure rests here, as we have seen, on the prior acceptance of certain persuasive definitions, that is, certain basic attitudes, on the part of our opponents. The moral reformer will thus find his enthusiasm dampened with regard to using the "rational" method of "giving reasons". He will find that the best he can do by using this method is to cater to some deep-seated attitudes that his audience already possesses. In order to carry his programme further, he will have to abandon reason even in this attenuated sense and resort to sheer persuasion.

Once we have granted the distinction between empirical evidence and reasons in ethics, our task becomes to explain a sense of 'reasons' more adequate than the one offered by Stevenson. Since Hume it has become customary to emphasize the close link between moral judgements and our "passions". Moral judgements speak to our feelings and attitudes and are thus capable of influencing human conduct. Hume never clearly explained what he took the nature of this link to be. He may have assumed that this link is of a causal sort. In Stevenson this assumption came into the open. But we saw that it must be rejected. It may be true that moral language serves as a kind of conductor through which the current of emotions passes from men to men. Some people have conceived of poetic language in a similar way. And in the case of a piece of arousing oratory one almost inevitably thinks of some such picture. But all this is quite immaterial to moral language as a structure governed by rules. Factual language, for that matter, may have its share of creating direct emotional repercussions, although it must be admitted that it is usually a great deal more, to use Hume's word, "indolent" in nature. But whether a stretch of linguistic behaviour is passionate or indolent has nothing to do with its logical nature.

III

STEPHEN TOULMIN

1. *The New Approach*

TOULMIN's approach to the problems of moral discourse was designed to overcome the difficulties to which the theories of both Moore and Stevenson had led. In his work he carefully took stock of and criticized the views of his predecessors. According to him these authors had not succeeded in giving a satisfactory account of moral discourse which would enable us to appraise moral arguments in practice. Therefore, before turning to our examination of Toulmin's own theory, we should do well to take a look at the disagreements voiced by him against our two preceding authors. These disagreements centred on the concepts of truth and validity.

Moore's views on the nature of moral terms led, as we saw, to the conclusion that we must either say outright that moral reasoning does not exist at all, or construe it in such a way that it ceases to be practical and we can no longer understand its relevance to human conduct. In the first case moral judgements would become blind; in the second, powerless. Stevenson was more impressed by the latter peril. He insisted that a theory of moral discourse must do justice to the practical function of moral judgements. However, his single-mindedness concerning this point had the effect that moral judgements became in his theory blind, not just in the sense of being the results of untestable intuitions, but in the sense of being sheer voicings of likes and dislikes, favourable and unfavourable attitudes that men find themselves having. In Moore's theory men turned out to have in matters of practical morality no other guides besides their intuitions, but he insisted that a moral intuition had an objective foundation—that it rested on the presence of a moral quality. Since Stevenson rejected the notion that there are such things as moral qualities existing independently of the wills and desires of moral agents, the acceptability of a moral judgement became a purely arbitrary and subjective matter. He was unable to preserve the distinction between what merely seems good, or obligatory, and what really is so. Moral argument and reasoning became a sheer battle between conflicting attitudes for which the notion of validity was said to have no relevance.

Although Toulmin agreed with Stevenson that moral judgements have the force to influence our actions and decisions, Stevenson's conclusion was quite unsatisfactory to him. It seemed to Toulmin that it is as certain as anything could be that there is a distinction between what seems and what really is good and that certain arguments which are put forward to support a moral conclusion are valid, while others are invalid. For him, there is "a sense of 'valid' (and the criteria of validity), which are already implicit in our ethical discussions" (PRE, 41), and the philosopher's task is to analyse that sense rather than raise the question whether or not the concept of validity is applicable to moral discourse at all. According to Toulmin, the source of inadequacy and paradox in the theory of a philosopher like Stevenson is that he has

too narrow a view of the uses of reasoning—he assumes too readily that a mathematical or logical proof or a scientific verification can be the only kind of 'good reason' for any statement. (PRE, 46.)

In moral reasoning, Toulmin claimed, a special kind of inference or argument is used, which he called "evaluative inference": an inference where "we pass from factual reasons to an ethical conclusion" (PRE, 38). Curiously enough the same words had also been written by Stevenson. He also claimed that "one of the peculiarities of ethical argument lies in the inference from a factual reason to an ethical conclusion" (EL, 153). But contrary to Toulmin, Stevenson held that such inference can never be properly called valid or invalid. Where these two authors differed was then in their views concerning the nature of this inference.

We recall that, as Moore had come to doubt that moral terms designate properties, he also contemplated in his later work the possibility that the mode of inference in moral reasoning is not strict logical entailment. Certain inferences, from judgements of intrinsic value to judgements of moral obligation and vice versa, were said to be admissible and valid though the connexion between those judgements fell short of analyticity. On the other hand, he seems always to have believed that if there were any valid arguments from *factual* premises to an ethical conclusion, the kind of inference exhibited by those arguments would have to be analytic entailment. Stevenson's views seem to have been based on a similar assumption. He probably thought that the kind of inference to which the notion of validity could be legitimately applied would have to be based on "linguistic rules" which, as we saw, he conceived as being like the formal rules of artificially constructed language systems. But since he believed further that (*a*) the kind of inference which is characteristic of moral reasoning does lead from *factual* premises to a moral conclusion, and that (*b*) no moral conclusions follow from factual premises just on the basis of such formal rules, he had to conclude that for moral reasoning the notion of validity is altogether irrelevant.

The ground for rejecting the relevance of validity to moral reasoning was, for Stevenson, the belief that moral judgements are fundamentally incapable of being true or false. Again, Moore had already mentioned the possibility that moral terms and judgements are non-descriptive. However, he did not work out this suggestion himself in any detail. To do so would probably have entailed radical changes in other parts of his theory about the truth of which he was convinced at least as strongly as he might have doubted the tenability of the notion that moral terms refer to and describe a certain kind of abstract entity. It seemed to him that if moral terms did not refer to a certain kind of property, moral judgements would not have any objective foundation and would be incapable of being true or false and contradictory to one another.[1] This was a conclusion Moore was not willing to draw. Stevenson, however, was willing to do exactly this. Moral judgements, since they do not essentially describe or refer to any states of affairs, were for him, at bottom, neither true nor false and incapable of logically contradicting one another.

We saw that in Stevenson's theory moral judgements are, in part, reports or expressions of our attitudes, in part, like imperatives.

[1] See *The Philosophy of G. E. Moore*, Schilpp, ed., pp. 540 ff.

We also saw that, for him, the imperative element is by far the more important and characteristic one. Consequently, he held, the question of verification—of truth and falsity—does not, except in a rather trivial sense, arise with respect to moral judgements. To verify or to falsify a moral judgement is simply to show that the speaker does or does not happen to have a certain attitude towards the object in question. Beyond this, the question of truth and falsity is simply not relevant. Toulmin, on the other hand, claimed that with regard to moral judgements questions of verification, truth and falsity, are always quite proper and meaningful (*PRE*, 52). But he also claimed that in order to call moral judgements true and false, we need not think of moral terms as referring to non-natural properties. All that is required is that there be a distinction between "good and bad reasons" by which moral judgements are supported. Toulmin agreed with Stevenson that ethical terms do not refer to objective properties. But he claimed that Stevenson was, in a way, not radical enough at this point and that, besides his narrow views on inference and validity, he still shared another basic assumption with Moore. "The supporters of both doctrines" (that is, philosophers like Moore who supported an objective doctrine and philosophers like Stevenson who, according to Toulmin, partially supported a subjective doctrine), Toulmin wrote,

take it for granted that opposed ethical judgments can only be contradictory if they refer to a property of the object concerned; and that, unless they do refer to a property, such judgments must refer to some psychological state of the speaker—in which case they can never contradict one another at all. (*PRE*, 42.)

Toulmin described this assumption also as the idea

that, in order to be logically respectable, to be capable of being regarded as 'true' or 'false' or of being reasoned about, a sentence must be made up only of concepts *referring* to something either 'in the object' or 'in the subject'. (*PRE*, 57.)

And, he claimed, it was because of this lingering assumption that Stevenson came to the paradoxical conclusion that with respect to moral judgements the notions of truth and falsity are in the end not applicable at all. According to Toulmin moral terms never in any way refer to anything, be it objective or subjective.

There is no reason in the world why all our words should act as names for definite and unique processes—physical *or* mental: only some of them, in fact, are of such a kind that it makes sense to talk of such processes. And we can easily see that the class of concepts for which it does make sense cannot include ethical concepts. (*PRE*, 44.)

Similarly, he went on, the nature of moral disagreement and the manner in which two moral judgements may be opposed to each other must be interpreted in a radically different way.

We have come to realise what it is that people in ethical disagreement really do have to contradict each other about—nothing physically or psychologically 'concrete' or 'substantial', but something which, for logical purposes, is quite as solid and important—namely, whether or not there is a good reason for reaching one ethical conclusion rather than another. (*PRE*, 57.)

These two ideas,

(1) That with respect to moral arguments, as arguments from factual premises to a moral conclusion, we can quite properly speak of validity, and

(2) That moral judgements, although they do not refer to anything, are capable of being called true and false and contradictory to one another,

thus constitute what basically separates Toulmin from both Moore and Stevenson.

Toulmin claimed to be making another fresh start in moral philosophy. He believed that earlier writers, including Moore and Stevenson, had been preoccupied with the analysis and definition of ethical terms and concepts. According to Toulmin the right thing for the ethical theorist to do is to start not with moral terms, but, so to speak, from the other end, with moral arguments and reasoning. We must not ask questions like 'What is the definition of the term "good"?' or 'What is goodness?': the problem of moral reasoning must be attacked head-on by asking 'What reasons are good reasons for a moral conclusion?'

How far the latter question had been neglected in the past is a moot point. It seems far-fetched to say that any moral philosophers who have been concerned with the meanings of moral terms were, or thought themselves to be, engaged in an endeavour which had no relevance to questions of moral reasoning. Thus, for example, although it is true that Moore's main effort was directed towards being clear about ethical terms, this does not mean that he did not hold the problem of moral reasoning to be important. Moore held, as strongly as anyone, that the point of all discussion of ethical theory is, after all, to get in a better position to appraise our reasoning about moral matters. By becoming clear about the nature of moral terms Moore hoped to be able to judge better what can be accepted as proper evidence and as correct reasons for a moral judgement (PE, 6). And in the case of Stevenson, we saw that his views on the nature of the types of argument by which moral conclusions can be supported were a direct result of his theory of the two types of meaning of moral terms. As we saw in the two preceding chapters, both Moore and Stevenson offered theories not only of moral terms, but also of moral reasoning. Nevertheless, the theories of Moore and Stevenson provided no *solution* to the problem of how moral arguments are to be appraised. Their theories turned out to be such that no guidance could be got from them with regard to how we are to distinguish between good and bad, valid and invalid moral arguments in practice. It was to this anomaly that Toulmin's theory of good reasons purported to offer a remedy.

2. *The Theory of "Good Reasons"*

According to Toulmin, some cases of moral reasoning are quite straightforward and simple. Sometimes, when we are in doubt about whether a given course of action is the morally right one, all we have to do to settle the issue is to determine whether it conforms to the accepted moral code. In that case the only reason we need to give for a judgement that the action in question is a morally right action is a factual classification of it (PRE, 144-6). Moral reasoning of this kind has, then, the following pattern:

X is Y

∴ X is right,

where the conclusion follows from the premise on the basis of the principle that whatever is Y, is right which is accepted in the moral code. We must notice that 'X is right' follows from 'X is Y', not on the basis of the *meanings* of these two statements; 'X is Y' is merely what Toulmin calls the *reason* for 'X is right', and not a part of its meaning. That 'X is right' follows from 'X is Y' is a matter of morals, that is, it depends on what in fact the accepted moral code is.

So far, what Toulmin has said is not an advance over Stevenson; the psychological idiom is simply lacking. We saw that for Stevenson, a moral judgement follows from a factual reason both as a matter of psychology and as a matter of morals, that is, it follows in terms of an appropriate persuasive definition. To accept such a persuasive definition is the same thing as to have the disposition to respond with a certain attitude to a belief as a stimulus which was then said to constitute the "reason" for the moral judgement in question. And to accept such a persuasive definition is also to take sides with regard to a normative ethical issue. An accepted moral code would be for Stevenson simply a set of persuasive definitions which a society subscribes to.

Toulmin has not yet shown us that the connexion between a moral judgement and its reasons is a logical one. He will not be able to show this unless he is willing to say that a moral code is a kind of logical organon. But to say this would be extremely problematic. It would tend to eradicate the difference between the logical tools by which a subject matter is investigated and that subject matter itself. A moral code is a set of prescriptions or rules governing human conduct; a set of logical rules, on the other hand, can govern human conduct only indirectly, by governing the discourse about conduct. There is therefore at least an apparent initial wrong-headedness about saying (as also Stevenson was in effect saying) that which instances of moral reasoning are valid, is itself a moral matter. What valid forms of inference there are for ethical inquiry seems to be a question which is quite different from the question of what principles there are for determining what is ethically right and wrong. The purpose of ethical inquiry is to arrive at well-founded judgements of what is ethically right or wrong. Such judgements can be concerned with particular actions but also with whole classes of actions. In the latter case one's concern would be with ethical principles. But if ethical principles are themselves the result of ethical inquiry, they cannot be identical with the principles or rules of inference used to conduct that inquiry.

Our interpretation of what Toulmin intended as his first pattern of moral reasoning seems nevertheless correct in the light of such assertions on his part as that there is a "form of argument peculiar to ethics'. A quite different pattern naturally suggests itself for the first sort of case that Toulmin considers. It may be claimed that what Toulmin took to be the form of the most simple sort of moral argument is really an enthymeme which, when fully written out, would become:

> Whatever is Y, is right
> X is Y
> ∴ X is right.[1]

When viewed in this manner, moral argument does not seem to exhibit any special form of inference. What are Toulmin's reasons for rejecting this pattern in favour of his own? His reasons become evident when we examine his views on the nature of more complex cases of moral reasoning.

Toulmin claimed that many moral issues are more complicated and cannot be decided simply by appealing to the accepted moral code. There are cases in which our contemplated action does not fall unambiguously under an accepted moral principle. In those cases, he claimed, we must turn to estimating the social merit of the consequences of our actions by having in mind the "function of ethics" as the harmonization of people's interests (*PRE*, 148 ff.). There are then, according to Toulmin, moral arguments also of a different pattern:

> X is conducive to social harmony
> ∴ X is right,

where the relevant rule of inference is the principle of social harmony: whatever is conducive to social harmony, is right.

---

[1] Cf. Hare's review of Toulmin's *The Place of Reason in Ethics* in *Philosophical Quarterly*, vol. i. 1951.

How should we interpret this latter rule? Is it just another moral principle on a par with such things as the keeping of promises, truthfulness, &c.? If this were the case, we can again say that what Toulmin has given us is not a new form of inference but an enthymeme. We would say that the argument written out fully would be:

> Whatever is conducive to social harmony, is right
> X is conducive to social harmony
> ∴ X is right.

We could also say that Toulmin's theory is still no advance over Stevenson's. From the factual premise 'X is conducive to social harmony' the ethical conclusion 'X is right' follows not as a matter of logic but as a matter of morals. Whether the conclusion follows from the premise is thus still itself a normative moral issue. This, we may argue, becomes evident if we put the principle of harmony where it belongs—in the position of the major premise. But Toulmin seems to have thought that the case before us now is really quite different, that the principle of harmony is not just another moral principle at all. He claimed that if you justify an act by saying, for example, that it is a case of promise keeping, you cannot go on to justify it further by saying that it is conducive to social harmony. What you can justify in the latter fashion is a moral principle or social practice, not a particular act. According to Toulmin, there are two kinds of moral reasoning each having its own logical criteria (*PRE*, 148 ff.). In one sort of case, he seems to be saying, the logical criteria are moral principles—in the other, the logical criterion is the social merit of our principles and general practices.

However, what exactly Toulmin did say at this point is not quite clear. He also claimed that there are arguments about individual actions in which no principle is involved and the decision whether the action in question is right depends on such considerations as whether the action has consequences which meet another's need (*PRE*, 147). Furthermore, he claimed that there are certain test cases wherein the difference between the two types of moral reasoning vanishes. In such cases the pending decision about the rightness of an individual action is made into a matter of principle, and the issue is no longer solely the rightness of that individual action but the rightness of a principle or social practice.

It seems that if we try to give a consistent interpretation to Toulmin's theory, we are confronted with a choice between two alternatives. On the one hand, we could interpret Toulmin as saying that in the second type of moral reasoning no principles whatever are employed and the whole matter depends on the nature of the consequences involved. But then the question arises: what features must the consequences have in order to be relevant for deciding the issue? And in order to get an answer to that question some principles are obviously needed. The other interpretation would be that in both types of moral reasoning there are principles involved, but the principles are radically different in kind. In the second type of moral reasoning, we might say, we use the principle of social harmony as a second order principle. According to Toulmin, that principle describes the "function of moral discourse"; it is what "makes a judgement ethical", sets the "limits of ethical reasoning", and determines the "scope or framework" of ethics (*PRE, passim*). If we adopt this interpretation, we can describe Toulmin's theory as follows: if the argument in question is about a test case, it will contain two stages:

I. X is Y
∴ X is right,

which inference is backed by the moral principle: whatever is Y, is right. That principle in turn is justified by:

II. ϕ is conducive to social harmony
∴ ϕ is right,

which inference, in its turn, is backed by the second order principle: whatever (principle or practice) is conducive to social harmony, is right. If the argument in question is about the rightness of a (first order) moral principle or social practice, it contains just the step schematized by II.

Thus even if Toulmin would grant that when an ordinary first level moral argument is used, no special form of inference is needed since the principle involved may just as well be put into the position of the major premise, he could still claim that arguments about the moral rightness of principles themselves, and those involved in test cases, are different. Here no first order principles are any longer available and the inference cannot be rendered analytic by supplying an appropriate major premise. We can get from the premises to the conclusion only by considering the principle of harmony as a second order principle and letting it do duty as a rule of inference. But what can we mean by calling the principle of harmony a second order principle? How is it discovered? And why should we accept it, rather than some other? These are some of the questions that we must still consider.

3. *Truth and Validity*

Toulmin, as we saw, rejected the correspondence theory of truth. Moral judgements are capable of being true or false, but this, according to him does not require us to say that moral terms and judgements aim to refer or to correspond to anything. With regard to validity we found him taking an equally unorthodox view. The notions of formal consistency and analyticity were, for him, quite irrelevant with regard to the kind of validity to be found in moral reasoning. We must now take a closer look at Toulmin's own positive views on truth and validity.

He held, in effect, that truth and validity in moral discourse are not two questions but one. To say that a moral judgement is true is to say that there are good reasons which support it and this in turn amounts to saying that there is a valid inference from certain factual premises to that moral judgement. Truth, in so far as it applies to moral judgements, is thus more complicated and indirect than one might think. The truth and falsity of a moral judgement, Toulmin seems to have maintained, can become a meaningful problem only relative to some descriptive or factual statements the truth of which has already been ascertained. The question 'Is this moral judgement true?' amounts really to the question 'Is this moral judgement true in relation to such and such true factual statements?' And a moral judgement *is* true if, and only if, there is a valid inference from such statements to that judgement.

In making the points just mentioned Toulmin was, in a way, drawing renewed attention to the phenomenon which had been discussed by earlier authors as the supervenience or dependence of goodness and other ethical predicates. Moore, we recall, had pointed out that an object can be good only by virtue of other character- istics which it possesses. It makes sense to talk about the presence or absence of a non-natural property only in relation to the natural properties of the thing in question. Toulmin's claim that to speak of the truth or falsity of a moral judgement is always and necessarily to speak of its relation to certain factual statements or "reasons" is indeed very similar to all this. But his disagreements with Moore soon became evident. Moore's further point was that, in spite of the fact of supervenience, it was nevertheless not the case that goodness was simply identical with certain natural properties or that 'good' can be defined in naturalistic terms. There is a dependence between goodness and natural properties, but this dependence is peculiar: it is somehow weaker than analytic and stronger than causal dependence. What then *is* the nature of this dependence? To that question Moore had no satisfactory answer to give and consequently he could not explain how moral judgements can be supported by reasons. Stevenson made a renewed effort to get to the bottom of the relation between facts and values in order to explain how reasons operate in ethics. His theory concerning this relation was not metaphysical like Moore's, but psychological and causal. But his theory, as we have seen, could not explain adequately the place of reason in ethics either. Moore, in order to explain moral reasoning, was looking for a "real" relation between facts and values; Steven- son, in the Humean fashion, claimed that the relation was merely psychological association.

The novelty of Toulmin's approach lay in his claim that, in order to explain moral reasoning, we do not have to look for *any* sort of relation between facts and values on which ethical inferences are founded. All we have to do is to get clear about the rules by reference to which such inferences are drawn. It is in this connexion that his claim that to say that a moral judgement is true is simply to say that it has good reasons has to be understood. A moral judge- ment does not reflect a fact of some sort, something existing in its own right. For Moore and Stevenson it does. For Moore this fact, this something existing in its own right, was the presence of a non-natural property in an object, for Stevenson it was a psychological state in the subject. According to Toulmin, all this was superfluous and misleading "theorizing". All we have to do is to pay careful attention to the conventional links between moral judgements and factual assertions which are embodied in the practice of moral reasoning and everything will fall into its place. Toulmin claimed that what we need is not a theory of truth of moral judgements but only to get clear about the method which we in fact use for deciding which of these judgements are worthy of belief. He was thus interested only in the criteria of truth which men actually employ in ethics.

According to Toulmin a moral judgement is true if there is a good reason for it. Now P is a good reason for J only if P itself is true and the inference 'P, consequently J' is valid. By assuming that P is true, we are thus left with the validity of the inference 'P, consequently J' as the criterion for the truth of J. The validity of moral argument and the truth of a moral judgement thus come, in practice, to the same thing. Toulmin did not claim that to say that a moral judgement is true is exactly the same thing as to say that it has good reasons. If a moral judgement has good reasons, then we merely have a good reason for *saying* that it is true. Thus what Toulmin has to say concerning the truth of moral judgements is really compatible with any theory of truth including the correspondence theory. The holder of that theory *may* hold that although to say that S is true is to say that it corresponds to facts, the criterion or reason for *saying* that S is true, that is, that it corresponds to facts, is its having a good reason. But Toulmin would find this rather uninteresting; he believed that the search for a theory or definition of truth had been a misguided philosophical task (*PRE*, 72–74). Instead of asking 'What is truth?' or 'What does "true" mean?' he recommended that we ask a question like 'What kinds of things make a conclusion worthy of belief?' (*PRE*, 74). In other words, what are needed are criteria of truth and not "philosophical theories" of truth. His conclusion with regard to truth is thus very much like his conclusion with regard to goodness: we must not ask what goodness is or what 'good' means but what are the criteria or good reasons for saying such things as 'This is good'.

In order to appreciate the full force of Toulmin's views, we must follow his arguments in some detail. He believed that we can throw some light on the nature of moral reasoning through the analogy with a word game.

In my childhood, we used to play a game with the following rule: starting from the letter A, and working through the alphabet, one had to make up sentences of the form:

> I love my love with an A, because she is artful;
> I hate her with an A, because she is arch;
> I take her to the 'Anchor'
> And feed her on artichokes;
> She comes from Aberdeen,
> And her name is Agnes Anstruther.

. . . .

According to the rule of the game, only some of the possible reasons one might give for 'loving-with-an-A', or 'hating-with-an-A' are to be accepted. That your love is 'bashful' or 'comic' is a bad reason to give, either for 'loving-her-with-an-A' or for 'hating-her-with-an-A'; that she is 'awkward' or 'ambidextrous' is a good reason for either. Good reasons and bad reasons, correct and incorrect inferences, sound and unsound arguments, all are decided in this case by the rule of the game. (*PRE*, 81.)

Let us see how, *à la* Toulmin, the question of truth and falsity may be decided with regard to the utterances made in the course of such a game. "Statements" like 'I love my love with an A', 'I hate her with an A', &c., are "true" if there are "good reasons" for them. A good reason for an assertion is, we have said, one that is itself true and from which that assertion follows via a valid inference. In this game, the reasons: 'she is artful', 'she is arch', &c., in order to be good reasons, must be true in the sense of being meaningful or grammatically correct as English phrases. If we did not use meaningful and correct English, the game could not even get started. This corresponds to the idea that the truth or falsity of a moral judgement can be meaningfully questioned or asserted only if reference is made to some true factual premises. Without any facts at our disposal, moral reasoning would be vitiated from the very beginning. Within the framework of Toulmin's game, questions like 'Is "I love my love with an A" true?' (or 'Is there a good reason for "I love my love with an A"?') thus boil down to questions like 'Is "She is artful", therefore "I love my love with an A" a valid inference?' And those questions are answered by finding out whether the "inferences" in question are in accordance with the rules of the game or not. 'Is "I love my love with an A" (or some other such "statement") true?' is thus, in the end, decided with reference to the rules of the game.

Let us now apply this analogy to Toulmin's theory of moral reasoning as we have outlined it in the preceding section. 'Is the moral judgement J true?' By making the assumption that we know the relevant facts (P), this becomes 'Is there a valid inference from P to J?' If the case clearly comes under an established moral principle, the answer is quickly given. In doubting that answer, one would be behaving like a person who, in the above game, after it has been pointed out to him that 'artful' does begin with the letter 'A', still insisted that 'I love my love with an A' is not "true" because 'she is artful' is not a "good reason" for it. He would simply put himself out of the game. On the other hand, if our case did not clearly come under an established rule and constituted a test case, or if our case concerned the moral rightness of a maxim or principle itself, we would have to evoke the principle of harmony. But, Toulmin declared, the question *is* decidable. Once we have found out that the contemplated action or the principle in question is conducive to the harmony of interests, there is no more room for further (moral) argument. To suppose otherwise, so Toulmin claimed, is again, to put ourselves out of the game.

Now, even if moral reasoning is a language game in the sense that the truth of moral judgements is a matter settled by reference to rules, I shall argue that where Toulmin went wrong was in the choice of these rules. There is no reason to believe that in not accepting the principle of harmony as the ultimate rule for moral discourse, we are putting ourselves outside of morality. In the guise of presenting a logical thesis about moral language Toulmin was either merely making an empirical generalization about social practices or offering a moral recommendation of his own.

4. *The Function of Moral Discourse*

Toulmin pointed out that the rules of the above word game are "comparatively arbitrary" since the whole game is "comparatively pointless". But, he went on to say, "all our more typical modes of reasoning are far from pointless, and the rules for distinguishing 'good' reasoning from 'bad' are correspondingly far from arbitrary" (*PRE*, 82). According to Toulmin there is an "intimate connection" between such rules, that is, the "logic of a mode of reasoning", and the point which that mode of reasoning has or the function or purpose which it serves. His method in trying to discover the logic of moral discourse was therefore to consider its point, function, or purpose. As opposed to the "narrow" views of truth and validity which, according to him, underlaid the theories of Moore and Stevenson, Toulmin advocated the doctrine of the "versatility of reason", and held that

every mode of reasoning, every type of sentence, and (if one is particular) every single sentence will have its own logical criteria, to be discovered by examining its individual, peculiar uses. (*PRE*, 83.)

These last points are ambiguous. Two separate questions may be raised about the use, function, or purpose of a mode of discourse. One is logical, the other empirical and factual. If, for example, we said that the use, function, or purpose of moral judgements or moral discourse is non-descriptive, this would be a logical point. If what we said is true, there would be nothing that any individual could do to change this circumstance. He could not decide to use moral language in some other way. If he tried to use words like 'good' and 'ought', and sentences like 'X is good' or 'A ought to do Y', exclusively for describing objects or situations and was successful in his attempt, he would not have changed the use or function or moral language; he would have merely stopped using moral language.

On the other hand, we can talk about the use, function, or purpose of a mode of discourse in a quite different sense. Having once agreed upon the logical features of the type of language we want to call moral, we can then go on to make statements about the aims and purposes which people try to promote by using that language. It is also possible to proceed to such considerations without first having the answers to questions about the logical use and function of moral language. Moral language could be ostensively identified simply as the language in which terms like 'good', 'right', 'ought', 'moral obligation', &c., function in conspicuous and crucial ways. But in either case, our statements about the use, function, and purpose of moral language might be only contingent empirical generalizations. How well established such generalizations are would depend on how much, and how firmly, people agree in their interests and aims which they try to promote by using moral language. But it is always possible that an individual, contrary to all general practices, will use moral language for promoting aims not shared by others. We do not misuse moral language merely by being non-conformists, that is, by not promoting the same purposes and aims as others do. On the other hand, it is possible for an individual to misuse moral language regardless of his purposes. What would be wrong in that case would be his language and not necessarily his aims. He could be misusing moral language for any aim or purpose. It is conceivable that a whole community, or even the better part of mankind, would lapse into a misunderstanding concerning moral language and begin logically to misuse it. And if this misuse is radical enough, then, in one sense, morality could be said to have disappeared from that community or from the face of the earth. But at the same time, people could still continue having certain uniform purposes, interests, and aims, although they could not any longer use moral language to pursue them.

We can clarify this distinction between the two senses of 'use' by applying it to Toulmin's word game. The language of that game, that is, the sentences uttered in accordance with certain rules, have, logically speaking, a use or function in the sense that they constitute the way to play that particular game. Uses and functions are in this sense determined by rules and perhaps there is no harm in illustrating this by saying that 'because she is arch' has the use of or functions as a reason for 'I hate her with an A'. But the language of "Loving my Love with an A" may have uses and serve purposes in quite another sense. I may say, for example, 'I feed her on ammonia' with the purpose of provoking laughter or in order to insult someone. And this use of my words would have nothing to do with the rules or conventions of the game. These two types of use involve two entirely different kinds of impropriety or failure. Whether 'I feed her on ammonia' is a good or bad "reason" depends on the rules of the game. Whether I manage to be funny or insulting depends on the psychology of the other players.[1]

In this second sense of 'use' the whole game may have a use or purpose. Ordinarily we would play the game for amusement, but we may play it also with the purpose of annoying someone. And in so far as our game has such an external purpose, it is true that its rules are not arbitrary. A given game is a good game for a given purpose only if it in fact serves that purpose well. But what is a good game in this sense is not determined by further rules but depends on the facts of human psychology and what not. And whether or not we have in a given case succeeded in picking the right kind of game hinges not on how well we have conformed to some rules but on such things as our ingenuity, experience, and care.

Now when we compare moral discourse with a word game, it is clear that the harmonization of people's interest can be said to be only an external purpose of that discourse. Such a purpose is not specified by the rules that determine what can and what cannot

---

[1] Toulmin seems to have noticed this distinction but surprisingly did not see its relevance to his own theory. Thus on pp. 198–9 of *PRE* he reproduces the following *Punch* joke:

VICAR (observing Jenkins the grocer, bent over the counter, alternately chewing the end of his pencil and scrawling illegibly on a flour-bag): 'Ah, Jenkins! Engaged on a complex arithmetical computation, I see!'
JENKINS (straightening up and scratching the back of his head): 'No, y'r Rev'rence, 't bain't anything loike thet. Oi be jest reck'ning Mrs. Will'ums's groc'ry bill.'
VICAR (exploding with laughter and leaving the shop in a hurry): !!!

and remarks about it:

What makes Jenkins' scrawling an 'arithmetical computation' is the way in which he manipulates the symbols, not the purpose for which he does so.

legitimately, that is, correctly, be said within moral discourse. Similarly, the use of a moral judgement can be said to be to contribute to the harmony of people's interests only in the sense in which the use of the words 'I feed her on ammonia' within Toulmin's word game may be to be funny or insulting. In trying to harmonize people's interests, I am concerned with bringing about real results, I am not merely trying to follow a set of rules or conventions.

If our aim is to amuse ourselves we may or may not do well by choosing to play "I Love my Love with an A". This depends on what in fact amuses us. Similarly, if our aim is to promote social harmony we may or may not do well by engaging in moral discourse. This depends on what in fact promotes such harmony. Perhaps it is true that if we want to bring about social harmony, we *would* do well to use moral language as a means for accomplishing that purpose. People no doubt have regarded moral language as a good means for promoting social harmony; this may account for its persistent and widespread use. It may even be that moral language was developed for the very purpose of promoting social harmony. But the concern with social harmony may only explain the genesis and the continued occupation with moral language; it cannot be a part of the rules or conventions of that language. It may explain why the conventions of moral language are what they are and why men engage in linguistic performances in accordance with those conventions, but it is itself not one of those conventions.

Consequently, when our aim is to bring out what are the conventions or rules which determine the uses which utterances within moral language have, our concern should be with entirely different matters. We should then be anxious to point out and discuss such things as that moral judgements are used for praising and blaming, prescribing, commending, &c. As opposed to these uses of moral language, its use for the promotion of social harmony is something external to it. This fact becomes evident once more when we reflect that, for example, the descriptive language of science can also be used for promoting social harmony. In fact, in some situations it may be the case that the chances for a harmonious coexistence among men would be greatly enhanced if men were willing to meddle less with the affairs of others by the use of moral language: in other words, if they were to abstain from moral praising and blaming, prescribing, commending, and condemning.

5. *Toulmin's Thesis is not a Logical Thesis*

As against Moore, and in agreement with Stevenson, Toulmin held that goodness and rightness are not properties. Toulmin agreed with Stevenson that moral judgements are not used essentially for describing, but for influencing behaviour. Thus he wrote:

> It is a wicked man who beats his wife; but to say that he is wicked is not just to say that he beats his wife—or, for that matter, to assert any other fact about him. It is to *condemn* him for it. (*PRE*, 55.)

. . . .

> If I say 'meekness is a virtue' . . . I am encouraging my hearers to feel and behave differently. (*PRE*, 55.)

With such remarks Stevenson could easily agree. Toulmin, in fact, goes even further in his agreement with what he misleadingly calls the imperativist but really is the emotivist doctrine:

> Unquestionably, many of the facts to which our philosopher [i.e., the "imperativist"] will draw attention in presenting his case are true and important. In practice, moral exhortation is often no more than straight persuasion or intimidation. Ethical remarks are, indeed, made with the intention that hearers should act or reflect on them. Certainly they evince our feelings: what we call 'wicked' horrifies us, the 'admirable' gratifies us. (*PRE*, 49.)

However, for Toulmin, this was not the end of the story:

> Ethical words are used, at one extreme, in fully developed, logically complex judgments designed to harmonise the aims and actions of the members of a community. At the other extreme, they appear in unpondered, logically crude interjections—exclamations and commands—which release the emotions of the speaker, or act like goads upon the hearer. (*PRE*, 166.)

We are now in the position to spot easily the confusion contained in the above three passages. In discussing the functions of ethical language Toulmin is mixing up two things which we have seen it is essential to keep apart. On the one hand there is the use of ethical terms in linguistic acts or conventional performances; on the other, there is the use of those terms in bringing about real effects in the minds and actions of men. In discussing the logical features of moral language only the former sort of thing is relevant. The following two lists compiled from the three quotations above point out Toulmin's confusion:

I	II
assert	persuade
condemn	intimidate
encourage	evince
command	horrify
exhort	gratify
	harmonize
	exclaim
	release emotions
	goad

Only the first of these lists mentions performative uses or illucutionary acts; the second list is made up instead of names for things done with language only indirectly, for causal uses or perlocutionary acts.[1]

Stevenson, we recall, was guilty of the same confusion. While he ought to have been discussing the kinds of conventional or rule-governed linguistic acts which we perform in using moral language, he was talking about the sorts of causal effects often produced by the use of that language.[2] The contrast we ought to point out in

---

[1] Cf. pp. 27–29 above.

[2] Strictly speaking, Stevenson and Toulmin are not guilty of *exactly* the same confusion. What we have called the causal uses of language (Austin's perlocutionary acts) presuppose what we have called the performative uses of language (Austin's illocutionary acts). Toulmin's harmonization of interests is a causal use of moral language in this sense. It presupposes the performative uses of that language for praising, blaming, commending, prescribing, &c. For Toulmin the purpose of moral language is to promote social harmony by praising, blaming, commending, &c. Stevenson, on the other hand, speaks of the *direct* production of effects on the minds of men through the emotive "impact" that moral terms have. For this reason we said that it was hard to see how Stevenson, particularly in his discussion of "independent emotive meaning" was talking about the use of language in any sense since no element of convention and rule, of "understanding" would enter in at all. But perhaps this distinction cannot be rigidly observed. It is hard to see how absolutely "brute" facts can have any effect on the minds of men; perhaps a degree of rule, convention,

criticizing Stevenson's views is the one illustrated by our two lists. Toulmin, however, had an entirely different point in mind. He concentrated on things mentioned solely in our second list, that is, the causal uses of moral language, and was anxious to single out what is merely one sort of causal effect that can be brought about by using that language. All sorts of effects may be brought about by using moral language, but, so was Toulmin's claim, ultimately all these things must serve the harmonization of human interests. For Toulmin, fully developed moral judgements are designed to have a *certain kind* of final effect on behaviour—namely, the harmonization of "the aims and actions of the members of a community". Therefore, so Toulmin argued against Stevenson, when somebody says (in the full moral sense) 'X is right', then to show that he in fact did like or have a pro-attitude toward the act in question is not to exhibit the only reason which that assertion is capable of having. Eventually, when the occasion requires, we must "prove" that assertion by showing that the thing in question (an action or a social practice) contributes to the harmony of interests in the whole society. According to Toulmin, a person would not be in the legitimate position to pass a moral judgement unless he is able, in principle, to deliver such a proof.

But how did Toulmin arrive at the conclusion that the kind of proof which is required in order to support a moral judgement consists in showing that an action or practice contributes to social harmony? He claimed that this conclusion was reached by studying the purpose or function of moral language. The nature of the moral proof, Toulmin claimed, is determined by the function or purpose

"interpretation" has to be always present. An interesting borderline case between causal use of language (properly speaking) and the direct production of an emotional impact is provided by Wittgenstein:

> 498. When I say that the orders "Bring me sugar" and "Bring me milk" make sense, but not the combination "Milk me sugar", that does not mean that the utterance of this combination of words has no effect. And if its effect is that the other person stares at me and gapes, I don't on that account call it the order to stare and gape, even if that was precisely the effect that I wanted to produce. (*Philosophical Investigations*, New York: Macmillan, 1953 [Oxford: Blackwell]).

In what way is the other person's gaping the effect of my use (performative, illocutionary) of language? Yet, it involves language (rule, convention, "understanding") in a way in which my producing just a big noise would not have.

which moral language serves. It is in this step of his argument that the fatal confusion is involved.

There is a sense in which the logic of expressions is determined by their functions or purposes. The formula 'I approve X', for example, is used by the speaker for the purposes of approving, endorsing, backing, entitling, &c. The rules which constitute the "logic of approval" are just those rules or conventions which enable us to use the words 'I approve X' for these and similar purposes. If I observe those rules, then, as a matter of course, I am using the expression, 'I approve X' for the purpose of expressing approval, giving an endorsement, &c. But there is nothing in those rules which would guarantee that if I observe them, I am using the expression 'I approve X' for approving or endorsing rightly, or for approving certain things rather than others, or for promoting social harmony. To use the expression 'I approve' for the latter purposes involves choice and effort; to use it for expressing approval does not. Consequently, the observance of linguistic or logical rules alone does not guarantee that a given approval is justified or supported by good reasons. In order to justify or "prove" a given approval, rules and principles of an entirely different sort are needed—rules and principles which are concerned with substantive matters of human conduct and not just with linguistic propriety.[1]

Parallel remarks can be made about expressions like 'This is good', 'This is right', or 'You ought to do that'. They are used for approving, endorsing, praising, prescribing, entitling, imputing obligation, enjoining, admonishing, issuing behests, exhorting, &c., &c. We are not at the present concerned with what exactly are the performative forces of such expressions in their moral or in their non-moral senses. But for whatever kinds of linguistic acts or uses such expressions do have a potential, they must be given a further direction which is not already there by virtue of their simply being parts of language as a system of communication. If I use these expressions correctly, that is, in accordance with linguistic rules, I will have used them for the purpose of endorsing or issuing a

---

[1] This point has been made very clearly by Hare and we shall discuss it again when we come to his views in the next chapter. How the expression 'I approve X' can be supported by reasons will be discussed in detail in chapter 5.

behest or exhorting, but the correctness of their use does not require that I have used them for the purpose of endorsing certain things rather than others, issuing certain behests rather than others or exhorting people to do this rather than that. Or, conversely, in order to realize the purpose of endorsing, issuing a behest or exhorting, that is, in order to perform these linguistic acts at all, I must conform to certain linguistic or logical rules. But in my effort to endorse one particular thing rather than another, issue a certain behest rather than another, exhort someone to do this rather than that, I do more than merely try to conform to such rules. It is clearly this latter sort of thing I am doing if I use moral language for the purpose of promoting social harmony. And the question of whether in so doing I am justified in a given case goes beyond the question of linguistic propriety. It is a substantive question of proper conduct and not a mere question of using moral language correctly.

We may clarify what we have just said through an analogy. Words and expressions are like tools. A tool or an instrument has its own proper use or function; so does a word or expression. The micrometer is used for measuring minute distances; the expression 'I approve' is used for approving, the expression 'You ought' for exhorting or what not. In one sense, in order to use the micrometer at all, we must use it for measuring minute distances. Of course, we can use a micrometer as a paperweight, or as a doorstep, but that would not be using a micrometer in the same sense; it would not be using it for what it is designed to be used for. If we use a micrometer as a doorstep, then, in a sense, we are not really using it at all. We would not be using it *as* a micrometer; we would not be using it for the purpose it is conventionally used for. In the same sense we would not be really using a book if we used a book for pretending that we are not paying attention—and held it upside down. There is a sense in which it is necessary to use the micrometer for measuring minute distances. It is the sense in which it is not necessary to use it for whatever it *can* be used for through its being a mere physical object of a certain shape and weight. It is also the sense in which it is not necessary to use the micrometer well or efficiently or for doing good rather than harm.

Similarly, in order to use the expression 'I approve', it is necessary to use it for approving. Again, there is a sense in which we would not be using that expression at all unless we used it for approving: approving is what the expression is, or is meant to be, used for. In this sense it is not necessary to use that expression to make a line in a poem rhyme with the next which ends with 'move', or in order to give an example of an English phrase. Nor is it, in that sense, necessary to use the expression 'I approve' for approving rightly or modestly, or for approving certain things rather than certain others. Using the expression 'I approve' in these latter sorts of ways involves our choice in a manner in which using it for approving does not. And again, similar remarks would be true, *mutatis mutandis*, of expressions like 'This is good' or 'You ought'.

It is thus evident that harmonization of interests cannot be the purpose or function which belongs to expressions like 'This is good' or 'You ought to do that' necessarily, in the above sense of that word. It is a contingent matter that such phrases are sometimes used for the purpose of harmonizing interests: it is certainly possible to use these expressions without using them for this purpose.

Toulmin, as we saw, seems to have been aware of the distinction which we have drawn between the two senses in which a mode of discourse may be said to have a purpose, but he certainly failed to realize its full importance for his own theory. The following passage involves what we have called the logical sense in which a type of language or discourse may be said to have a use or purpose.

Although factual reasons (R) may be good reasons for an ethical conclusion (E), to assert the conclusion is not just to assert the reasons, or indeed anything of the same logical type as R. It is to declare that one ought to approve of, or pursue, or do something-or-other. It is a wicked man who beats his wife; but to say that he is wicked is not just to say that he beats his wife—or, for that matter, to assert any other fact about him. It is to *condemn* him for it. (*PRE*, 55.)

Moral judgements are then of a different "logical type" from factual statements because they are used for such things as "declaring that one ought to approve of, or pursue, or do, something-or-other", and for condemning people as opposed to asserting facts about them. But to say that the use or function of moral judgements is sometimes condemning people has only a contingent connexion with the notion that the use or function of moral judgements is to harmonize people's interests. We may condemn people without condemning them for not contributing to social harmony. Uses or functions like condemning, commending, prescribing, and "declaring that one ought to approve of, or pursue, or do, something-or-other" may mark off the logical type to which moral judgements belong, but harmonizing interests cannot be said to do the same sort of thing at all.

What is contained in the last passage quoted is virtually all Toulmin said that can be looked upon as dealing straightforwardly with the use and purpose of moral discourse in a logical sense. His central thesis about moral language, on the other hand—the thesis that the use, function, or purpose of that language is to bring about social harmony, or "the least conflict of interests attainable under the circumstances" (PRE, 224)—cannot be looked upon as a logical thesis at all. I shall argue that this thesis must be interpreted either as a contingent empirical generalization about the aims or goals which people in fact have in mind and try to pursue when they use moral language, or as a recommendation concerning the criteria of application of such words as 'good' and 'right'. In the first case Toulmin's thesis would merely amount to a description of the standards on which social morality is in fact often based; in the second it would constitute a normative but dogmatic prescription of moral standards for which, as a morally normative claim, Toulmin offers no arguments at all. In neither case can it be looked upon as a theory about the logic of moral discourse. We shall discuss each of these possible interpretations in turn.

Toulmin seemed to accept the idea that moral terms and judgements are non-descriptive in character. This idea first came into prominence, as we saw in the preceding chapter, with Stevenson, who called the non-descriptive element of such terms and judgements their emotive meaning. Since then not only have new names been coined, but the whole idea of a special brand of meaning has itself undergone a significant transformation. Philosophers are still willing to speak of descriptive meaning of moral terms for which other names are cognitive meaning and factual meaning. But they have by and large abandoned the term 'emotive meaning' because of its psychological sound. They are more apt to speak of evaluative, prescriptive, or normative meaning. The important point that this shift in terminology reflects is the recognition that in talking about linguistic meaning of any kind we are always talking about some-thing governed by rules. Stevenson's emotive meaning was a thing to which the concept of rules was quite irrelevant. We have seen that the inadequacies of Stevenson's theory stemmed largely from his purely psychological conception of meaning. Because of that conception, he could give no satisfactory answer to the question of how the two types of meaning are related and consequently in his theory, moral judgements became incapable of being supported by reasons in a logical sense.

Toulmin's starting-point was more promising. He did not, or at least claimed not to, overlook the importance of rules. In a general way he seems to have agreed with Stevenson that moral language is very different from descriptive language. But his manner of trying to bring out this difference was quite unlike Stevenson's. We saw that he criticized Stevenson because, according to him, the latter still adhered, although perhaps in a merely vestigial form, to the notion that ethical terms have meaning because they refer to something.[1] Toulmin, on the other hand, professed to conceive of the meanings of moral terms in the Wittgensteinian manner as their uses in the "language-game" of ethics and explicitly rejected the referential theory of meaning as applicable to them. The Wittgen-steinian view of the nature of language is very similar in spirit to the one developed in greater detail and more systematically by Austin and which we ourselves are trying to make use of throughout this book. It may be characterized briefly as follows. The meaning of a speech-act or utterance is its use, the function that it performs in communication. To speak of kinds of meaning would be there-fore to speak of kinds of uses to which an expression or a form of words may be put. And since the use that an expression has depends on the rules or conventions which connect it with other expressions, or with bits of verbal as well as non-verbal behaviour, we can, in a

[1] See pp. 100–1 above.

derivative sense, speak of the meaning of a form of words or expression as the set of rules which govern it. Through such rules utterances as well as non-verbal acts are woven into whole activities or "language games".[1]

In effect, what Toulmin tried to do was to characterize the language-game of ethics, to spell out its rules and to distinguish it from such language games as scientific description and explanation. Such an approach can indeed be illuminating, but in Toulmin's hands it became seriously misleading. He claimed that the rules of moral discourse are fixed by its purpose, but we have seen in detail how this claim involved a serious confusion.[2] In general, Toulmin expected to get more out of rules than they can yield. Following linguistic rules, just as following the rules of a game, assures success only in the sense of correctness of procedure. I may be following the rules or criteria of application which govern the application of the expression 'horse', and still make mistakes. I may not have been in a good position to make good use of those criteria: I might have been careless, the light might have been bad, someone may have been deliberately deceiving me, &c. Following the linguistic rules governing the application of empirical terms does not automatically assure the truth of our assertions. There are rules of a different kind, rules of scientific procedure or of common sense, the following of which may avoid some of these eventualities. But surely, there can be no set of rules that would guard against all of them. Furthermore, the rules of language and of method themselves

[1] See Wittgenstein, *Philosophical Investigations.*
[2] The necessary distinctions we made in the course of our discussions, (1) between the internal and the external purpose or use of a language or mode of discourse and (2) between the performative (illocutionary) use and the causal (perlocutionary) use of expressions, are also pointed out by Wittgenstein as, for example, in the following passages:

492. To invent a language could mean to invent an instrument for a particular purpose on the basis of the laws of nature (or consistently with them); but it also has the other sense, analogous to that in which we speak of the invention of a game.

496. Grammar does not tell us how language must be constructed in order to fulfil its purpose, in order to have such-and-such an effect on human beings. . . .

497. The rules of grammar may be called 'arbitrary', if that is to mean that the *aim* of the grammar is nothing but that of the language. . . . (ibid.)

are not fixed once and for all. Adjustments may be required in our criteria and methods by recalcitrant experiences.

Similarly, the following of the logical rules that govern moral language does not assure that we will always call only those actions right which really are right. The sort of thing that linguistic rules tell me is that 'right' is applied to "voluntary" actions, that in saying 'This is right' I am commending, &c. Beyond this I must make use of rules of a different sort—moral rules. Following these rules, perhaps comparable to rules of scientific procedure and of common sense, will guarantee some measure of success. But here, even more so than with purely factual terms, the rules cannot guard against all possible ways of still going wrong. Moral rules are notoriously full of gaps and often inconsistent with one another. There are many cases where the rules themselves must go on trial. There is no set of rules that can assure the soundness of all our moral judgements. Philosophers have often tried to sum up in a formula the rules that assure just that. And Toulmin's principle of social harmony is to be understood as another attempt in this direction. People have largely given up the belief in the possibility of a perfect scientific organon. It is strange that such a belief still lingers on with regard to morality. If anything, such a belief is wildly more hazardous here.

Toulmin, although he granted, or even emphasized, that moral judgements are essentially non-descriptive, claimed that they are nevertheless capable of being supported by (logical) reasons; but in the process of developing his theory he really neglected the evaluative or normative force of these judgements. His theory of good reasons, as we have already pointed out, concerns merely the criteria of application of moral terms. That something was left out by his account seems to have been recognized by Toulmin himself:

> Of course, 'This practice would involve the least conflict of interests attainable under the circumstances' does not *mean* the same as 'This would be the right practice'; nor does 'This way of life would be more harmoniously satisfying' *mean* the same as 'This would be better'. But in each case, the first statement is *a good reason* for the second: the 'ethically neutral' fact is *a good reason* for the 'gerundive' moral judgement. (*PRE*, 224.)

The meaning of the term 'right' is not identical with the meaning of the phrase 'involves the least conflict of interest attainable' and the meaning of the term 'good' is not identical with the meaning of the phrase 'harmoniously satisfying'. How do we know then that statements containing the latter phrases are good reasons for moral judgements containing the term 'right' and 'good' respectively? What is the connexion between, say, 'right' and 'involves the least conflict attainable'? Why should we settle on 'involves the least conflict' and 'harmoniously satisfying' as the criteria of application of moral terms and not on some others such as 'performs efficiently as a member of its species', 'comes later in the course of evolution', 'is approved by most members of the society', 'is conducive to the welfare of the lower classes'?

Toulmin's choice has the air of being not just one alternative among many others. This may be in part due to his use of words like 'harmony' and 'least conflict' in formulating it. Such expressions, it may be maintained, are themselves value-expressions. But apart from this, what makes Toulmin's choice special is its intimate connexion with a fundamental sociological fact. It is quite possible that, say, the term 'duty' is often applied only to those modes of action that are conducive to social harmony. In fact, if the only moving and cohesive force in society is "interest", then what is called an individual's social duty always follows the utilitarian principle; nothing will be called 'duty' in the name of the society if it does not contribute to the satisfaction of the interests of its members. We must agree with Toulmin that socially accepted morality is always, or at least usually, determined by the principle of harmonization of interests. But certainly, this is not a logical point about moral language. It is possible that the recognized social duties might be quite different in nature. It may be true that often in trying to show that X is somebody's duty, we argue that X is conducive to social harmony. But there is nothing inevitable in this. Clearly, there are (and have been) societies in which the recognized duties are such that they undermine harmony in the interests of their members. In fact the only society in which this would not happen to any degree, would be an ideally utilitarian one. But it would be indeed odd to assert that only in such a society would people know how to use moral terms and arguments properly.

Toulmin claimed that his answer to the question "What is it in an ethical discussion that makes a reason a good reason, or an argument a valid argument?" did not constitute a "theory of ethics" (*PRE*, 160). He claimed that he simply "tried to describe the occasions on which we are in fact prepared to call judgements 'ethical' and decisions 'moral', and the part which reasoning plays on such occasions" (*PRE*, 160). His philosophy was not a "theory", but a "description of facts", of the "familiar, unquestionable facts of usage" (*PRE*, 144). And one of the things which, according to him, followed from these "facts of usage" was that moral language has for its purpose or function the harmonization of interests.

Is Toulmin's thesis that the function or purpose of moral discourse is the harmonization of interests then a contingent empirical generalization about the aims and goals which people often pursue by using moral language? If so, the pursuit of harmony of interests is just another fact about human behaviour in societies which might well have been otherwise. And it would be a fact which conceivably *ought* not to exist. We are free, with good reason or not, to say that people ought not always to pursue the harmony of interests. This gets us into the second alternative for interpreting Toulmin's thesis, namely, that it is itself a moral recommendation.

6. *Science and Ethics, Toulmin's Thesis as a Moral Recommendation*

Toulmin believed that his thesis that the purpose or function of moral discourse is to harmonize people's interests was a logical one. We have claimed, to the contrary, that it was either an empirical generalization about the aims which people in fact often pursue when they use moral language, or that it was itself a moral recommendation. In the preceding section we have been concerned with the first of these alternatives. Before turning to the second, let us take a look at the analogy which, according to Toulmin, exists between science and ethics.

In both science and ethics, he claimed, there is a contrast between "fully-fledged judgements" and "direct reports of experience" (*PRE*, 123-4). In science this contrast was explained as follows:

The fully-fledged scientific judgment, 'This stick is really straight', is therefore in sharp contrast to the more-or-less exclamatory expression of surprise at what you see, feel, smell, or taste. And, to be 'true', it must follow correctly from a theory which accounts for all normal people's sense-experiences in similar situations—'accounting for them' here having the force of 'showing that they were to be expected'. (*PRE*, 123.)

Toulmin went on to claim that the counterpart of this distinction can be found in ethics:

The fully-fledged moral judgment can similarly be contrasted to an immediate, unconsidered report or exclamation. A pleasant surprise, for example, may lead us to exclaim in any of five equivalent ways: 'Hurrah!', 'Good!', 'I am pleased', 'That seems good news' and 'That is good news'. The differences between these five remarks again depend on the balance reached between rhetorical force and articulateness. The first is more forceful than articulate, vigorously evincing our feelings; the last more articulate than forceful, expressing a quieter satisfaction. Logically, however, they are equivalent: all act as direct reports of our feelings, and all lead an observer to the same conclusion—that, provided we are not dissembling or making a verbal mistake, the news pleases us. (*PRE*, 123-4.)

The central point about the distinction between "direct reports" or "exclamations" (Toulmin seems to lump these two together in spite of their at least seeming differences) and "fully-fledged judgements" was, according to Toulmin, that while the former are "incorrigible", the latter are not. He claimed that utterances like 'Hurrah!', 'Good!', 'I am pleased', 'That seems good news', and 'That is good news',

like the direct reports of our sense experience, . . . are 'incorrigible': no question of truth and falsity, evidence and reasoning, can arise over them. (*PRE*, 124.)

And, by contrast, he maintained,

The fully-fledged moral judgment, like the fully-fledged scientific judgment, is far from 'incorrigible'. It also is (in some sense) the fruit of all our experience . . . and can be disputed accordingly. It, too, will have (in some sense) to 'account for' all our relevant experiences, enabling us to sort out those cases in which things that seemed to us good (or right) were really good (or right) from those in which our feelings were a bad guide, what seemed good being really bad, and what seemed wrong being right. In ethics, as in science, incorrigible but conflicting reports of personal experience (sensible or emotional) are replaced by judgments aiming at universality and impartiality— about the 'real value', the 'real colour', the 'real shape' of an object, rather than the shape, colour or value one would ascribe to it on the basis of immediate experience alone. (*PRE*, 124–5.)

The points gathered from here and other similar passages, may be summarized as follows. In science, we start with direct incorrigible reports or expressions of sense-experiences and construct a theory or system which has the aim of "correlating" or "accounting for" them by showing that those experiences "were to be expected". And a "fully-fledged" scientific judgement is true only when it follows from such a theory or system. In normative ethics, again, we start with direct incorrigible reports of experiences, this time, however, not of sense-experiences but of feelings of pleasure and displeasure, of satisfaction, rightness, obligation, &c. We then develop a theory or system—an ethic—which "accounts for" and "correlates" these feelings and similarly, a "fully-fledged" moral judgement is "true" if it follows from such a theory or system. In ethics, however, the purpose that we have in mind is not prediction but social harmony.

Because of this last point, Toulmin seems to have been forced to say, the "direct reports of experience" relevant for ethics are not, after all, quite as incorrigible as those relevant for science. There is, he claimed, a significant difference between science and normative ethics. A scientific explanation, which shows what or how an object really is, will not change the "corresponding experience": the object will continue to *look* just as before. But the type of reasoning which provides an answer to a question like " 'Is this *really* good (right, obligatory)?'—may . . . change the corresponding experiences (our feelings of satisfaction or of obligation)" (*PRE*, 127). I shall attempt to show that Toulmin's whole manner of making a comparison between science and ethics is misleading.

First of all there are some ambiguities to be cleared up. There have been many philosophers who have held that there are incorrigible sentences. However, these philosophers held that 'incorrigible' means 'certainly true and incapable of being shown to be false'. Toulmin's view, on the other hand, seems to be that 'incorrigible' means 'incapable of being true or false'. One class of sentences which many philosophers have held to be incorrigible in the former sense are variously called "sense-datum statements", "atomic propositions", or "protocol-sentences". These were held to be incorrigible because they are direct or immediate reports of bits of experience. They are nevertheless reports, that is, statements about or descriptions of experience and therefore capable of being assessed as true or false; although the one and only criterion for assessing them in this way is whether someone or another candidly has asserted them.

Toulmin does not distinguish between reports and exclamations. Now exclamations, such as 'Hurrah!', 'Good!', 'Gosh!', 'Good grief!' cannot be incorrigible in the sense that what they report or describe cannot be contested. They do not report or describe anything. They are incorrigible in the sense of being neither true nor false. With regard to them the concept of truth and falsity is irrelevant altogether. Toulmin does not argue the point but it seems that he is assuming that it makes good sense to speak of incorrigibility only in this latter sense. Sense-datum statements and protocol-statements, *if* they are incorrigible, are on a par with exclamations, or are perhaps not statements at all but themselves exclamations. Such a claim would receive some plausibility from the notorious difficulties attached to finding examples of sense-datum statements. Sometimes philosophers have resorted to such artificial constructs as 'Brown here now' which themselves sound like exclamations.

Another ambiguity, bound up with the first, is involved in Toulmin's claim that in both science and in ethics we attempt to replace reports of what merely seems (looks, appears) with assertions concerning what really is.

In both, one encounters a contrast between the 'appearance' and the 'reality'—the scientist distinguishing between the 'apparent' colour of the sun at evening and its 'real' colour (quite apart from atmospheric refraction and so on); the moralist distinguishing those things which are 'really' good, and those actions which are 'really' right, from those things which we simply like and those actions which we simply feel like doing. (*PRE*, 84–85.)

Toulmin claimed that the incorrigible statements or reports which are relevant to science are concerned with what appears, whereas those relevant for ethics are concerned with what seems: 'appears' goes with, for example, colour, but 'seems' goes with value and obligation (*PRE*, 125). In order to keep the parallelism explained in the above passage straight, we must therefore assume that, for Toulmin, what "we simply like" is identical with what seems good and what "we simply feel like doing" is identical with what seems obligatory. But in all this there is a great deal of confusion. "That which is *seemingly* the case", Toulmin himself remarked, "carries with it a strong air of deception, unreality or fraud." But he also said that expressions of what we like and feel are incorrigible. Now how can they be incorrigible if they are "logically equivalent" to saying that it *seems* that this is good or obligatory and if the latter ways of speaking suggest "deception and fraud"?

Let us approach this more systematically. In one sense, phrases like 'X seems (to me) so-and-so' (or 'X looks, appears so-and-so') may be taken to be reports of certain experiences (although, as I shall argue, they can never be taken to be incorrigible reports). In that sense of the words 'seems' and 'looks' it is true that scientific reasoning is not concerned with altering what seems or looks to be the case. But similarly, moral reasoning would then be irrelevant, would not make any difference, to what seems or looks good or obligatory. After I have accepted a scientific explanation, the stick in the water will still *look* bent to me. But also, after I have accepted a moral argument, I might still *feel* reluctant to return the money.

The type of reasoning which provides an answer to a question like 'Is this *really* good (or obligatory)?' need not have anything to do with "changing the corresponding experience". After it has been proved to me that X is good or that Y is obligatory, I can still go on feeling dissatisfaction towards X or still not feel like doing Y.

After such a proof I can no longer be in doubt or uncertain about the goodness of X or the obligatoriness of Y, but such certainty can be quite compatible with any feelings that I might have. In this sense feelings are wayward. Moral reasoning is practical in the sense that it leads to certainty which entails or even constitutes decision. If I know, that is if I am certain, that Y is obligatory, I have, in one sense, decided to do Y.[1] Nonetheless, such a decision does not causally or psychologically determine the whole of my ego. My decision might have been weak and my knowledge shaky. If phrases like 'it looks or seems or appears to me' are taken to be reports of certain atomic incorrigible internal experiences, then scientific reasoning cannot alter what looks or seems to be the case; but similarly moral reasoning cannot then make any difference to what looks or seems good or obligatory.

But to seem to be good need not be to be the object of a certain feeling. And to appear to be bent need not be to be the object of a certain sensory experience. Phrases like 'X seems so-and-so' may be taken in a different sense altogether. They may be taken to express uncertainty and lack of conviction and to contrast with phrases like 'I know' or 'I am certain'. And in that case looks and appearances can be dispelled in both science and ethics. After I have accepted a scientific explanation I shall no longer think that the stick in the water is bent, although it still looks bent. Similarly, after I have accepted a moral argument I shall no longer think that I need not return the money, although I might still feel reluctant to do so.

In so far as 'X seems good' contrasts with 'I know that X is good' (and with 'X is (really) good') it means 'I think X is good'; it expresses a degree of uncertainty and does not report a feeling. To say that X seems good is normally not to say that X is the object of a certain feeling such as pleasure. 'X is pleasing' or 'X pleases me' may be (one type of) evidence for X being (really) good, but to say that X seems good is not to state that evidence. In saying 'X seems good' we merely indicate that there is *some* evidence for saying that X is good but that that evidence is only slight and perhaps unreliable.

---

[1] Cf. Stuart Hampshire and H. L. Hart, 'Decision, Intention and Certainty', *Mind*, vol. lxvii, no. 265 (January, 1958).

In one sense, therefore, the parallel between science and ethics is more thoroughgoing than Toulmin suspected. If phrases like 'X seems so-and-so' are taken to be reports of certain experiences, neither science nor ethics is concerned with changing the mental states that they indicate. On the other hand, if such phrases are taken to express uncertainty or lack of knowledge, then both scientific and ethical reasoning are designed for and indeed capable of "changing the corresponding experiences".

Toulmin claimed that in both science and ethics we start with "incorrigible direct reports" and eventually replace these with "fully-fledged judgements" which are "far from incorrigible". Since, as we saw, Toulmin explained that the incorrigible reports which are relevant to science concern what appears, whereas those relevant to ethics concern what seems, we may list as two candidates for being "incorrigible reports" the following: (1) 'This appears red' which belongs to science and contrasts with 'This (really) is red' and (2) 'This seems obligatory' which belongs to ethics and contrasts with 'This (really) is obligatory'. Now at first sight there seems to be no reason to suppose that either 'This appears red' or 'This seems obligatory' are incorrigible. 'This appears red' may be a way of saying that if certain special circumstances did not prevail, the thing might not look red, and that because of these circumstances one is prevented from knowing its real properties. 'This seems obligatory', in its turn, may be a way of saying in a hesitant manner that the act under consideration is obligatory. It implies that one cannot say, definitely, 'This is obligatory'. Toulmin himself, as we saw, went as far as to suggest that "That which is seemingly the case carries with it a strong air of deception, unreality or fraud."

In order to be at all inclined to think that 'appears' and 'seems' have anything in common (namely the required idea of "incorrigibility" that Toulmin had in mind), we must, as he perhaps did, assimilate them both to 'looks'. But even that will not do. In one sense 'This looks red' is indistinguishable from 'This seems red', in that it expresses or implies hesitancy and is therefore not incorrigible. But it cannot be denied that it also has another sense. It may be taken just to describe the (visual) look of the object and mean 'This has a red look'. Are we now nearer to incorrigibility? I don't think so. We might not be at all happy about 'red' as describing the thing's look. We may feel that it has a warmth, a blush, not rendered by 'red'. We may want to say 'sanguine', or 'coralline', or 'rosy' instead. We are not at all sure exactly what to say. (What *is* the apparent colour of the sun at evening?)

It may be objected that given a sample, say, a ripe strawberry, we can then say for certain whether the object under consideration is like or unlike that sample. 'This looks red', it may be maintained, is to say 'This looks like things (for example, strawberries) which (really) are red'. From this, however, it would also follow that 'This appears red' is not incorrigible. 'This appears red' is now, *ex hypothesi*, equivalent to 'This looks like that which (really) is red', but the latter sentence contains as one of its parts 'That (really) is red'. Therefore, if 'That (really) is red' is not incorrigible—as Toulmin agrees that it is not—then 'This looks like that which (really) is red', and consequently also 'This appears red', cannot be incorrigible either.

Similar remarks apply to 'This seems obligatory' if we try to interpret it as 'This looks obligatory'. If the latter sentence does not imply hesitancy—if it does not say, roughly, 'Either this is obligatory or I am wrong'—it must be a description of the "moral looks" of the contemplated act. But what are "moral looks"? Presumably they are certain feelings and emotions. But are not such feelings even more inscrutable and hard to describe than sometimes the colour of an object is? Suppose I am contemplating an act of revenge. The act seems obligatory. But what then is its "moral look"? Is it an act which I "simply feel like doing"? Clearly not. A contemplated act of revenge (say, murder) could not look the same as the prospect of staying in bed a little longer. Is it a feeling of compulsion? But why do I then hesitate? Is it then a feeling of moral obligation? But what kind of feeling is that? Is that the feeling caused by the prospect of actions which are morally obligatory, only weaker? Are we not thus led to say that we often do not know, we cannot tell, we are uncertain, what such moral feelings are and when we have them? Finally, to say that 'This seems obligatory' means 'This looks like that which (really) is obligatory' would not make it incorrigible either. In that case, 'This seems obligatory' is incorrigible only if, for example, 'Honesty (really) is obligatory' is, but the latter, as Toulmin himself insisted, is not.

Looks, for example, colours, are often taken as indefinable or primitive in science, but this is so not because they are incorrigible. What is basic in science is simply what is taken to be so in a certain system.[1] Science is, largely, system building. But is ethics or morality? Certainly in a much lesser degree. What is to be taken to be basic, atomic, indefinable, in a system of ethics? "Moral looks", that is, our attitudes and feelings concerning objects and human conduct? I shall argue below that the study of moral attitudes and feelings is indeed illuminating for ethics but it is extremely doubtful that it could yield a system of ethics comparable to anything found in science. Apart from the fact that our moral feelings are elusive and hard to identify, moral judgements, as Toulmin himself pointed out, constantly correct them. But there is no reason to believe that these judgements correct our feelings only in the direction of social harmony.

The scientist, Toulmin said, in order to develop a coherent system, either "tightens up" the criteria of our everyday concepts, or "discards" those concepts altogether and "replaces them" with new ones (*PRE*, 91). In a sense, a similar thing happens when a moral code is adopted. Terms like 'good', 'ought', 'right', and 'duty' acquire certain meanings which are held more or less constant as long as the moral code survives. This concerns mainly the descriptive part of their meaning, that is, their criteria of application, but different moralities may also have their different brands of emotive or evaluative meanings. We shall have to discuss this matter in greater detail later. But the meanings of moral terms are never frozen completely. Moral language is not an artificial language; it possesses all the characteristic flexibility and "open texture" which belongs to a non-scientific or pre-scientific language. Different moral codes can thus come into contact, and the possible conflict between them can itself be a moral issue.

---

[1] For a fuller treatment of the question of what is to be taken as basic in formal systems see, for example, Nelson Goodman, *The Structure of Appearance*, Cambridge, Massachusetts: Harvard University Press, 1951 (Oxford University Press).

Moore's views had led to the consequence that moral discourse and reasoning have no direct logical connexion with human conduct. Toulmin came to a conclusion which was equally absurd. Moral reasoning does have practical import—to influence human conduct is its whole point; but, and this is the absurdity, it influences people to one and only one purpose—namely, to the purpose of harmonizing their interests. For Moore there was nothing in the logic of moral discourse which made it practical; for Toulmin one practical point constituted its whole logic. Moral arguments, Toulmin claimed, are best characterized by saying that they form part of the process by which we "correlate our feelings and behaviour in such a way as to make the fulfilment of everyone's aims and desires as far as possible compatible' (*PRE*, 137).

We have seen that one alternative for interpreting this claim is to regard it as a piece of sociology—as an empirical generalization of facts which could well have been otherwise. It seems that Toulmin himself thought of his thesis in a stronger sense. He argued, for example, that "The only context in which the concept of 'duty' is straightforwardly intelligible is one of communal life", and that there is a close *logical relation* between moral concepts such as duty and harmonization of interests (*PRE*, 133). But as we have pointed out, and as Toulmin himself admitted, in actual practice the meanings of moral terms are certainly not identical with the meanings of such phrases as 'conducive to social harmony'. The principle of social harmony points only to one set of possible moral standards or criteria for applying terms like 'good', 'right', and 'ought'. To say that the purpose of moral discourse is to serve social harmony is thus itself a proposal or recommendation to adopt one set of moral standards among alternative ones.

There is nothing to prohibit Toulmin to assume the role of the moralist. However, if Toulmin's thesis is a normative proposal, the manner in which it is presented is too dogmatic. Moore wrote that since the term 'good' is indefinable, "nobody can foist upon us such an axiom as that 'Pleasure is the only good' or that 'The good is the desired' on the pretence that this is 'the very meaning of the word' " (*PE*, 7). We can adapt Moore's words and turn them against Toulmin by saying that since not even the criteria of application of such words as 'good', 'right', 'ought', and 'duty' are always identical with conduciveness to the harmony of interests, nobody can foist upon us such an axiom as that 'morality is what contributes to the harmonization of people's interests' on the pretence that this is 'the very function or purpose of moral language'.

R. M. HARE

1. *Imperatives and "Phrastics" and "Neustics"*

HARE agreed with Stevenson that one of the most characteristic things about moral judgements is their intimate connexion with human conduct. But whereas Stevenson had held that this connexion is of a causal or psychological sort, Hare claimed that there is an important difference between making or getting someone to do a certain thing and telling him to do it. The former is merely a psychological matter, the latter is not. We have discussed the inadequacy of the psychological approach to moral language and the absurdities into which it led, not the least of which was the paradoxical conclusion that the concept of validity is not applicable to moral reasoning. Hare's abandonment of Stevenson's psychologism was therefore another genuine advance in twentieth-century ethical theory.

Hare, just as Stevenson, emphasized the imperative character of moral judgements, but, in opposition to Stevenson, he insisted that an imperative or command is not a kind of verbal shove.

> In ordinary parlance there is no harm in saying that in using a command our intention is to get someone to do something; but for philosophical purposes an important distinction has to be made. The process of *telling* someone to do something, and *getting* him to do it, are quite distinct, logically, from each other. (*LM*, 13.)

Telling someone to do something is to engage in a linguistic, and therefore conventional and rule-governed, performance; getting someone to do something is to produce a real effect on the mind or behaviour of someone. I may get someone to do something without telling him to do it and I may tell him to do it without seriously trying to get him to do it.

For Hare, "the language of morals is one sort of prescriptive language" (*LM*, 1). By that he meant that moral judgements are characteristically one kind of value-judgement and that they "entail" imperatives or commands. That all value-judgements have this character was for him a matter of definition:

> I propose to say that the test, whether someone is using the judgement 'I ought to do X' as a value-judgement or not is, 'Does he or does he not recognize that if he assents to the judgement, he must also assent to the command "Let me do X"?' (*LM*, 168–9.)

His "substantial" claim was that moral judgements are value-judgements in the above sense:

> The substantial part of what I am trying to show is this, that, in the sense of 'value-judgement' just defined, we do make value-judgements, and that they are the class of sentences containing value-words which is of primary interest to the logician who studies moral language. (*LM*, 169.)

The study of moral language was thus, for Hare, closely connected with the study of imperatives or commands. What, then, is the nature of imperatives? Stevenson had claimed that moral judgements, in so far as they contain an imperative element, possess "emotive meaning" and are used for persuasion, that is, for causally influencing men's attitudes and actions. For Hare, on the other hand, imperatives and moral judgements are used not for persuading, but for prescribing. And, he claimed, prescribing and persuading, just as making a statement and making someone believe it, are quite different from each other. Thus although both Stevenson and Hare lay stress on the imperative nature of moral language, there is a most significant difference between the theories of these two men. Hare rejects the notions of emotive meaning and the persuasive use of moral judgements and substitutes for them the concept of the prescriptive and commendatory uses or functions of such judgements. According to him it is very important to realize that moral judgements are used for telling people to do or to prefer something, but, he claimed, this is very different from persuading them.

Telling someone to do something, or that something is the case, is answering the question 'What shall I do?' or 'What are the facts?'

When we have answered these questions the hearer knows what to do or what the facts are—if what we have told him is right. He is not necessarily thereby *influenced* one way or the other, nor have we failed if he is not; for he may decide to disbelieve or disobey us, and the mere telling him does nothing—and seeks to do nothing—to prevent him doing this. But persuasion is not directed to a person as a rational agent, who is asking himself (or us) 'What shall I do?'; it is not an answer to this or any other question; it is an attempt to *make* him answer it in a particular way. (*LM*, 15.)

By again making use of the notion of a linguistic performance, with which we are by now familiar, we may amplify this distinction as follows. Telling someone to do something, that is, prescribing a form of conduct, is a linguistic performance, but persuading someone to do something is not. The distinction in question becomes evident when we reflect on the fact that for prescribing and stating there are explicit performative formulas whereas there is nothing comparable for persuading. To utter the words 'I prescribe . . .' (or 'I tell you to . . .') is to prescribe, and to utter the words 'I state that . . .' is to state. But we do not have the form of words 'I persuade that . . .' or 'I persuade you to . . .' at all and to say 'I persuade . . .' (or better, 'I am persuading') is not to engage in persuading but in stating, or more precisely, in describing, an activity of mine which I may be carrying on by using language but also by other means.[1] Prescribing and persuading exemplify two entirely different sorts of ways of doing something with words or two entirely different sorts of uses of language. To prescribe is to use language performatively, to persuade is to use it causally.[2]

---

[1] Cf. Hare's contribution to the symposium: 'Freedom of the Will', *Aristotelian Society*, Supp. vol. xxv, 1951. The fundamental point here was made by Austin; see his essay 'Other Minds' in *Philosophical Papers*, and *How to Do Things with Words*, especially Lecture I.

[2] As we recall, in discussing Stevenson and Toulmin we have already observed this contrast between the two different kinds of uses of language in some important cases; still further ones will come up below. A fuller and more systematic treatment of this distinction can be found in Austin. Once again it should be pointed out that my use of 'performative' differs from Austin's. Austin was first anxious to contrast "performatives" with "constatives" or statements. But in the later lectures in *How to Do Things with Words* he developed the concept of an "illocution" which embraces both performatives and statements so that the contrast between the two is considerably softened and "performative" seems to designate primarily a phrase through

There is another essential difference between prescribing and persuading. A performative speech-act, besides possessing a performative force which can be isolated and made explicit by such phrases as 'I prescribe . . .', 'I tell you to . . .', 'I order you to . . .', 'I state that . . .', is further characterized by being governed by criteria of application, that is, by possessing a sense and a reference. Thus 'I tell you to shut the door', 'I order you to shut the door', 'I state that the door is shut', 'I predict that you are going to shut the door', &c. all make reference to something in the world or in experience. By contrast, persuading has no criteria of application, no sense and reference, any more than, say, boxing someone's ears does. Let us see how Hare makes this point in his own terms.

Hare claimed, then, that in order to get clear about moral language, we must get clear about imperatives. But, he claimed further, imperatives, unlike anything Stevenson suspected, are not just persuasive devices but bear a significant similarity to such fully "cognitive" utterances as factual statements. Imperative and indicative sentences are both similar to and different from each other:

> Both are used for talking about a subject matter, but they are used for talking about it in a different way. The two sentences 'You are going to shut the door' and 'Shut the door' are both about your shutting the door in the immediate future; but what they say about it is quite different. An indicative sentence is used for telling someone that something is the case; an imperative is not—it is used for telling someone to make something the case. (*LM*, 5.)

The distinction described in the passage above is superficially reminiscent of Stevenson's distinction between emotive and descriptive meaning. What a sentence "is about", or its "subject matter", seems to correspond to what would be indicated by Stevenson's descriptive meaning, and what a sentence "is used for" seems in some ways to correspond to the sort of thing that can be done with a sentence through what Stevenson called its emotive meaning. But what Hare had in mind, *at this point*, is really quite

which the "illocutionary force" of utterances, including statements, is made explicit. I go even further and use 'performative' interchangeably with 'illocutionary'.

different from Stevenson's distinction between the two kinds of meaning. This becomes evident if we follow Hare's discussion of the similarities and differences between imperatives and indicatives in terms of his theory of "phrastics" and "neustics". The theory went briefly as follows. The two sentences

(1) You are going to shut the door, and
(2) Shut the door,

may be rewritten so that each of them can be seen to contain a "phrastic" and "neustic". The phrastic of a sentence is a phrase which "refers" to what the sentence is about or to its subject matter. (1) and (2), Hare explained, have a common phrastic, they are both about the same thing—namely,

(3) Your shutting the door in the immediate future.

But the sentences (1) and (2) "convey" something more than what is contained in (3).

What we have so far tells us quite clearly what the sentences are about. It does not, however, tell us what the speaker is saying about it. We do not know whether he is stating that your shutting the door in the immediate future is what is going to happen or be the case, or whether he is telling us to make it the case, or something else. (*LM*, 17.)

The parts of the rewritten sentences which tell us *that*, Hare called the "neustics". A neustic is a phrase which "indicates" (here Hare does not say "refers to") what is said about what the phrastic refers to. In our case one of the neustics must indicate that (1) is used to make a statement, the other that (2) is used to give a command. Hare believed that the words 'yes' and 'please', respectively, could serve this purpose so that (1) and (2) when rewritten out fully become:

(4) Your shutting the door in the immediate future, yes.
(5) Your shutting the door in the immediate future, please.

The analysis of sentences into phrastics and neustics is a complicated matter and I shall not try to give a full discussion of all the problems that it entails. Nevertheless, a few comments must be made. For our purposes let us notice first of all that the apparent parallel between Hare's notions of the phrastic, or "what a sentence is about", and the neustic, or "what it is used for saying", and Stevenson's notions of descriptive and emotive meaning is illusory. These distinctions are really drawn on different levels. Stevenson's distinction was made between two kinds of meaning. If we think of meaning as something conveyed by complete speech-acts we would have to say that, for Stevenson, a moral judgement consists of two speech-acts performed jointly and existing side by side: a factual statement and a command. In uttering a sentence of the form 'X is good', we are doing two things at once—describing and commanding. And each of these things can be done equally well in isolation from the other. We can describe without commanding, and we can command without describing. On the other hand, the distinction between phrastics and neustics is not a distinction between two kinds of (sentential) meaning. This distinction is drawn, so to speak, on a sub-sentential level. We cannot *say* anything with a phrastic or with a neustic alone; they are not separate sentences, but only incomplete elements of these. If we think of meaning as belonging only to complete speech-acts, in isolation, phrastics and neustics would have no meaning.

It seems quite unlikely that anyone would want to maintain that what Hare called neustics could, by themselves, have meaning. Hare said that what the neustic of a sentence indicates is the "nodding" or "asserting" that sentence (*LM*, 18–19). And surely just to "nod" or "assert" without nodding or asserting anything would have no meaning. Just the same, Hare might have, at times, thought of neustics as conveying a kind of meaning in its own right. He claimed, as we shall see, that the commendatory use of the term 'good' is what essentially makes up its meaning and commendatory use would seem to be the sort of thing which is indicated by the neustic of a sentence. What Hare had to say about phrastics leaves the issue even more open. He wrote that the neustic element makes the difference between "merely mentioning a sentence in inverted commas", and "using it in earnest", and that it is "something essential to *saying* (and meaning) anything" (*LM*, 18). Phrastics by themselves, we are thus led to think, would not say or mean anything. But there are other passages in Hare's work which suggest that there is a sense in which phrastics are capable of having meaning in isolation. For example, he wrote:

> The imperative and the indicative moods also have in common, because of their common phrastic element, everything to do with their reference to actual or possible states of affairs. There is a possible state of affairs referred to by the phrastic 'Your shutting the door in the immediate future'. This reference is not affected by what comes after. Both imperatives and indicatives have to refer to the state of affairs which they are about. (*LM*, 22.)

This passage implies that sentences as wholes, as well as simple phrastics, both refer to states of affairs. In this sense, then, phrastics seem to be capable of having a meaning of their own. But what Hare says needs clarification. If what is referred to is a state of affairs, as opposed to a thing or object of some sort, it may make a difference whether we talk about full sentences or phrastics alone as doing the referring. Sometimes a state of affairs is talked about as that which makes a sentence true, but since phrastics are neither true nor false, there cannot be states of affairs corresponding to them in this sense.

Perhaps we can straighten matters out as follows. Let us say that it is the full sentence, or rather, the speech-act (or if we are particular, the person who performs the speech-act) that refers and that it does because the sentence, or the speech-act, contains a phrastic element. Let us say further that, when we talk about reference to states of affairs, the phrastic of a speech-act refers always to a possible state of affairs—to a "sheer possibility", to a state of affairs in a possible world, if you like—and that it is the full speech-act, phrastic *cum* neustic, that says something about this possible state of affairs. The full speech-act, through its neustic, says either that the possible state of affairs, indicated through its phrastic, is the case (actual) or that it is to be made to be the case.

It is at this point that we shall have reason to disagree with Hare. Why should we limit the number of neustics to two—the indicative and the imperative? There clearly are speech-acts which say neither that a certain state of affairs is the case nor that it is to be made to be the case. Asking a question is an obvious example. But there are others. In issuing a warning I am talking about a state of affairs, but I neither say that that state of affairs is actual nor that it is to be made actual. Promising is a further example. In saying, on the 3rd of September, 'I promise to return the money tomorrow', I refer to my returning the money on the 4th of September, but I say neither that that is the case nor that that is to be made to be the case. Suppose that on the 4th of September I do not return the money: that will have made me guilty neither of a mistake nor of disobedience. There are many other speech-acts which do not fit into the imperative–indicative mould: challenging, protesting, envisaging, favouring, approving, &c. I shall try to show that, correspondingly, neustics are countless in number and that this fact has very important consequences with regard to the analysis of moral judgements. Since Hare seems to have assumed that there are, essentially, only two neustics, he maintained that those judgements contain somehow both an indicative and an imperative neustic. He was thus led to making the same disastrous distinction as Stevenson between the two kinds of meanings of moral judgements—a distinction which, as we shall see in greater detail, his own theory of phrastics and neustics initially provided a way of avoiding. I shall argue that moral judgements have neustics peculiar to themselves and that if we realize this we are no longer tempted to claim that in such judgements there are two meanings existing side by side. That claim, as I have tried to indicate throughout this book, has dominated much of recent ethical theory but has also been a source of serious difficulties.

We have claimed that the natural thing to say seems to be that Hare's phrastics do not have meaning in their own right and that it is rather the full speech-act or a sentence (we do not have to insist here, as Hare does not either, on the difference between these two really distinct things) that has meaning and perhaps that, at bottom, it is really the person who performs such an act who is the prime carrier of meaning. But here we actually have a choice. On the one hand, meaning can be regarded as being constituted by both the performative force and the sense and reference of a speech-act or sentence. And since it seems clear that Hare's neustic is exactly what indicates the performative force of a sentence and his phrastic exactly what gives its sense and reference, in one sense, only phrastics *cum* neustics would have meaning. There is, however, a narrower, and traditionally dominant, sense of meaning in which meaning is identical with just sense and reference, in other words, with the phrastic element alone. In that sense, then, phrastics car have meaning in their own right. There is, perhaps, even a further sense of meaning. Instead of identifying meaning with sense and reference, we may identify it with performative force. This, as we shall see, is just the way in which Hare seems to conceive of it when he is contrasting the meaning of the term 'good' with its criteria of application or sense.

There is nothing wrong with speaking of meaning in any of these senses as long as one keeps them separate. Some of the recent controversy concerning whether meaning is use or reference is misled because it is assumed that it has to be either one or the other. The judicious course is clearly to allow different senses of meaning or, perhaps better, to distinguish between different levels of meaning. If we do this, we can then say that on the level of sense and reference phrastics do have meaning and that so do neustics on the level of performative force. But we must also realize that on one level—on the level of sentential meaning—phrastics and neustics are incomplete and constitute only elements of meaning.

It is not on the level of sense and reference, nor on the level of performative force, that recent ethical theorists have claimed that moral judgements possess two kinds of meaning. To say that an utterance, sentence, or expression has more than one meaning on the level of sense and reference is to say that it is ambiguous with regard to the objects of which it is true or to which it refers. And to say that an utterance, sentence, or expression has more than one meaning on the level of performative force is to say that it is ambiguous with regard to the sort of linguistic act it constitutes or is used for. We shall see that the expression 'I approve of . . .' may be ambiguous in this way: it may be used for giving one's approval but also for reporting one's favourable state of mind. Characteristically, both of these two types of ambiguity or multiplicity of meaning are something we attempt to eliminate. They are considered flaws in our speech if left unresolved. The alleged multiplicity of meaning of moral judgements is of an entirely different nature. It is not a flaw or shortcoming but supposedly an integral part of the proper functioning of language. There is no need nor possibility of eliminating it. It must be made use of rather than shunned. Furthermore, it is presumably a multiplicity of meaning on the level of whole sentential meaning. To utter a moral judgement is, according to these authors, to perform two full speech-acts at once, to say two complete and separable things in the same breath.

We are now in the position to see what may well be two of the sources of this misguided doctrine. The distinction between the two kinds of meaning of moral judgements was, we have said, propounded explicitly for the first time by Stevenson. But Stevenson, it should be by now amply clear, was confused as to what may be considered legitimately a use or function of language from a logical point of view. If we think, as Stevenson did, that something like persuading can be part of the meaning of a speech-act, we may easily come to believe that there are utterances which have a double meaning. As a matter of fact, almost all utterances have causal effects, that is, psychological repercussions of one sort or another. If we count these repercussions as part of their meanings, elements or types of meaning can be multiplied quite easily. By issuing a warning I may also startle someone. My utterance will thus have two meanings. By describing a situation, I may make someone sad. Again, my utterance will thus have two meanings. By reporting an experience, I may convince someone that his theory is wrong. And what I said will again have had two meanings. What Stevenson did was to notice that moral judgements often have emotional repercussions of one sort or another and thus a whole new brand of meaning was called into existence. All this, we realize now, is based on a confusion: the psychological effects of a speech-act are not part of its meaning and in so far as our speech produces such effects we are not engaged in using language in the performative or logical but in the causal sense. But we can see how Stevenson came to the doctrine of dual meaning. To say that a moral judgement incorporates two kinds of meaning is to say that passing it involves doing two things, performing two linguistic acts, at once. And describing and persuading are the sorts of thing which *can* be, and sometimes are, done at the same time and in one breath.

But once we realize that persuading is not a linguistic job in the required sense and cannot therefore constitute a kind of meaning, we should be a lot less inclined to embrace the doctrine of the duality of meaning. Hare, we saw, did realize this point about persuading; it is therefore surprising that, as the next section will show, he nevertheless went along with Stevenson's basic idea that moral judgements have two kinds of meaning. Hare claimed merely that the other kind of meaning, besides descriptive meaning, is not persuasive or emotive meaning, but prescriptive or evaluative meaning. Now, describing and persuading are, we said, things of the sort that can be properly done at once, in one utterance. But are describing and prescribing? If in uttering a sentence I am both describing and prescribing, I would be, to use Wittgenstein's phrase, playing two "language-games" at the same time. And this, instead of being something to be engaged in freely and exploited, would be an ambiguity and flaw. It would produce bafflement and confusion: how could such a protean form of speech be evaluated? Describing and prescribing obviously have different standards of assessment. We always want to know how we should take an utterance. Questions like 'Is this an order or a piece of advice?', 'Are you condemning me or warning me?', and 'Is this a description or prescription?' seem in principle always in order. And the proper answer seems never to be 'I am doing both'. But in Hare's theory this would have to be the only proper answer if someone were to ask 'Are you describing or prescribing?' with regard to a moral judgement.

The second source for the doctrine of dual meaning which we may do well to point out in a preliminary way at this time is the following. We have seen that sentential meaning or meaning in the full sense has two levels: there is the level of sense and reference and the level of performative force. Therefore, there is a temptation to say with regard to utterances such as moral judgements, in which meaning on both levels is equally important and conspicuous, that they contain two kinds of meaning. But these two elements of meaning do not exist side by side in a full speech-act; the latter presupposes or builds on the former. I can perform the linguistic act of, say, commending only if my words, first of all, have a sense and a reference. I shall argue that the dogma of the duality of meaning of moral judgements is in part due to confusing these two levels of meaning with the notion of separate kinds of meaning. A level of meaning does not constitute a kind of meaning. It is true that a moral judgement, like any speech-act, involves (1) certain criteria of application (the phrastic element, sense and reference) and (2) a performative force (the neustic element), but from this it does not follow that it involves two meanings existing side by side.

Hare's theory of neustics and phrastics has genuine merits; one only wishes that he had made more thoroughgoing use of it in developing his views on the nature of moral language. If he had, I think he would have abandoned the dogma of the duality of meaning. The merits of the theory of phrastics and neustics are the following. First, it is comprehensive and tries to do justice to all the aspects of an utterance or speech-act. It has now become clear that the traditional preoccupation on the part of philosophers with statements and descriptive discourse has led to a one-sided view of language. The belief that the business of language is, basically or in so far as it is "cognitive", to describe or report features of reality or experience had brought with it the notion that the only interesting and worth-while question with regard to an utterance is the question of its sense and reference. Wittgenstein, in his own oblique way Stevenson, and more recently Austin have brought to our attention another equally important question, concerning the use, point, or force of an utterance. Clearly, sentences and expressions have more uses than just to describe or report features of the world. And this fact is particularly important for ethical theory. Hare's doctrine thus has the virtue of recognizing and making explicit both sides of what is involved when we are engaged in saying anything. The concept of a phrastic takes care of what has been traditionally called meaning, that is, sense and reference; the concept of a neustic is designed to elucidate the recently discovered or emphasized element of performative use.

Second, the theory of phrastics recognizes the unity of a speech-act. Stevenson's descriptive and emotive meanings were two isolable things which could exist in their own right quite independently of one another. They were tied together in an utterance by a mere external and contingent psychological bond. Phrastics and neustics, on the other hand, are internally related and could not perform their function in separation. In any full speech-act both elements must always be present.

However, as we have already intimated and shall see more fully in the next section, Hare failed to apply his promising theory of phrastics and neustics consistently to problems of moral language. He quickly lapsed into talk about two kinds of meaning of moral judgements and thus became heir to the difficulties that beset Stevenson's views.

2. *Criteria of Application, Performative Force, and Kinds of Meaning*

Hare agreed with Moore that naturalism, if by that we mean the doctrine that "there is a set of characteristics which together *entail* a thing being good" (*LM*, 81), cannot be right. But Moore had, at least initially, maintained that this is so because of the peculiar non-natural character of goodness as a property. In order to avoid the unrewarding consequence of the notion of goodness as a property, Hare sought to put his case against naturalism in purely linguistic terms. For him,

What is wrong with naturalist theories is that they leave out the prescriptive or commendatory element in value-judgments, by seeking to make them derivable from statements of fact. (*LM*, 82.)

.   .   .   .

Value-terms have a special function in language, that of commending; and so they plainly cannot be defined in terms of other words which themselves do not perform this function; for if this is done, we are deprived of a means of performing the function. (*LM*, 91.)

Hare went on to elaborate on these points by making a distinction between what he called the meaning of value-terms and their criteria of application. In the case of a value-term like 'good', meaning is distinct from criteria of application; in the case of a descriptive term like 'red' or 'sweet' they are the same. To explain the full meaning of the word 'red' is just to explain its criteria of application, but it is not so with the term 'good' (*LM*, 94–98). The meaning of that term is quite distinct from its criteria of application: it is its evaluative or, more specifically, commendatory use.

However, it is not quite clear what exactly Hare did hold on this point. He claimed that the criteria of application of the term 'good' nevertheless specify part of its meaning (*LM*, 117–18). Perhaps the best way to sum up Hare's views on this point is that in the case of a value-term the criteria of application never make up the *whole* of its meaning. This negative point leaves him free to recognize that *part* of the meaning of value-terms is specified by their criteria of application. The central idea is that value-terms, and value-judgements, have two kinds of meaning—(1) descriptive meaning, determined by criteria of application, and (2) evaluative meaning, made up of commendatory or prescriptive use—and that they therefore contrast with descriptive terms and factual statements which have only one—viz. descriptive—kind of meaning (*LM*, 117–18).

This distinction between the two types of meaning (or between criteria of application and evaluative use) bears a close similarity to Stevenson's distinction between descriptive and emotive meaning. Consequently, as we shall see, it raises the familiar problem. The crucial question regarding Stevenson's theory, we recall, was how the two kinds of meaning which moral judgements were said to have are related. Since Stevenson could not give a satisfactory answer to this question, his whole theory faltered. The problem of finding the bond that binds together the two separate meanings of a value-judgement would not have arisen for Hare if instead of their two kinds of meaning he had spoken of their phrastic and neustic elements. We have seen that phrastics and neustics are sub-sentential elements and therefore have, in one sense of the word, no meaning in isolation. But Hare thought that value-judgements are more complex than indicative and imperative sentences. Before we can analyse value-judgements in terms of phrastics and neustics, we must first break them down into indicatives and imperatives.

Each value-judgement is thus really two sentences in one. It consists of (*a*) an indicative sentence which gives it its descriptive meaning, and (*b*) an imperative, or imperative-like, sentence which gives it its evaluative meaning. A value-judgement contains two sorts of sentential meaning and its full analysis would therefore yield two phrastics and two neustics and not just one of each. Hare himself did not attempt any actual analysis of value-judgements in terms of phrastics and neustics, nor did he say that such an analysis is even possible. What exactly is the relevance of these concepts to an investigation of the nature of moral language is an issue which he left largely up in the air. However, his talk about phrastics and neustics on the one hand, and about descriptive and evaluative meaning on the other, leads one to believe that the analysis of value-judgements really involves two stages. On the level of sentential meaning a judgement of the form 'X is good', for example, would yield, to follow Stevenson for a moment:

(*a*) I approve of X.
(*b*) Approve of X also.

But when we penetrate below the level of (sentential) meaning, (*a*) and (*b*) reveal a further structure and are seen to be each made up of a phrastic and a neustic:

(*a'*) My approving of X, yes.
(*b'*) Your approving of X also, please.

The theory of two types of meaning when combined with the theory of phrastics and neustics will thus show value-judgements to have an unexpected and peculiar complexity. Furthermore, it would be a kind of complexity that would make, as we shall see, moral reasoning impossible. There is, however, really no reason to believe that value-judgements are more complex than other speech-acts in that they contain two kinds of meaning and are thus really two speech-acts in one. We are able to pronounce value-judgements, just as commands, statements, &c., in one breath, without a hiatus noticeable anywhere, and, as I shall argue, the phrastic–neustic distinction is directly applicable to them.

Hare claimed, then, that in some instances—in the case of descriptive terms and judgements—criteria of application determine the whole of meaning. But, he claimed also, there are other instances—value-terms and value-judgements—in which meaning is not (wholly) determined by such criteria. Value-terms and judgements also have an evaluative use. There are various things wrong with these claims. First of all, it may be doubted whether meaning is ever wholly determined by criteria of application. As we have pointed out before, what has meaning in a primary and full sense is a complete utterance or speech-act, such as informing, describing, warning, commending, ordering, promising, and so on. All these speech-acts are governed by rules in addition to criteria of application and the full meaning of none of them is completely determined by criteria of application. On the other hand, on one level, on the level of sense and reference, meaning is always, and not just in some instances, that which is governed by criteria of application.

Before we can complete an act of communication, such as informing, describing, warning, commending, ordering, proposing, promising, and so on, something must have occurred previously: certain vocables must have been correlated with certain things in the world, they must have been taken to have a certain reference or a certain sense. Does correlating vocables with things in the world constitute a separate kind of speech-act? In one sense it clearly does. I may say 'I define X as Y' or ' ". . ." means . . . ' or 'By "the lady" I was referring to . . .' or 'By "him" I meant . . .' or 'By "noise" I meant . . .', and so on. These would be acts of linguistic legislation. In using a natural language we find that the phase of linguistic legislation is largely over, but there is still ambiguity and vagueness and there is the occasional need to introduce new expressions.

There is another sense, however, in which correlating words with things in the world is not a separate kind of speech-act. At any rate, in this sense, it is not an explicit act. It is like entering into a contract by tacit consent. In using a sentence to inform or to warn or to order someone, I use that sentence also in the sense that I correlate certain vocables with certain things in the world, but I do not use that sentence *to* correlate those vocables to those things in the world.[1] I cannot inform without correlating words and things,

---

[1] Cf. pp. 27 ff. above.

without applying words to things. But to inform is not to correlate or to apply. I can inform someone only if my words have a certain sense and reference, but to inform is not to give sense and reference. So even if correlating words with things in the world, or applying them, is an act we perform, it is not an act on the same level with such acts as informing, ordering, warning, and so on, unless by correlating and applying we mean the explicit acts of linguistic legislation such as defining and eliminating ambiguity and vagueness. The differences between the three types of thing we have been trying to distinguish from one another may perhaps be made clearer through an analogy with an (old-fashioned) apothecary: he (1) labels his jars, (2) "reads" the labels, and (3) prepares drugs. The analogy is the weakest with regard to (1) since he has to get the right labels on the jars with the right contents; he is thus not exactly "legislating". (2) and (3), however, fit quite well: in preparing drugs he reads the labels, but he does not prepare the drugs to read the labels.

The above remarks may throw light on the claim often made recently under the influence of Wittgenstein that meaning is never reference. What is valid in this claim is that correlating words with the world or applying them or name-giving is not, as Wittgenstein would say, a move in a language-game in a sense in which informing, warning, ordering, and so on are moves in a language game. Applying words or referring is not anything in its own right. It is like labelling and by merely labelling his jars the apothecary has not yet become engaged in carrying out his trade. Labelling jars is not a complete "form of life" in the sense in which preparing and dispensing drugs is. In a similar sense, applying words to the world is incomplete as compared with such things as informing, describing, warning, promising, and prescribing. Labelling jars is only preparatory; and so is giving sense and reference. Furthermore, the jars really *bear* labels only in so far as they are used in a further activity. Similarly, a term has a sense or referent, singles out something in reality, only in so far as it functions in a complete act of communication.[1]

Correlating or applying words to such and such things, or from

---

[1] Cf. Wittgenstein, *Philosophical Investigations*, especially sections 22, 27, and 49.

the hearer's point of view, taking words as being correlated or applied to such and such things, is a matter governed by rules—by criteria of application. But just as applying is only ancillary to such full speech-acts as informing, warning, commending, and so on, criteria of application are only a preamble to further rules. There are thus (at least) two types of linguistic rules, each operating on a different level. There are criteria of application—as Hare calls them —and there are rules of informing, warning, ordering, and so on. Hare was quite willing to grant that *some* speech-acts—"value-judgements" as he called them—are governed by rules which go beyond criteria of application. But the truth of the matter is that all speech-acts—factual statements as well as value-judgements— must be governed by rules of two different sorts. This does not, however, mean that all speech-acts have two kinds of meaning, or that any of them do.

There are (at least) two sorts of linguistic rules and meaning may be said to be determined by either one or the other of them, or by both together, but in each case we would have a different sense of meaning. In the first case we would have meaning as sense and reference or meaning as it belongs to the phrastic elements of sentences. In the second, we would have meaning as performative force or meaning as it belongs to the neustic elements of sentences. In the third, we would try to conceive of meaning in a more comprehensive manner as covering both sense and reference and performative force or as belonging to full sentences. But we cannot say, as Hare in effect does, that sense and reference, on the one hand, and performative force, on the other, constitute two kinds of meaning perfectly on the same level and comparable to one another.

How did Hare, and before him Stevenson, come to have the mistaken notion that value-judgements and, more specifically, moral judgements contain two kinds of meaning? The source of this mistake seems to have been that they noticed and emphasized a very interesting fact about language but failed to understand it fully. There are types of sentences or speech-acts in language where the preponderance of what is communicated depends on rules governing sense and reference or criteria of application. These are the types of sentences and speech-acts that make up what is some-times referred to as "descriptive discourse". There are, however, other types of sentence or speech-act where the most salient feature is rather their performative force. Since previous writers on ethics, including Moore, had paid relatively little attention to that feature of language, they had come up with rather one-sided theories of moral language. Stevenson and Hare set out to remedy this situa-tion and based their theories on the exaggerated claim that there is an altogether peculiar brand of meaning belonging to moral judgements. The truth of the matter is that neither sense and reference nor performative force constitute a kind of meaning; rather, as we have shown, they constitute different levels of meaning. It is natural to assume that they both do constitute a kind of meaning since depending on the kind of speech-act at hand either one or the other of these features is more in prominence and there are speech-acts and contexts in which one of them looms so large that it almost obliterates the importance of the other. There are contexts—science, ordinary statements of fact, reports of hap-penings of all sorts, and so on, in short, "descriptive discourse"— where what is said or communicated is almost exclusively deter-mined by criteria of application and we are therefore tempted to identify criteria of application with "descriptive meaning". Never-theless, to do so would be a mistake. Criteria of application, as we have seen, concern only the phrastics of sentences and a sentence constitutes a description only if it contains also a neustic. Applying words, like labelling, is an act of communication only if it takes place within a broader context. There is no communicative context which may be called applying as such.

Now it is true that when for a stretch of time or space the com-municative context remains the same—in the case of a fiscal report, for example—we have to pay little or no attention to performative force, and have to heed only the sense and reference. But even within "descriptive discourse" there are shifts from one type of linguistic performance to another and it is important to be clear whether a given utterance is to be taken as a report or prediction, for example. Such things would make a difference, with regard to the question of what constitutes valid evidence for a given claim.

It is for this reason that we find, within in a broad sense descriptive language, explicit performative phrases like 'I state . . .', 'I predict . . .', 'I report . . .', 'I postulate . . .', and so on. But most basically, a bit of descriptive discourse would not be what it is—a piece of information, a report, a prediction, and so on, an assertion concerning a topic and not a mere mentioning of a possible state of affairs or "entertaining" of a thought—without being governed by conventions which go beyond mere criteria of application. Therefore, if by 'descriptive meaning' we mean what a full descriptive utterance or speech-act has, descriptive meaning must involve more than just criteria of application.

Let us now consider the background of the claim that the performative force of value-judgements (or what Hare calls their "use") constitutes by itself a kind of meaning. Stevenson, as we saw, was impressed by the fact that imperatives do not describe anything but nevertheless have meaning. He concluded therefore that they must have a different kind of meaning from descriptive utterances. And since he found it useful to analyse moral judgements as being in part imperative utterances or commands, he concluded further that moral judgements possess, in part, a special kind of meaning. Hare's train of thought was very similar although his theory of how imperatives enter into moral judgements was, as we shall see, much more complicated and subtle. The fault in the arguments of both Stevenson and Hare lies, however, in the assumption that an imperative as a whole possesses a peculiar kind of meaning. All that is peculiar to an imperative is its neustic. And the neustic of an imperative sentence by no means makes up the whole of its meaning; it makes up its meaning only on one level. An imperative still contains, as Hare himself pointed out, a phrastic and is therefore governed by criteria of application.

Austin has shown that there are a number of other speech-acts besides the ones in which we characteristically use the imperative mood which are different from descriptive speech-acts or statements. The words 'I promise . . .', for example, he pointed out, do not state or describe what I am doing; their utterance in appropriate circumstances rather constitutes my doing a certain thing, that is, giving a promise. But while in his earlier writings he had thought that this difference is a complete difference and that what he called 'performatory utterances' have nothing in common with statements, in his later work (*How to Do Things with Words*) he abandoned this sharp distinction and substituted for the doctrine of performatory utterances the doctrine of the "locutionary meaning" and the "illocutionary force" of speech-acts. He still held that the words 'I promise . . .' are not used to state or describe anything, but he no longer claimed that therefore 'I promise . . .' is a completely different kind of speech-act from such speech-acts as a statement. Promises and statements are different in that their performative or illocutionary forces are different, but, the new doctrine implied, they are nevertheless similar in that they both include sense and reference, they are both governed by criteria of application, that is, by conventions of sense and by conventions of reference. In saying 'I promise to return the money to you tomorrow', that is, in promising a particular thing, I am singling out certain things in the world exactly in the same sense in which I am doing so when I make a statement such as 'The money which you gave me yesterday is now in the First National Bank'. As a matter of fact, I cannot give a promise without singling out certain things in the world. If the words 'I promise to return the money to you tomorrow' did not have any sense or reference, were not governed by criteria of application, I could not have, in using them, promised the *specific* thing I did promise. Of course, I may just say 'I promise' but that would be a complete speech-act only if it is clear from what has gone before what it is that I am promising.

Now all this seems pretty obvious. How then does it happen that philosophers have nevertheless said that moral discourse exemplifies an altogether separate kind of meaning? At least part of the explanation is that instead of talking about full utterances or speech-acts their favourite topic of discussion has often been moral *terms*, such as 'good' and 'ought'. But surely the meaning of single terms is an abstraction: what has meaning in the primary sense, constitutes a unit of communication, is the utterance of a full sentence, although there are of course one word sentences. It may well be that there are words and expressions which have no sense or reference, are not governed by criteria of application. But it does not follow that because of this they lend a special kind of meaning to the discourse or speech-acts in which they figure. 'I promise', 'I command', 'Do', 'I will', considered in isolation, have no criteria of application, but we do not have to say that since they are not, after all, nonsense syllables, they must possess a different kind of meaning. We may look at them rather as being like Hare's neustics. Thus the sentence 'I promise to return the money to you tomorrow' may be analysed into a phrastic and a neustic as 'My returning the money to you tomorrow, promised'. 'Jump into the lake' or 'I command you to jump into the lake' would go into a phrastic and a neustic as 'Your jumping into the lake in the immediate future, commanded (or do or please)', and so on.

Moral terms like 'good' and 'ought' may be very similar in this respect to 'I promise', 'I will', 'Do', and so on. And if they are, it would be clear that they do not lend a separate kind of meaning to moral judgements. They would lend these judgements only a peculiar performative force. Furthermore, the contrast of performative force would exist not only between moral judgements and descriptive statements but also between moral judgements and commands, warnings, promises, questions, and so on. The bifurcation of language into descriptive and evaluative sorts of utterances is essentially just as crude and misleading as the Positivist notion that the only really meaningful bits of language are verifiable descriptive statements of fact. What is needed is a more subtle analysis.

The bifurcation of meaning led to the idea that a moral judgement is a peculiar hybrid in part used for describing and giving information, in part used for prescribing. This, aside from being intuitively repugnant and reflecting a mistaken notion of language, had serious consequences for Hare's further theories. If criteria only go with describing, evaluating as such will seem to have no criteria at all. It would follow that we can give no reasons for our evaluations. In order to escape this undesirable consequence, we must then search for the connexion between descriptive criteria and evaluative use or force of expressions.

This last problem, as we shall see, proved as insoluble for Hare as it had been for Stevenson. The problem would not have arisen, had Hare not fallen victim to the old prejudice that criteria of application, that is, the conventions governing sense and reference, are basically or at least in the first instance relevant only to the descriptive uses of language. In fact, he mistakenly identified criteria of application with descriptive meaning. Had Hare realized that criteria of application or rules of sense and reference have a place in all contexts and not only in descriptive ones, he would have been able to develop a much more satisfactory theory of moral language. To apply a term or to correlate it with something in the world is only preparatory to making a real move in language. Application, as we have seen, concerns only what Hare himself called the phrastic element of sentences and before we have really said anything, produced a full unit of communication, the neustic must be added. By descriptive meaning, on the other hand, Hare meant something that belongs to a full unit of communication as a whole. Therefore, to identify criteria of application with descriptive meaning was a disaster. A moral judgement contains both descriptive and evaluative meaning, so Hare claimed, but if criteria of application are involved only in descriptive meaning, what is their relevance to moral judgements in so far as these are evaluative judgements and possess evaluative meaning? The answer which Hare was to give was in an essential way the same as Stevenson's and equally paradoxical: the relevance of criteria of application to our moral evaluations is, on the one hand, itself a matter of morals, and on the other, simply a matter of psychology.

3. *Prescriptivity, Criteria, and Reasons*

Throughout his work Hare has been anxious to emphasize two things: (1) that moral judgements are prescriptive, and (2) that moral judgements are supported by reasons. Unfortunately, he believed that we can do justice to these two points only if we accept the dogma of the two kinds of meaning of moral judgements. This dogma seems to be an inextricable part of his writings. Nevertheless, there are things he says concerning the two points just mentioned which are relatively independent of this dogma. Like Stevenson before him, Hare discussed the prescriptivity of moral judgements largely in terms of imperatives. But while the former had claimed that the analysis of moral terms shows that a moral judgement simply contains an imperative sentence as part of its meaning, for Hare the relation between moral judgements and imperatives was more complicated. He did say that a moral judgement, if it is used evaluatively, entails an imperative, but his whole account of the matter was more subtle. Even Stevenson had said that a moral judgement really *is* not, in part, an imperative but is only, in part, *like* an imperative. Hare explained where the relative dissimilarity lies. (See particularly *LM*, chapter ii.)

Moral judgements involve universality in a way in which ordinary imperative sentences do not. When I give the command 'Jump in and pull the man out' I do not imply that anyone in exactly the same circumstances as the addressee is to jump in also; in fact I am designating a particular person, and no one else, to perform the task. On the other hand, if I pass the moral judgement 'You ought to jump in and pull the man out' I do imply that anyone in the same circumstances would have that obligation also. In other words, an 'ought'-judgement makes reference to reasons and general principles in a way a simple command does not. Of course the person to whom I said 'Jump in and pull the man out' may also ask for reasons, but I may refuse to give them in a way in which I cannot refuse to give reasons for my 'ought'-judgement. If I do not recognize that there must be a general 'ought'-principle of which my 'ought'-judgement was an instance, I had no business using the word 'ought'. An 'ought'-judgement already *is* a general issue, but a simple command may only be *made* into a general issue, in which case, in a sense, it ceases to be a simple command.

From such considerations, which I have rendered very briefly and in my own words, Hare concluded that the imperative mood, if it is to be serviceable for the analysis of moral terms, must be "modified" and "enriched" "in order to be able to frame in it proper universal sentences" (*LM*, 181 and 187). Hare summed up the differences between the ordinary imperative sentences and 'ought'-judgements as follows:

The reasons why proper universal sentences cannot be framed in the imperative mood are two. In the first place this mood is confined, with a few exceptions which are apparent only, to the future tense, whereas a proper universal sentence has to apply to all times, past, present, and future (e.g. 'All mules are barren' has to apply to all mules at all periods of the world's history if it is to be a proper universal; we have to be able to derive from it, in conjunction with 'Joe was a mule', the sentence 'Joe was barren'). Secondly, the imperative mood occurs predominantly in the second person; there are some first person plural imperatives, and some third person imperatives in singular and plural; there is also a form 'Let me . . .' which serves as a first person singular imperative. But these persons are of different form, in English, from the second person, and may be of a somewhat different logical character. More serious is the difficulty that there is no means of framing an imperative sentence beginning with 'one' or with the impersonal 'you': there is nothing in the imperative mood analogous to the indicative sentence 'One does not see many hansom cabs nowadays' or the value-judgement 'One ought not to tell lies'. It is obvious that, if we are to be able to frame proper universal imperatives, they must be such that, with the aid of the appropriate minor premises, we can derive from them imperative sentences in all the persons, as well as in all the tenses. The imperative mood, therefore, has for our purposes to be enriched in order to make it possible to frame sentences in all persons and all tenses. (*LM*, 187–8.)

These deficiencies, Hare claimed, can be eliminated by making use of the method of analysing sentences into phrastics and neustics with which we are by now familiar. Phrastics, since they are common to indicatives and imperatives, are as universal as we please. So by adding an imperative neustic to a properly universal phrastic, Hare explained, we get an artificial but enriched imperative, for example:

(1) All things that are said being true, please. And this imperative is then presumably quite close in meaning to the 'ought'-judgement:

(2) One ought always to speak the truth. (*LM*, 189.)

One cannot help but have serious doubt about this procedure. First of all, in what sense can (1) be said to be still an imperative, artificial or otherwise? Hare's answer would be: it has an imperative neustic. But one should think that 'please' was chosen by Hare to designate the imperative neustic on the ground that it is a word which often figures in such speech-acts as commands, entreaties, appeals, pleas, petitions, requests, and so on. Now all these speech-acts look to the future and are person-directed and the word 'please', when it figures in them, serves exactly to emphasize this. In other words, it is not just that ordinary imperatives do not possess universal phrastics whereas 'ought'-judgements do, but the neustic of an 'ought'-judgement is also radically different from the neustic of an imperative. An imperative does differ from an 'ought'-judgement by having certain restrictions on its criteria of application: an imperative is not properly universal, we cannot, for example, single out by it something in the past; but this is so because imperatives and 'ought'-judgements differ also with regard to their performative forces. The difference between the two is a total difference.

The fact that Hare made a mistake in seeing even a partial similarity between 'ought'-judgements and imperatives, and in trying to equate the performative force of the two, can be seen in still another way. The trouble is that once we have "modified" and "enriched" the imperative mood along Hare's lines, we have done in one way too little, in another too much. If we ignore the difficulties concerning the proposed neustic 'please' mentioned before, general 'ought'-principles can be satisfactorily translated into the new imperative mood:

(1) One ought always to speak the truth.
(2) All things that are said ought to be true.
(3) All things that are said being true, please. (Cf. *LM*, 191.)

But singular 'ought'-judgements, Hare himself pointed out, provide difficulties. Let us, for example, take 'You ought to tell him the truth'.

(1') You ought to tell him the truth.
(2') The thing you are about to tell him ought to be true.
(3') The thing you are about to tell him being true, please.

With this procedure we end up with (3') which is indistinguishable from a singular imperative and therefore does not imply that there is a general principle which constitutes the reason for it. (1′), however, does imply that there is such a general principle. (1′) commits me to saying that if anyone is in the same situation, he ought to tell the truth also; (3′), on the other hand, does not commit me to saying that. This translation of the singular 'ought'-judgement into an explicit phrastic and an explicit neustic will therefore not do. The analysis of singular 'ought'-judgements, Hare explained, is really very complicated, but for the above example he seems to have proposed the following:

(4) If you do not tell him the truth, you will be breaking the principle 'All things that are said being true, please' and I hereby subscribe to that principle. (cf. *LM*, 193.)

But the trouble is now that (4) is not by any stretch of imagination an imperative of any kind or even like one, artificial or not. It rather points out the important fact that in passing a moral judgement I am, or may be, among other things, subscribing to or enunciating a principle of conduct.

The conclusions we want to draw from the above discussion are the following. One of the main reasons for Hare's claim that moral judgements possess what he called "evaluative meaning" was that in some important ways they resemble imperatives and that the imperative neustic 'please' is what epitomizes this kind of meaning. But we have seen that Hare himself has much to say on how *dissimilar* moral judgements and imperatives really are and we pointed out that the dissimilarity is even a great deal more thorough-going than he believed. In uttering an imperative I may say 'please', but hardly in uttering a moral judgement. Comparison with imperatives thus in no way supports the doctrine of the evaluative meaning of moral judgements.

The comparison of these two types of utterances, 'ought'-judgements and imperatives, served for Hare another purpose: it was to lend support also for the claim that moral judgements possess "descriptive meaning" as well. Here Hare emphasized dissimilarities rather than similarities. A moral judgement, unlike an imperative, makes reference to general principles: it implies that there is a reason behind it and that if it is the case that I ought to do a certain thing, then anyone in the same circumstances must have the same obligation. Therefore, Hare concluded, moral judgements must have some descriptive meaning. But he agreed with Stevenson that what the descriptive meaning of a moral judgement is cannot be gathered simply from linguistic rules. The descriptive content of a moral judgement is rather determined by the moral rules to which the person passing that moral judgement subscribes. What the descriptive meaning of a moral judgement is, and therefore what would count as a reason for that judgement, was thus made itself a matter of the morals of the individual in question. This would indeed raise doubts concerning how moral reasoning in a serious sense is at all possible. However, this is a topic which we have reserved for the next section. Our question for the present is: do we have to assume the existence of descriptive meaning in moral judgements in order to account for their universality and the fact that they make reference to general principles?

In his second book, *Freedom and Reason*, Hare himself seemed to be uneasy about the account which he had given of the descriptive aspect of moral terms in *The Language of Morals*. He now approached the problem largely in terms of what he called the "universalizability" of evaluative judgements. Descriptive and moral judgements are alike, he said, due to the fact that they are both universalizable (*FR*, 12). And by universalizability he simply meant that if a person attributes a predicate to an object, then he must attribute that predicate to "anything which was like it in relevant respects" (*FR*, 11). Only if a judgement is universalizable in this sense can it have reasons and be other than arbitrary (*FR*, 21). But we can easily agree with Hare that moral judgements are universalizable in this sense, and therefore based on reasons, without having to conclude that such judgements possess descriptive meaning. All that is required for moral judgements to be universalizable and capable of being supported by reasons is that they involve criteria of application. Hare nevertheless urged in *Freedom and Reason* (and before in *The Language of Morals*) that evaluative terms and judgements, including moral terms and judgements, possess two *kinds* of meaning and that what makes evaluative judgements similar to descriptive judgements is that both of them contain descriptive meaning. It is just that evaluative judgements possess something in addition—namely, evaluative or prescriptive meaning. The point is, however, not that value-judgements do something in addition to describing. Such judgements do not describe at all, although it is true that both passing a moral judgement and describing involve criteria of application. Hare believed that we can explain how moral judgements can be supported by reasons only if we say that such judgements incorporate two kinds of meaning, evaluative (or prescriptive) and descriptive. But, as a matter of fact, if we do say this it becomes difficult to understand how it is logically possible to give reasons for a moral judgement at all.

To say that moral judgements possess two kinds of meaning, descriptive and evaluative, and leave it at that would obviously be unsatisfactory. If we did not explain how these two meanings are logically related, we would not understand how it is possible to give reasons for a moral judgement. A reason for a moral judgement is presumably a descriptive statement. It is easy to see how such a statement could be a reason for another descriptive statement: S is a reason for S' if, and only if, S is true and S' logically follows from S. But a moral judgement, Hare has told us, is not just a descriptive statement. It is also, and primarily, an evaluative judgement. If so, we can see how a moral judgement can be supported by a descriptive statement as its reason only in so far as it contains descriptive meaning, that is, to the extent to which it itself is a descriptive statement. But what about that part of the moral judgement that is evaluative? The distinction between the two kinds of meaning in moral judgements has created a gulf which no logic can bridge. It can be bridged only, Hare will have to say, by a decision for which no reasons can be given.

We have already expressed our suspicion that the situation is hopeless. It is hopeless due to Hare's failure to notice that properly speaking criteria of application and descriptive meaning are not one and the same. Criteria of application and descriptive meaning are not identical and there is therefore no reason to believe that only descriptive utterances, or utterances in so far as they are descriptive, have criteria. If we do believe that, the problem of moral reasoning becomes insoluble from the start. To describe and, say, to commend, are both to do more than to apply words. To apply words is simply to correlate them with something in the world. By having done this, we have not yet said or communicated anything. It is therefore difficult to give a direct verbal example of this activity. Perhaps Hare's phrastics will do as well as anything for this purpose. 'This being blue' applies the words 'this' and 'blue', that is, it correlates them with a particular object and a colour. There are conventions which must be obeyed if the act of application is to come off; it would be a misfire if, for example, what I intended to single out is in Africa and not a colour but a shape. If this act of application does take effect, we would not yet have anything that can be called true or false, right or wrong, justified or unjustified. Still, we would be on our way. 'This being blue' says nothing, but what it accomplishes must be accomplished as something preparatory to saying anything. That preliminary act is involved in anything that I say. It is involved in my saying 'This is blue', that is, in a descriptive statement: I have now added the descriptive neustic. And it is also involved in my saying 'Is this blue?', that is, in a question: I have now added the interrogative neustic. It would also be involved in the order or command 'Paint this blue': I have now added the imperative neustic; although here additional matters of application come in also. Finally, suppose that I am in a painter's studio commenting on his work in progress, and say 'This is a good blue'. Again application, that is, the act of evoking a sense and reference by relying on certain criteria, must be accomplished if I am to have succeeded in having said anything by adding the evaluative neustic. If I am to succeed in the act of commending, I must first of all have secured proper initial uptake of my words by observing certain criteria of application, that is, rules by which words are correlated with things found in the world and experiences. This is of course not all I have to do; in order to commend I must observe further rules. The hearer has to understand not only *what* I am commending but also *that* I am commending. And this is possible only by reference to further conventions.

Furthermore, the observance of the proper criteria of application, together with the further rules on which the felicitousness of an act of commending depends, does not of course secure that my commendation was right or justified.[1] But neither does the observance of criteria of application secure the truth of the descriptive statement 'This is blue'. All I have to do to observe criteria of application is to mean by 'blue' blue. Once I have done this, I can go on to perform the further acts of describing, ordering, commending, or what have you. It is only after I have performed one of these further acts that there will be anything that is capable of being appraised as true or false, right or wrong. Truth and falsity, rightness and wrongness, require in any case more than just managing to say what one means, that is, to observe the proper conventions.

'This is blue' and 'This is good' both have criteria of application or a sense and a reference. The difference is merely that one of them is also a descriptive or factual statement and the other, let us say, a commendation. There is of course the further question whether the term 'good' by itself possesses criteria of application or just commendatory force. But with this question we need not yet be concerned. I have merely been trying to argue that Hare was wrong in claiming that only descriptive judgements or judgements in so far as they are descriptions have criteria of application whereas imperatives, commendations, prescriptions do not, and that therefore we must assume that moral judgements, if they are to be capable of being supported by reasons, must themselves be, in part, factual or descriptive judgements. This assumption, I have claimed, instead of making it easier to give a satisfactory account of how moral judgements can have reasons, makes such an account impossible. Had Hare not made this assumption and not given up the distinction between phrastics and neustics in favour of the distinction between descriptive and evaluative meaning, he would have probably been more successful. If we view criteria of application in the manner which I have indicated above, it does become possible to make sense of how moral judgements can be supported by factual reasons. The relation that allows a factual statement to be a reason for a moral judgement is not a relation between two sorts

---

[1] 'Felicitousness', or rather its opposite 'infelicity', is Austin's term. See his *How to Do Things with Words*. The two dimensions, adumbrated here, in which our speech-acts may be appraised will be discussed more fully in the next chapter. Austin also has a good deal to say on this subject.

of meanings. A factual statement is a reason for a moral judgement by virtue of a relation between their respective criteria of application. If the criteria of application of a factual statement overlap the criteria of application of a moral judgement, then it is a reason for that moral judgement. And a moral judgement is fully supported by reasons and hence justified or right only when there is a set of (true) factual statements such that the criteria of application of that set contain the criteria of application of that moral judgement. There is no need to assume that a moral judgement is itself in part a factual statement.

Hare recognized that if moral judgements are to have reasons there must be a logical connexion between description and evaluation. He claimed that this connexion is not one of "entailment", but that it nevertheless "seems to be" a "logical" one (*LM*, 111). But as we shall see, it turns out in Hare's theory that the connexion is not really a logical one after all. He argued that the assertion 'This is a sweet strawberry' can serve as a reason for the assertion 'This is a good strawberry' only if we have the appropriate "major premise", that is, the specification of sweetness as one of the standards of goodness in strawberries (*LM*, 111). But what such standards or, as Hare called them, "principles of choosing" (*LM*, 134) are, is in his theory a matter to be ultimately settled by a decision. The description 'This is a sweet strawberry' is thus, according to Hare, linked to the evaluation 'This is a good strawberry' only through the decisions that we happen to make. Hare explained that sometimes there is a direct logical connexion between the assertion 'This is a sweet strawberry' and 'This is a good strawberry', but in those cases the assertion 'This is a good strawberry' is itself a mere description and so has no evaluative meaning. According to Hare, whenever assertions like 'This is a good strawberry' are genuinely evaluative, they have no logical connexion with any factual statements whatever. The connexion between evaluations and descriptions depends on standards and principles and those, in turn, on decisions. Such a conclusion is clearly unsatisfactory. Hare has told us that the most important thing about value-judgements is their prescriptive and commendatory force. Their function is thus to guide our decisions. But if the connexion between value-judgements and their reasons depends on our decisions, what is and what is not a well-supported value-judgement is itself a matter of decision. We are thus clearly going in a circle.

4. *Logic and Moral Reasoning*

Let us now turn to Hare's views on the nature of moral reasoning in greater detail. For him, to reason about moral judgements is in the end to reason about imperatives. Moral judgements were said to be one type of value-judgement and this meant that they entail imperatives (*LM*, 163). Thus a piece of moral reasoning always has for its ultimate end-product an imperative (*LM*, 39). The argument may be initially laid out in terms of value-judgements containing words like 'good', 'right', and 'ought', but the reasoning is not complete until all value-words have been eliminated and an explicit imperative is reached. Exactly what this imperative is in each case is a question which Hare did not discuss very explicitly and to which he gave no definitive answer. He believed, as we saw, that the analysis of "singular 'ought'-sentences", to which other value-judgements can be reduced, is "an extremely complex matter" (*LM*, 191). Throughout the remainder of *The Language of Morals* he seems to have taken a more simplified view and assumed that the imperative entailed by a moral judgement of the form 'A ought to do X' can be arrived at simply by eliminating the words 'ought to' from it, so that it becomes 'A, do X' (*LM*, 168-9).

Hare agreed with Toulmin that in ethics there is a difference between valid and invalid arguments, good and bad reasons. But he did not think that the concept of validity in ethical reasoning is different in type from that in deductive reasoning: for him moral reasoning was deductive and analytic. He claimed that all logical relations are analytic in the sense of depending on the meanings of words, especially on the meanings of logical words such as 'all'. If someone were to refuse to admit a valid argument he would thereby simply be displaying his ignorance of the meanings of such words. Thus, for example,

if someone professed to admit that all men are mortal and that Socrates was a man, but refused to admit that Socrates was mortal,

the correct thing to do would be . . . to say 'You evidently don't
know the meaning of the word "all"; for if you did you would *eo ipso*
know how to make inferences of this sort'. (*LM*, 33.)

Toulmin, we recall, maintained that there are valid inferences in
moral reasoning which are not analytic. With this Hare definitely
disagreed. For him logical relations in ethics, as elsewhere, were
synonymous with analytic relations. Hare tried to substantiate this
claim by arguing that logical relations are essentially a matter of
the phrastic element of sentences. The logical sign of negation; the
logical connectives 'if', 'and', 'or'; and the quantifiers 'all' and
'some', should be treated, he claimed, as parts of phrastics (*LM*,
20–21). And since phrastics are independent of the mood, or as
we should say, the performative force, of the sentences in which
they occur, Hare concluded that imperatives just as indicatives,
and commands just as statements, follow logical rules and may
contradict and entail one another (*LM*, 24–25).

  Do these consequences really follow? If we view logic exclusively
as a matter of phrastics, then it does follow in Hare's view that the
phrastics of imperatives are capable of contradiction and entailment.
The same thing does not, however, follow with regard to full
imperative sentences and commands. What is true of phrastics need
not be true of utterances into which phrastics enter as parts. If we
construe logic as concerned merely with phrastics, the question of
what entailment relations exist between our utterances in so far as
they contain further elements besides phrastics would simply
cease to be a purely logical question. Hare, of course, believed
that there are logical entailments between full sentences, and he
described the conditions under which they hold as follows:

A sentence P entails a sentence Q if and only if the fact that a person
assents to P but dissents from Q is a sufficient criterion for saying that
he has misunderstood one or other of the sentences. (*LM*, 25.)

So long as we speak of sentences which are all either indicatives
or imperatives it does not matter whether we think of logical
relations as existing only between the phrastics of those sentences
or between those sentences as wholes. It does not matter since,

as long as we remain exclusively in the realm of either indicatives or imperatives, the required neustics would all be the same. However, the sentences in moral reasoning are clearly of a mixed sort. The characteristic cases of moral reasoning must depend on logical relations existing between sentences which are not homogeneous, that is, do not have the same neustics or performative force. We infer a *moral* conclusion, which is not a statement, from *factual* premises, which are statements. Hare formulated two rules, of such heterogeneous inferences, the second of which, he claimed, is of paramount importance to ethics:

(1) No indicative conclusion can be validly drawn from a set of premisses which cannot be validly drawn from the indicatives among them alone.

(2) No imperative conclusion can be validly drawn from a set of premisses which does not contain at least one imperative. (*LM*, 28, Hare's italics omitted.)

Now these rules do not of course deal only with phrastics. Should they then be called logical rules? This would be just to quibble about words. There is excellent reason for calling logical relations those relations which have to do only with the phrastic elements of sentences or utterances. Criteria of application, or sense and reference, or what Hare called the phrastics of our speech-acts, are what traditionally logicians have been mainly concerned with. But there is a wider usage for the term 'logic' in which it includes also the study of the uses of language for making assertions, giving commands, asking questions, and so on, and of the interrelations between such full speech-acts. It is clearly this wider sense of 'logic' which is particularly relevant for moral philosophy. Therefore, when Hare argued that since moral reasoning is concerned with matters of substance, what moral conclusion follows from a factual premise cannot be decided by logic alone, we should probably understand him as using 'logic' in this broader sense.

This claim about the relation between factual premises and moral conclusions is what, according to Hare, separates his theory from naturalism and we find it reasserted in his later book *Freedom and Reason*. In it he wrote:

My theory, indeed, allows for our normal use of non-moral facts as part of the ingredients of a moral argument; but unlike naturalism, it says that they cannot be the sole ingredient besides logic. (*FR*, 198.)

There are thus two assertions which are central to Hare's theory of moral reasoning:

(1) the logic of moral reasoning is deductive and analytic, and
(2) moral reasoning concerns "matters of substance" in the sense of having "as its end-product an imperative of the form 'Do so-and-so'". (*LM*, 39.)

According to Hare, the first of these assertions meant that the conclusion of a piece of moral reasoning can contain nothing which is not "from their very meaning, implicit in the conjunction of the premisses" (*LM*, 32). Consequently, from (1) and (2) together it followed that in a moral argument the premises themselves had to contain an imperative—a universal imperative or general principle of conduct. We cannot draw a prescriptive conclusion from purely factual premises. Since the function of moral reasoning is to guide conduct, its premises cannot be purely descriptive.

The contrary view, we recall, was upheld by Toulmin. By what Toulmin called evaluative inference, we can proceed from purely factual premises to genuinely moral, that is, prescriptive, conclusions. Hare disagreed with Toulmin. He claimed, at least in *The Language of Morals*, that moral reasoning typically has the pattern of a syllogism. In a "moral syllogism" the major premise is a "general principle of action", an example of which is the universal imperative 'Never say what is false'. And from this universal imperative in conjunction with a factual minor premise, we can infer a particular evaluative conclusion. As the pattern of the last stage of moral reasoning, that is, the stage in which terms like 'ought' and 'good' have been eliminated in favour of explicit imperatives, we thus have, according to Hare, the following:

> Never say what is false
> S is false
> ∴ Do not say S

In contrast, Toulmin's position as viewed by Hare is the following (*LM*, 45 ff.). The conclusion 'Do not say S' can be got from the factual premise, 'S is false', directly with the aid of a rule of inference corresponding to the major premise, 'Never say what is false'. We might schematize this as follows:

$$S \text{ is false}$$
$$\therefore \text{ Do not say } S$$

Hare gave the following reasons for preferring his own theory to Toulmin's:

> To hold that an imperative conclusion can be derived from purely indicative premises leads to representing matters of substance as if they were verbal matters. (*LM*, 46–47.)

. . . .

> Suppose that I say 'Don't say that, because it is false'. Are we to represent this argument as follows:
>
> $$S \text{ is false}$$
> $$\therefore \text{ Do not say } S$$
>
> or shall we add the imperative major premiss 'Never say what is false'? If the latter, the inference is valid by the ordinary rules of logic; but if the former, we have to have a special rule of inference, which will be just this imperative major premiss in another capacity. Does it matter which of these alternatives we choose? Surely it does if we are concerned to distinguish between on the one hand general principles about our conduct, which have content, and tell us to do, or to refrain from, certain positive acts in our external behaviour, and on the other logical rules, which are rules, not for behaving correctly, but for talking and thinking correctly, and are . . . not about actions, but about the meanings of the words used. (*LM*, 48–49.)

This, I think, is a perfectly valid criticism although the phrase "meanings of the words used" is ambiguous. Our own discussion of Toulmin's views revealed that he was guilty of a confusion between questions of logic and questions of morals. We saw that, contrary to his views, neither the accepted moral principles of a society nor Toulmin's own supreme principle of social harmony can be regarded as logical rules governing inferences from factual premises to normative moral conclusions. It may be that there is no ironclad and absolute difference between the "analytic" principles of logic and the "synthetic" principles concerning matters of fact or matters of morals. But surely with regard to any given discourse of some complexity there is a vast relative difference between the principles concerning the subject matter of that discourse and the principles governing that discourse itself. It is true that Hare has not offered us a fully fledged theory on the basis of which we can always separate logical principles from principles of other sorts. Such a theory is perhaps too much to hope for from anyone at the present time. We must take his remark that logical rules are "about the meanings of the words used" on the strength of traditional views. And these views may no longer be adequate. As we pointed out, traditionally, logic has been concerned exclusively with the sense and reference of what we say and communicate, in other words, with matters relating to the phrastics of sentences. A logic which would be serviceable for ethics, on the other hand, would have to pay attention to and systematize relations between full sentences or speech-acts, in other words, between sentences or speech-acts as wholes containing not only sense and reference but performative forces or neustics as well. But ethical theorists in the twentieth century have not yet advanced to the point where a detailed development of such a logic is possible. The debate among them concerns, at the present time, only rudiments and foundations. Let us then continue our examination of Hare's contribution to this debate.

5. Decisions and Principles

Another reason which Hare gave for rejecting the view that moral reasoning is not deductive and analytic but based on a special kind of evaluative inference was that that view, "leaves out of our reasoning about conduct a factor which is of the very essence of morals. This factor is decision" (*LM*, 54–55). Logical laws do not determine everything about moral reasoning. A moral argument is essentially a kind of syllogism and we therefore need major premises. These, Hare claimed, are supplied by our decisions. According to him, if I decide to make an exception of a principle like 'Do not say what is false', I am making what he calls a 'decision of principle'. In that case my choice is not merely between observing or not observing that principle; what I decide will in effect create a new principle. Whenever an exception is made to a moral principle, and whenever a moral principle is broken, that principle is modified.

Hare went even further. Not only is a principle created whenever an exception is made to an already existing principle, but all decisions, whether to observe or to break principles, are creative acts, creating, or recreating, principles. "All decisions", he wrote, "except those, if any, that are completely arbitrary are to some extent decisions of principle. We are always setting precedents for ourselves" (*LM*, 65); and

> In order to act on principle it is not necessary in some sense to have a principle already, before you act; it may be that the decision to act in a certain way, because of something about the effects of acting in that way, *is* to subscribe to a principle of action. . . . (*LM*, 59.)

> . . . it is not clear what is meant . . . by speaking of moral principles 'existing'; but even if they (in some sense) exist, I am sure that they do not always exist *antecedently*, so that all we have to do is to consult them. . . . Nevertheless, when we do make up our minds, it is about a matter of principle which has a bearing outside the particular case. (*FR*, 38.)

Such passages are not entirely unequivocal. There are two things which are clearly implied by them: (*a*) that it is decisions that create principles, and (*b*) that sometimes principles do not exist before we decide to act on them. What is not so clear is whether Hare held the stronger beliefs: (a_1) that my decision to act in a certain way creates the very principle which serves to justify my decision to act in that way, and (b_2) that principles never exist before we decide to act on them.

To make these stronger claims would certainly be to go too far. Toulmin seemed to have this matter straight when he distinguished between the ordinary and the test cases of decisions. Sometimes, in order to justify my decision, all I have to do is to show that it was part of an established practice incorporating certain accepted principles. But there are unusual situations in which my decision becomes a test case for the rightness of a whole practice itself. What Hare seems to suggest at times is that all our moral decisions constitute test cases. But there seems to be no reason to deny that sometimes my task of justifying my decision is done once I have cited an accepted principle of conduct which my decision exemplifies. If I decide to act in a certain way, I may be doing just one thing at the time: choosing a course of action. I need not, at the same time, be setting up a principle. And in those cases where my decision becomes a decision of principle, I cannot of course refer to that very principle by way of justifying that decision. In so far as I can justify my decisions by principles, my principles must keep one step ahead of my decisions. In that sense it is, contrary to what Hare claimed, necessary "in order to act on principle . . . to have a principle already, before you act".

It may be that the justification we offer for our decisions in terms of principles would have to rest, ultimately, on further decisions for which no ready-made principles are available. It may also be that, ultimately, principles "exist" only in so far as they are incorporated in and sustained by our decisions. But Hare's account of the relation between decisions and principles and of the whole matter of moral reasoning and justification has, nevertheless, deficiencies. First, he does not pay enough attention to the fact that quite often an ultimate justification is not called for and it is enough to refer to a principle which exists in the sense that it is generally accepted or follows from a more general principle which is generally accepted. Second, and this is far more serious and will occupy a great deal of our attention, Hare does not explain how the more momentous and ultimate decisions—the decisions of principles—can themselves be defended by reasons. From Hare's writings we get inevitably the impression that they really cannot be defended at all and that morality rests on decisions and commitments for which rational justification is out of place.

According to the account which Hare gave of moral reasoning in *The Language of Morals* the possibility of moral argument rested on there being general moral principles. The problem of moral justification was conceived largely as the problem of moral principles. The view expressed in that book was that moral reasoning is deductive and general moral principles serve as major premises in practical syllogisms. Now as he himself pointed out (*LM*, 40–41), in a syllogism, whatever certainty the conclusion has depends on the certainty of its premises. In

> All mules are barren
> M is a mule
> ∴ M is barren,

the certainty of the conclusion 'M is barren' rests on whatever grounds there are for asserting the premises 'All mules are barren' and 'M is a mule'. Similarly, in

> Never say what is false
> S is false
> ∴ Do not say S,

the certainty of 'Do not say S' depends on whatever grounds there are for holding 'Never say what is false' and 'S is false'. But conversely, whatever uncertainty there may be about the conclusion of a syllogism must be reflected in its premises. Let us suppose that in a particular instance I am in doubt whether or not to assent to the conclusion not to say S. I must then also be in doubt about either 'S is false' or 'Never say what is false'. If I am in doubt about 'S is false', the issue is factual or empirical. If, however, my doubt concerns the major premise, I have to decide whether I should observe or break the principle 'Never say what is false'. But if, as in Hare's theory, 'Do not say S' is analytically *entailed* by 'Never say what is false' together with the factual minor premise, what *reasons* can I then have for doubting 'Do not say S' *before* I doubt 'Never say what is false'?

Now Hare argues with great force that moral principles are not self-evident nor can they be deduced from more general principles which are (*LM*, 39). The "Cartesian" approach, that is, starting with premises that cannot themselves be questioned, is as impossible in ethics as it is in science. According to Hare, general moral principles are therefore like empirical generalizations or hypotheses such as 'All mules are barren', and we can therefore be in doubt about moral judgements and imperatives as well as about general moral principles which entail them just in the same way as we can be in doubt about singular empirical statements and the empirical generalizations which entail them. Is Hare able to make good sense of this analogy? We may be in doubt concerning a singular empirical statement which a hypothesis entails if it does not square with observation. An empirical statement of fact may be deducible from general principles, but it must also be borne out by observation. Neither its deducibility nor its relation to experience is an absolute criterion, but if we have made sure that the observer is operating under normal conditions and is in a good position to deliver a verdict, then his verdict will count towards confirming or disconfirming the hypothesis. According to Hare, moral judgements and imperatives are, just like singular statements of fact, deducible from general principles. But what does he put in the place of experience and observation in the case of moral judgements and imperatives? This remains in the framework of Hare's theory extremely puzzling. Hare argued that the consequences of an action have just as much relevance to moral judgements as principles do and that moral principles must themselves be justified by the consequences of observing them. But since he insisted that "No imperative conclusions can be validly drawn from a set of premisses which does not contain at least one imperative" (*LM*, 28) and that, more generally, no value-judgements or normative statements are implied by factual premises, this relevance and justification can be no simple matter. Or at least, it is a matter which Hare failed to explain.

Hare might have pictured the process of justifying general principles of conduct as follows. The statement 'All mules are barren' is an empirical generalization, and the degree of confirmation that it possesses depends on the particular empirical statements which it entails. Similarly, the support that a general moral principle has depends on the particular moral judgements or imperatives entailed by that principle. Now the truth-values of particular empirical statements which are capable of lending a degree of confirmation to empirical generalizations are determined by experience. What would correspond to experience in the case of general moral principles? Well, Hare seemed to be saying, the fact that decisions of a certain kind are made. Just as we make statements like 'All mules are barren' on the basis of past experience, we lay down moral principles on the basis of past decisions. Something like this seems to be presupposed by the following passage:

But suppose that we were faced, for the first time, with the question "Shall I now say what is false?" and had *no past decision*, either of our own or of other people, to guide us. How should we then decide the question? Not, surely, by inference from a self-evident principle. . . . (*LM*, 40, my italics.)

Let us then interpret Hare as having said in *The Language of Morals* that just as empirical generalizations are confirmed by facts, general moral principles are confirmed by decisions. But could Hare consistently say that general moral principles or moral judgements are confirmed or disconfirmed if people *as a matter of fact* in relevant circumstances decide in certain ways and not in others? Such a view would have been incompatible with his claim that no normative or prescriptive statements are implied by factual statements. What 'Never say what is false' entails, according to Hare, is not statements like 'If confronted with the choice between saying or not saying S, which is false, you as a matter of fact, will not say S', but statements like 'If confronted with the choice between saying or not saying S, which is false, you should not say S'.

Now perhaps Hare could try to remedy this by saying that it is decisions as decisions of principle and not as mere factual settlements of a choice which serve as "evidence" for a general moral principle. But we are stretching our imagination. Moral principles are not self-evident; in Hare's theory they are like empirical generalizations. But it is difficult to make good sense of this analogy. Can we, for example, say that one moral principle or moral judgement is more probable than another? Do two favourable decisions give a greater degree of confirmation to a principle than would only one? Since a decision is always a "decision of principle", should not any one of them be just as conclusive as any number of them together? We may thus prove any moral conclusion we please, since by our decision we can always create the appropriate principle to serve as the major premise. Moral reasoning depends on moral principles and these, in turn, on our decisions. We are thus, from a moral point of view, free to decide as we please. Hare wrote:

I gave in the preceding chapter reasons for holding that no moral system whose principles were regarded as purely factual could fulfil its function of regulating our conduct. In this chapter I have shown that no moral system which claims to be based on principles which are self-evident can fulfil this function either. . . . It is not surprising that the first effect of modern logical researches was to make some philosophers despair of morals as a rational activity.

It is the purpose of this book to show that their despair was premature. (*LM*, 44–45.)

But if we make morals, as Hare (in effect) did, exclusively a matter of decisions, it seems that there is cause, if not for despair, then at least for some uneasiness and concern. To refer the matter to decisions is not enough, since the crucial question is, 'Why are some decisions more right than others?' Clearly, if moral reasoning is to be practical—that is, have relevance to our actions—it must have a connexion with our decisions. But it cannot be the case that what principles and rules we adopt is a matter merely of the decision we happen to make in any given case.

In the next chapter I shall try to show that if we are to make use of an analogy between the justification of empirical hypotheses and general principles of conduct, we must concentrate on a matter mentioned in passing earlier. If an observational statement is to have any weight in confirming or disconfirming a general hypothesis, it must be the result of careful or veridical observation. We must make sure that the observer was in the position to deliver his verdict. Similarly, a decision or a judgement concerning moral issues carries weight only if the person in question was in a good position to make that decision or pass that judgement.

We saw that Hare's theory concerning the nature of moral language was definitely an advance over Stevenson's. Instead of talking about moral terms as psychological instruments by which men's emotions are stirred, he concentrated on their prescriptive and commendatory functions. He pointed out rightly that prescribing and commending as linguistic acts need not be "highly coloured with emotion" (*LM*, 119). He saw clearly that there is a difference between the causal and the conventional connexions that exist between words and psychological phenomena. That ethical terms are causally connected with such things as emotions was not, however, all that Stevenson said about moral language. His further claims were that there is no logical connexion between the evaluative and descriptive meanings of a value-judgement. And with this paradox Hare must in the end agree. For both of these authors assertions like 'You ought to do this' or 'That is good' contain two kinds of meaning. These meanings we communicate in the same breath, but how this happens remains a mystery. For Stevenson the only tie between the two meanings in a value-judgement was a psychological accident: such and such descriptive dispositions go with such and such emotive dispositions and this is all that can be said about the matter. For Hare, a similar consequence follows: what descriptive and evaluative meanings belong together is merely a matter of decisions which in the business of living we are simply forced to make.

How then can moral judgements be supported by reasons? For Hare, the answer to this question depended on which moral principles we accept as the major premises in practical syllogisms, and this, in turn, on our decisions. Consequently, in the theory expounded in *The Language of Morals*, what reasons can be given for a moral judgement is a matter to be ultimately settled by the decisions we in fact happen to make—for no reason.

6. *Hare's Further Thoughts on Moral Reasoning*

In his *Freedom and Reason* Hare sought, among other things, to supplement the account of moral reasoning which he had given in *The Language of Morals* and on which we have concentrated so far. In his earlier book, as we have seen, he gave an account of the matter in terms of "decisions of principle" and the "practical syllogism" and put forth the thesis that we come to a reasoned moral conclusion concerning what we ought to do by deducing, as the ultimate end result, an imperative from a major and a minor premise, the first being a general principle of conduct, the second a particular factual statement concerning the contemplated action. But, he also said, whether there are any general principles of conduct which can serve as the major premises in such practical syllogisms depends on our decisions. Principles are indispensable for giving reasons for our decisions, but they are themselves derived from prior decisions of principle. We can have moral reasons for deciding to act in one way rather than in another only if we choose to accept them as reasons. Thus, it turned out, in the end reason in ethics must rest on purely non-rational commitments.

In *Freedom and Reason* Hare tried to offer a more well-rounded and less paradoxical doctrine. One may say that while in the earlier book he was anxious to defend the freedom of our moral decisions against what he regarded as the false demands of reason of the naturalistic variety, in the later one his concern was mainly to allot a more commodious place to reason without falling prey to naturalism. But, as we shall see, he was still unable to give a fully adequate account of the place of reason in ethics. It still turned out that reason plays a very subsidiary role in ethics: there are differences in our moral convictions which cannot be adjudicated by reason. This conclusion was merely hidden behind an ambivalent discussion of utilitarianism and what looks like the curious argument that since moral differences concern, ultimately, ideals, it is only what he called the 'fanatic' who would be anxious to try to eliminate them anyhow.

In *Freedom and Reason* Hare said that "it may be that moral reasoning is not, typically, any kind of 'straight-line' or 'linear' reasoning from premisses to conclusion" but is instead a kind of "exploration" (*FR*, 87). Nevertheless, whatever inferences are embodied in such reasoning were still held to be deductive and Toulmin's view to the contrary was still rejected. It is just that the whole matter was said to be more complex: moral reasoning is a kind of exploration like scientific reasoning which consists of "looking for hypotheses which will stand up to the test of experiment" (*FR*, 88). We saw that in *The Language of Morals* Hare was unable to make good sense of the presumed analogy between scientific and ethical reasoning. Let us see if in *Freedom and Reason* this idea yielded more satisfactory results. In it Hare said:

The rules of moral reasoning are, basically, two, corresponding to the two features of moral judgments ... prescriptivity and universalizability. When we are trying, in a concrete case, to decide what we ought to do, what we are looking for . . . is an action to which we can commit ourselves (prescriptivity) but which we are at the same time prepared to accept as exemplifying a principle of action to be prescribed for others in like circumstances (universalizability). If, when we consider some proposed action, we find that, when universalized, it yields prescriptions which we cannot accept, we reject this action as a solution to our moral problem—if we cannot universalize the prescription, it cannot become an 'ought'. (FR, 89–90.)

Suppose, then, that I find myself inclined to do a particular action X, but am wondering whether I *ought* to do X. In order to solve my problem, I must reflect in the following way. I ought to do X only if I am prepared to accept the universal principle that anyone in my position ought to do X. Am I prepared to accept that principle? Doing X has consequences for another person. But in prescribing X universally I must be ready for the eventuality that I myself will have to bear the consequences of someone doing X. In other words, the question I must ask is whether I would find the effects of X acceptable were I myself at the receiving end. If the answer is 'No', I ought not to do X (FR, 90–91). Let us call this manner of reasoning the universalizability argument.

Hare claimed that all this is nicely in parallel with the process of scientific reasoning:

Just as science, seriously pursued, is the search for hypotheses and the testing of them by the attempt to falsify their particular consequences, so morals, as a serious endeavour, consists in the search for principles and the testing of them against particular cases. Any rational activity has its discipline, and this is the discipline of moral thought: to test the moral principles that suggest themselves to us by following out their consequences and seeing whether we can accept *them*. (FR, 92.)

The difference between scientific reasoning and moral reasoning, Hare explained, is simply that while in science we do the testing in terms of "singular statements of fact", in morals we use "singular prescriptions" or imperatives (FR, 92). I must reject the provisional principle 'Everyone ought to do X' if, owing to my own inclinations, I cannot accept the singular prescription 'Let A do X to me'. One ingredient besides "facts" and "logic" in moral reasoning is, therefore, Hare claimed, "inclinations" (*FR*, 93).

How exactly do inclinations function in a moral argument? (1) 'Everyone ought to do X' entails (2) 'Let A do X to me', where A, Hare explained, need not be a specific existing person. Therefore if (2) is rejected, (1) must be rejected also. Now there are several ways in which looking at the matter in this manner may be misunderstood. First, in Hare's theory, (1) and (2) are both prescriptive utterances. Thus (2) does not report or describe an inclination, it is rather an "expression" of an inclination. To say anything else would go against Hare's anti-naturalism. We may refute the moral principle proposed by someone if we can show that in proposing that principle, he is, because his inclinations are what they are, inconsistent. But, Hare explained,

> It is not a question of a factual statement about a person's inclinations being inconsistent with a moral judgement; rather, his inclinations being what they are, he cannot assent sincerely to a certain singular prescription, and if he cannot do this, he cannot assent to a certain universal prescription which entails it. . . . If he . . . refused (as he must, his inclinations being what they are) to assent to the singular prescription, he would be guilty of a logical inconsistency. (*FR*, 109.)

Second, Hare insisted that for the logic of refuting (1) it is quite irrelevant that the person in question in fact fears or has a ground for fearing that someone will do X to him. The crucial case need not be a real one, a hypothetical one is sufficient. And this, Hare pointed out, is another difference between scientific and moral reasoning; in science only actual cases count. Our own actual fears or chances of having to suffer the consequences if everyone in the same circumstances were to do the sort of act we are contemplating may be irrelevant from the ethical point of view. In order to perceive the weight of a moral argument, we must be imaginative and sympathetic, capable of putting ourselves in other people's shoes.

> All that is essential . . . is that B should disregard the fact that he plays the particular role in the situation which he does, without

disregarding the inclinations which people have in situations of this sort. In other words, he must be prepared to give weight to A's inclinations and interests as if they were his own. This is what turns selfish prudential reasoning into moral reasoning. (*FR*, 94.)

. . . .

B has got, not to imagine himself in A's situation with his own (B's) likes and dislikes, but to imagine himself in A's situation with A's likes and dislikes. (*FR*, 113.)

It is therefore not just any inclinations which we happen to have that go to disprove contemplated moral principles; we must first become imaginative and sympathetic, and of course know the relevant facts. These remarks, as Hare himself points out, bring his views close to the "Ideal Observer Theories" of ethics. Before our inclinations, attitudes, and judgements count, we must put our-selves in a certain position and possess, as it were, certain credentials. I shall try to say a good deal more about this point in the following chapter.

Thus it seems that in *Freedom and Reason* Hare carried his account a great deal further: general moral principles are not just products of unarguable decisions, but are themselves subject to rational criticism. Still, puzzles remain and the appearance of genuine advance is largely deceptive. We saw that if Stevenson's theory were to include only "dependent emotive meaning" and no "independent emotive meaning", then we could understand how there can be something like argument in morals, but that at the same time we could then no longer understand how moral argu-ments could contribute to the changing and reshaping of attitudes. In that case moral language would merely cater to and reflect existing attitudes. If, on the other hand, we admitted "independent emotive meaning", then we could see how moral language can influence attitudes but, at the same time, argument in any usual sense would then become an impossibility. Or, to put this point differently, if we assume that all moral disagreement is rooted in disagreement in belief, moral reasoning would be possible. But then moral reasoning could never influence attitudes, it would have to presuppose a community of attitudes. If, on the other hand, we grant morality the active role of changing attitudes, we would have to say that moral "reasoning" is pure non-rational persuasion for which beliefs have no relevance. Hare leaves us with the same sort of dilemma. Moral arguments are possible in so far as there already is a uniformity of inclinations among men; but such arguments also have for their very task the elimination of disagreements in our inclinations, as it is exactly such disagreements that occasion moral arguments. In other words, the facts that make moral arguments possible make them also pointless and the facts that give such arguments their point, make them, at the same time, impossible.

That our inclinations may differ and thus occasion moral arguments was of course recognized by Hare. He made the point that two people may disagree about what ought to be done "because their different inclinations make one reject some singular prescription which the other can accept" (*FR*, 97). Indeed it would be odd for a moral philosopher not to acknowledge that fact. Morality would not be worth getting excited about if people's inclinations did not differ. But, in the tradition shared by many ethical writers, Hare also said that the inclinations of men are really basically very similar—"people's inclinations about most of the important matters in life tend to be the same (very few people, for example, like being starved or run over by motor-cars)". And, he claimed further, it is just this fact that makes moral reasoning possible (*FR*, 97).

Should we then say that, for Hare, morality is simply a matter of bringing the momentary and capricious inclinations of ourselves and others in line with the more basic inclinations which all of us share? If we did say this, we would make his view look too much like utilitarianism or Toulmin's theory of harmonization of interests. And both of these doctrines are rejected by Hare. Hare's view differs from utilitarianism first of all because, though anxious to preserve some of the spirit of utilitarianism, he construes the *form* of a moral argument quite differently. Perhaps according to him, the mutual harmonization of our inclinations and interests is what morality, if fully realized, would in fact accomplish; but a moral argument is for him not a deduction from the principle of utility as the highest major premise together with the factual statements about men's inclinations (*FR*, 108). Nor is it, as it is for Toulmin, a matter of deriving normative conclusions from such factual statements by using the principle of harmony as the ultimate rule of inference. Instead it consists of exploring, in the manner described above, what singular prescriptions the agent is willing to universalize on the basis of the inclinations which he has as an informed, imaginative, and sympathetic individual.

There is a further disagreement with utilitarianism and Toulmin. Hare points out that, in the end, there is no telling what inclinations the informed, imaginative, and sympathetic individual may sincerely claim to have. A man may be a firm believer in what Hare calls an "ideal". And this ideal may be such that in the name of it he would be willing to accept singular prescriptions which would frustrate all the inclinations and interests of others and also all the rest of his own inclinations and interests. On the basis of Toulmin's doctrine as well as straightforward utilitarianism it could be shown that such an ideal is morally wrong since it has consequences which are detrimental to general happiness. But what can be done with such a single-minded idealist or, as he calls him, a "fanatic" in Hare's own view? Can we find arguments against his ideal if we wish to do so? We may call him an eccentric or worse but are there any logical arguments against him?

Hare had to come to the conclusion that there really are none since it is "logically possible" to want *anything* (*FR*, 110). In order to refute the "fanatic's" ideal, we would have to show that in believing in it he is inconsistent since he would not really be willing to disregard some inclination of his which, in the name of his ideal, he is willing to disregard in other people. But if we could show this, the man would simply not be a genuine "fanatic".

However, Hare claims, the fact that we cannot in a situation like this use any arguments is no cause for despair, since there are really very few genuine "fanatics", that is, people with an all-consuming desire of a sort which would enable them to propose with perfect consistency courses of action which most other people would disagree with. "Men and the world being what they are", the "vast majority" will be able to accept, when confronted with the universalizability argument, only very much the same moral judgements. "In this respect", Hare concluded, "all moral arguments are *ad hominem*" (*FR*, 111).

In his discussion of utilitarianism Hare pointed out that there is particularly one inclination in human beings which assures that a very great majority of moral disagreements can be resolved by the universalizability argument—namely, the inclination or desire to have our interests or desires satisfied. We may safely assume that no man wants his desires to be frustrated. When in a particular case I find myself inclined to assent to the singular prescription 'Let me disregard that man's likes and dislikes', I find that I cannot universalize that prescription since I would then have to agree that my own likes and dislikes may be disregarded also and I find that I do not agree to that (*FR*, 113). Regard for another person's interests can be shown almost always to be a duty since all or almost all men desire the satisfaction of their interests.

The principle that everyone's interests are to be respected or that everybody is to count as one is thus established and morality again seems to become simply a matter of harmonizing the interests that we happen to have. Since all men want their interests to be respected, the universalizability argument can be generalized and does not depend on reference to a particular person and his desires. Something like utilitarianism (or Toulmin's theory of harmonization of interests) thus again seems to emerge.

But this, Hare argued once more, is not the complete story. There are, after all, people who are willing to prescribe universally a course of action although that course of action would frustrate the inclinations of others and also the inclinations which they themselves otherwise have. Hare, unlike Toulmin, is anxious to make room for such people in the moral community of men although he claims that they are "fanatics" and that it is impossible to conduct a moral argument with them. There is a part of morality, that made up of ideals, which goes beyond the simple harmonization of interests and which, therefore, may be impenetrable to rational argument.

Let us see once more how Hare came to this conclusion. Essential to his discussion of ideals is a distinction between inclinations, desires, likes, interests, &c., on the one hand and ideals on the other.

The distinction was drawn as follows. An inclination, desire, interest, &c. is not *in itself universalizable*:

To want to have something does not commit the wanter to wanting other people, in the same circumstances, to have it. (*FR*, 157.)

. . . .

. . . interests likewise are not universalizable; what it is in one person's interests to have, it is not necessarily in his interest that anyone else should have. (*FR*. 158.)

Because they are not in themselves universalizable, desires and interests are criticizable by the universalizability argument. Desires and interests are expressed by singular prescriptions, that is, by plain imperatives. These are not *in themselves* universalizable, but they are morally justified only if they can give rise to 'ought'-statements, that is, to the sort of thing that *is* universalizable. If a desire or interest is not capable of passing this test, it must be morally rejected. On the other hand, an ideal is already in itself universalizable. It is expressed not in an imperative but in a value-judgement. To express an ideal is to say that a certain thing is pre-eminently good or that a certain course of action ought to be followed. And to say that, is to commit oneself to saying that any other exactly similar thing is also good or that any other exactly similar course of action is equally obligatory. When a man expresses an ideal he has already taken the burden of universalizability on his shoulders and if he is fully clear about the matter he has already accepted the consequences, for himself as well as for others, that may go with everyone acting on that ideal. The argument from universalizability would shake him only if he is *not* clear about the full extent of his commitment. If he is fully clear about it, the argument from universalizability would not tell him anything new and he need not be moved by it.

Hare did not, of course, want to claim that ideals are never capable of being argued about. He was quite willing to accept the consequence that in so far as our ideals do not conflict with people's interests, "conflicts between ideals are not susceptible to very much in the way of argument" (*LM*, 155–6). As long as a man is consistent about his own ideals, there is really nothing that can be said to him in order to show that he ought to change them. And this, to an extent, is as it should be, since there is nothing wrong with a certain diversity in men's ideals (*LM*, 151 ff.). The situation changes when ideals come into conflict with interests: "it would indeed be a scandal if no arguments could be brought against a person who, in pursuit of his own ideals, trampled ruthlessly on other people's interests" (*LM*, 157). Was Hare able to tell us how to avert such possible scandal? In his effort to do so he emphasized the *similarity* between ideals and desires, inclinations, interests, &c.:

. . . to have an ideal is *eo ipso* to have an interest in not being frustrated in the pursuit of it. (*FR*, 160.)

. . . .

. . . ideals . . . are not just like desires; for there is no universalizability-requirement in the case of desires, whereas there is in the case of . . . ideals. But this does not prevent ideals . . . sharing with desires their characteristic of being dispositions to action; and indeed, if we use the word 'desire' in a wide sense, we can say that any evaluation, just because it is prescriptive, incorporates the desire to have or do something rather than something else. (*FR*, 169–70.)

An ideal thus incorporates a desire. How does this make it possible to argue about it? Well, we may apply the universalizability argument to the desire in question. We may ask whether the person who has the ideal is willing to accept the consequences if that desire were shared universally. But, as we pointed out, it would seem that if he is clear-headed, he has already done this. By expressing his ideal, if he is not confused, he is expressing a universalized desire, an 'ought' and not a plain imperative. He has then thought the matter through in terms of the interests and desires of others, as well as his own, and has in spite of it decided to adopt an ideal and therefore there would not be any possibility of arguing with him.

Hare says that moral reasoning consists of the universalizability argument; but, he would have to admit, a man with an ideal may be immune to that argument even if his ideal is such that it will make him "trample ruthlessly on other people's interests". In fact, it is exactly ideals of that outrageous sort that would tend to be unassailable on rational grounds since they are likely to be the products of "fanatical" minds. So, it would seem, the "scandal" cannot be averted and we must merely take comfort in the thought that, as Hare assures us, since "fanaticism" is rare, it does not occur often.

Hare says that we can test our decisions by moral reasoning by trying to work up from singular prescriptions to 'ought'-statements and general principles. However, he seems to be saying also, by a sort of leap human volition can always anticipate the results of such reasoning and thus nullify them. What really matter in morality in the end are not the particular desires and inclinations that people have, but the more general attitudes toward these desires. These general attitudes include in all or most cases the universal desire to have all one's own desires respected. Since there is this general desire, utilitarian type arguments are possible in morality and almost any man can be argued into respecting the desires of others as well. But the common existence of this desire is merely a "fortunate contingent fact" (*FR*, 172), and a man *can*, logically, decide against it. If he professes to have an ideal or general principle of conduct, then, if he is clear-headed, he is expressing a *general* desire, a desire *about* the desires of others and of himself. Normally, such a general desire includes the desire to have all one's other desires respected and a man can therefore, by the universalizability argument, be argued into respecting the desires of others as well. But it is always possible that a man's desire goes against any other desire or set of desires which he has. If this is, or were, the case, we may not be able to argue him into respecting any of the desires of others either. We may call him a fanatic and accuse him of having perverted ideals but we cannot defeat his reasoning. There are moral positions against which rational argument is helpless.

The difference between the views on the nature of moral reasoning which Hare expressed in *The Language of Morals* and those found in *Freedom and Reason* thus come to this. According to the earlier view moral reasoning depends on the availability of general principles of conduct which can serve as major premises. But what general principles are available depends on decisions for which no reasons can be given. According to the later view, moral reasoning is a process of exploring which singular prescriptions can yield universal 'ought'-statements or general principles of conduct. Owing to the "fortunate contingent fact" that human desires are basically similar and that all men desire that their desires be respected, a normal man would accept only certain general principles or ideals—namely those which do no violence to the desires of others. In a vast number of cases moral disagreement can thus be resolved by argument. But there is no logical limit to the singular prescriptions that a man may be willing to universalize. Therefore, when someone chooses a course of action, then no matter how morally outrageous his choice may seem to us, we may not be able to present arguments which ought to convince him that it is morally wrong. We can make him change his mind by moral argument only if we can show that his choice, when universalized, would lead, at least hypothetically, to actions on the part of others which are in conflict with his self-interest. But if he is clear-headed and willing to commit himself to the bitter end, then any choice that he may make would be rationally invulnerable.

It is plain then that for Hare, morality must still be, in the end, a matter of purely non-rational decision and commitment. In fact, the new theory, instead of making the rational or logical foundation of ethics more secure, really shatters it completely. Ideals, Hare is in effect saying, are incapable of being argued about when they (a) come strongly into conflict with the existing inclinations of people, and (b) are adhered to with a clear head and disinterestedly. Moral argument is concerned only with the harmonization of the existing interests of men, but ideals go beyond such interests. Morality, since it includes ideals, seeks sometimes to give new direction to our goals and interests; harmony between the existing interests of men is clearly only one moral ideal among others. It follows from all this that how great a role reason plays in morality must, for Hare, be itself a normative moral issue. If our supreme moral ideal is of a utilitarian sort, our morality would remain close to reason. But if our moral conscience is of a more radical and "fanatical" bent, it would leave the realm of reason behind. Thus arguments in ethics will have validity only as a matter of a *moral* commitment. Since the only form of reasoning in morals is the universalizability argument, I must find moral reasoning binding only if I happen to embrace the utilitarian ideal. If I decide against that ideal and take a different moral stand, which I am both morally and logically free to do, I have made myself invulnerable to rational criticism. In one blow I decide both a matter of morals and a matter of logic. Curiously enough, Hare himself, as we have seen, deplored such a confusion between logic and morality in his earlier book.

Thus Hare's new theory was really no improvement over the old: morality is in the end a matter of non-rational decision or commitment. Hare was anxious to argue that the non-rational residue in morals which remains in his theory is really rather insignificant. But how insignificant is it? It seems that we can say so only if we consider ideals themselves insignificant since it is when we come to them, Hare said, that the possibility of reasoning stops. Hare does not *say* that ideals are insignificant—in fact, since he devotes a great deal of space to discussing them, we are inclined to think that he regards them as being very important—but it seems that he would *have* to say this if he is to make good his claim that the alleged inarguability of ideals does not destroy reason in ethics. Ideals, Hare is in effect saying, when adhered to with a clear head and disinterestedly, although part of morality, cannot be criticized from a moral point of view no matter how strongly they come into conflict with people's interests and no matter how basic those interests may be. Moral argument is concerned only with the harmonization of existing interests of men, but ideals go beyond existing interests. This, as we have pointed out previously, is an integral part of morality and moral language; Hare called it "prescriptivity". Morality and moral language do not just reflect existing interests, their role is also to redirect them. The universal harmony of interests or least suffering is just one moral ideal among others. Therefore, it would seem, if the only argument available in morality is the argument of universalizability, then a very vital part of morality, and not an insignificant one, must lie outside reason.

Hare's chief argument for claiming that the universalizability argument does nevertheless cover all that can be and need be covered by reason in morals rests largely on his distinction between "fanatical" and "liberal" ideals. The "fanatic" shows no regard for the interests and ideals of others, whereas the "liberal" does; hence we can argue with the latter, although we cannot argue with the former. Only the fanatic raises his ideals so far above the existing interests of men that it becomes impossible to argue about them in the way in which Hare says we argue in morals; the liberal, on the other hand, does take into account existing interests, and hence allows moral reasoning about his ideals (*FR*, 177). But, as we pointed out, whether I am a liberal or a fanatic would depend solely on an ultimate moral commitment on my own part. Hare unmistakably declares his preference for liberal ideals. But this, we must take it, is itself an unarguable value-judgement of his.

Furthermore, if we say that we can argue about liberal ideals, we would also have to say that liberal ideals are, in Hare's view, hardly anything more than suggestions concerning how the existing interests of men can be best harmonized with one another. At least at times Hare certainly seems to think that liberal ideals are more than that: the gist of much that he has to say about ideals is that the role of all ideals, including liberal ones, is to go beyond the concern with the mere harmonization of existing interests of men. But in that case liberal ideals as well, and not just fanatical ones, must go beyond what Hare conceives of as reason and argument in ethics. In order to take care of that consequence Hare seems to argue that even if liberal ideals did go beyond reason, this would not make the realm of unreason in ethics into something that should cause despair. Sometimes he talks of liberal ideals as something like visions of what would go into making up the good life without seriously disrupting the existing fabric of human interests and inclinations (*FR*, 179). They are something to experiment with when the dangers and costs are not too high. There is further the suggestion that (some) liberal ideals are private or personal ideals: we are free to pursue them without interfering with the lives of others (*FR*, 179).

From these and similar reflections Hare seems to draw the conclusion that if liberal ideals cannot be argued about then this is not really a great misfortune, since we can afford to agree to disagree about them. And as to fanatical ideals, Hare's conclusion seems to be, the fact that they cannot be reasoned about is not a very great misfortune either. It would be a great misfortune if real fanaticism—the single-minded, unswerving, and ruthless pursuit by a man or group of men of what they consider as an improvement of the world even in the face of what is or would be, if that man or group of men were not the stronger party, to the detriment of all or some of their other interests—were widespread; fortunately, Hare says, it is not. But all this may be beside the point. Whether or not we should wish for more reason in ethics than Hare allows has nothing to do with the question of whether or not there *are* forms of reasoning in ethics which Hare does not explain. And, for that matter, more reason in ethics than Hare allows may be desirable in a time when more people decide to commit themselves to a "fanatical" morality and start advocating radical revisions and innovations in the structure of existing interests and goals.

V

SUMMING UP AND LOOKING AHEAD

1. *Towards the Proper Method*

IN the four preceding chapters we have followed a twofold aim. First we have sought to trace the main features of the development of ethical theory in the twentieth century by examining the views of four authors. Second, we have attempted to appraise these views and bring out in each case the central criticisms that may be levelled against them. By and large, we have tried to meet each of our philosophers on his own ground, although we have also made use of ideas and concepts not to be found in a fully explicit form in the writings of any one of them. In this chapter we shall pay less attention to the particular ways in which the chief doctrines of twentieth-century ethical theory were originally formulated. We shall (1) work towards a clearer overall view of the historical development, and (2) try to give an outline of a mode of analysis of moral language which we have previously alluded to only in passing. This mode of analysis, it will be seen, has not been fully employed by any one of our authors but the whole development of recent ethical theory has been leading towards it. I shall argue that it can also form a basis for further progress.

We have seen that one of the predominant trends in twentieth-century ethical theory has been towards a more purely linguistic method. According to Moore, "scientific ethics" seeks to give an answer to the question: what is good? (*PE*, 3.) And in one sense, in the sense in which ethics is distinct from "Casuistry" (and identical with what we have called ethical theory or meta-ethics), the answer to that question was to be given through the examination of the predicate 'good' (*PE*, xiii and 5). But since Moore conceived of this predicate as referring to a property, theoretical ethics became for him in the first place a study of the nature of that property. This was not the only way in which Moore approached the problem of the logic of moral discourse. Nevertheless, the spirit of this initial orientation remained characteristic of all his attempts at solving this problem. Moore's ethical theory thus involved a great deal of metaphysics.

At the same time, we noticed that his actual arguments were worked out largely without any explicit mention of or reliance on metaphysical concepts. There are many passages in *Principia* and elsewhere in which Moore remained on the level of straightforward linguistic analysis. In the light of his own labours, the problem of non-natural properties came to look like an impenetrable issue; he was much more successful in those portions of his work which were not directly concerned with that issue. It was the linguistic aspect of Moore's philosophy which appealed to later writers. There came to be less metaphysics in ethical theory, and more attention paid to the actual structure and workings of moral language.

This trend was clearly visible in Stevenson. While for Moore ethical theory had been concerned ultimately with non-natural properties, with Stevenson there was no need to move on to such deeper questions. Nevertheless for Stevenson too, ethical theory was not concerned exclusively with the grammar of ordinary moral language. Stevenson developed a psychological theory of meaning according to which questions like 'What is the meaning of this term or expression?' would in principle always be decidable by empirical investigation. The meaning of a word was for him the pattern of causal interaction between its utterances as identifiable sounds and the corresponding psychological processes, or, ultimately, the overt actions of persons who make or hear these utterances.

The relation between linguistic and non-linguistic events thus became more intimate and direct; there was no longer any need to include in it the extra step of grasping the "meaning" of a word as that to which the term refers or that which it names. The relation between words or expressions and the rest of the world was nevertheless still conceived by Stevenson as being an external one. According to him, utterances of words are connected through empirical laws with such things as beliefs, emotions, attitudes, and eventually actions. Basically, words and expressions are signs of psychological events or states in the same sense as clouds are signs of rain. When such and such words are uttered, then it is probable that such and such beliefs, emotions, or attitudes are present in the speaker; and this is all that can be said about it. It is not a matter of a logical necessity, of implication or presupposition, that if certain words are uttered, then certain beliefs, emotions, or attitudes must be present also. The connexions between the use of language and the rest of man's behaviour was thought of as being always empirical and never logical.

In the place of Moore's non-natural properties Stevenson put the psychological notion of attitudes and conceived of ethical language as causally reflecting and influencing the polarity exhibited by these psychological phenomena. While Moore conceived of moral language as a discourse about a non-natural subject matter, for Stevenson the use of moral language constituted a process through which we bring to bear psychological and causal influence on the attitudes and actions of others and presumably also of ourselves. It is possible, however, to think of moral language in a still different way. We may view it simply as a means of calculating and concluding what to do. It may be looked upon as a system of moves or operations which we perform with the aim of coming, eventually, to practical decisions.

In such a case, the relation between our utterances of moral words and sentences as linguistic events and our feelings, attitudes, intentions, decisions, and, ultimately, actions as non-verbal matters of substance, could be thought of as being the relation between different performances in a wider activity. And since this activity is governed by rules, we may say that the relation in question is not merely factual and causal, but logical. Roughly speaking, it is this view of moral language which underlies the theories of Toulmin and even more clearly so of Hare. The characteristic way in which these authors probed into the nature of moral terms and judgements was by asking: what is the use, role, or function of these terms and judgements in the activity in which they play a part?

If by the investigation into the nature of moral terms and judgements we understand an attempt to determine their use, role, or function, moral language would be viewed as a part of the moral life itself and not merely as a device for exerting causal influence on it. Nor would we then look at it narrowly as a "mere" linguistic activity, constituted by the handling of symbols or signs, which runs parallel to and reflects those things which make up the substance of morality. We call certain judgements moral because they are moves in a certain activity or practice and not because they concern a certain "subject matter" such as the property goodness or because they, in a causal sense, evince and evoke certain attitudes. Moral discourse and morality are a seamless web.

It may be claimed that this approach was explored already by Stevenson. And to some extent this claim would be justified. Stevenson, just like Toulmin and Hare, rejected the Moorean view that the significance of moral language derives from its relation to a non-natural subject matter. As opposed to this view Stevenson seems to have held that the significance of moral language consists in its use for evoking and expressing emotions and attitudes. In particular, one may maintain, Stevenson's theory of emotive meaning as formulated in the working models was an attempt to characterize the imperative or prescriptive function of moral terms. But such an interpretation would blur an important difference. We saw that Stevenson was not really talking about the imperative use of sentences like 'This is good' but rather about their disposition to set to work a subtle psychological "mechanism of suggestion". For Stevenson, the power of words like 'good' to evoke and express emotions and attitudes was determined by psychological laws of conditioning and not by linguistic rules which derive from convention rather than nature. According to his theory, linguistic rules merely combine signs with other signs and not with the occasions of their utterance. Emotive meaning was therefore viewed by him not as a matter of rules and conventions at all, but as a brute, although subtle and complex, fact of psychology. Consequently, if by the use or function of an utterance we mean something which is governed by conventions or rules, Stevenson's theory of emotive meaning cannot really be looked upon as an attempt to characterize the use or function of moral terms.

For the philosopher who does not share what we have called Stevenson's psychologism, the task is done once he has succeeded in exhibiting the use of moral terms and judgements. For him, to probe into the psychology of the matter would be to work overtime. After he had brought out the (logical) rules which govern these terms and judgements by specifying the occasions of their (correct) utterance, there would be no need for him to look further for the "meaning" of these terms in the psychological manner of Stevenson. He would grant that the use of moral, just as any other, terms has psychological accompaniments; but, he would insist, this fact is irrelevant to the ethical theorist. Consequently, when Stevenson says that in the case of moral terms in so far as they are "emotive", there are no such logical (or linguistic) rules, such a philosopher is apt to feel disappointed and retort that Stevenson is misled concerning his task as an ethical theorist. The fact is, this philosopher would say, that even in the case of purely "emotive" words, in so far as they are *words* at all, there are rules which govern their use, since it is possible to misuse them. He would admit that it is perhaps true that ethical terms are emotionally charged and that they share this feature with shrieks, laughs, and groans; but, he would insist, this fact is insignificant for the moral philosopher. Moral terms do not merely have the psychological force to evoke and to exhibit emotions and attitudes; they also possess a conventional use or function governed by linguistic rules.

Our last two authors, Toulmin and Hare, appreciated these points quite well and rejected the Moorean as well as the Stevensonian methods of approaching the problems of moral language and reasoning. For them, moral terms neither referred to non-natural properties nor did they, essentially, just evince or evoke attitudes and feelings. In the manner of Wittgenstein, these men concentrated instead on the uses, functions, and purposes that such terms have, or, to use terminology which we have freely borrowed from Austin, on the linguistic performances into which they enter. But, as it became clear in the preceding chapters, their success in carrying out this, we may call it, functional analysis was very imperfect. In Toulmin's case, there was a great deal of confusion concerning what the sort of thing is that may be called the use, function, or purpose of a term, sentence, or mode of discourse and what is the nature of the rules that govern it. In Hare's case the main trouble lay in his misunderstanding concerning the respective status of the criteria of application and the performative force of our utterances and the consequent espousal of the Stevensonian dogma of two types of meaning. With these stumbling blocks put aside, we can hope to develop a more fruitful functional analysis of moral language.

2. *Reasons and Linguistic Performances I*

In spite of the fact that Stevenson conceived of meaning in psychological terms and cannot therefore, properly speaking, be said to have been concerned with the performative uses of moral terms at all, but only with their different types of psychological cause and effect, his theory of emotive meaning can nevertheless be looked upon as leading, in an oblique way, to the study of moral judgements as linguistic performances. Stevenson said that what he called the emotive meaning of moral terms is best understood by comparing it with exclamations like 'Blast it!' or 'Hurrah!' Such exclamations are not statements about or descriptions of anything psychological or otherwise, but contrary to what Stevenson himself sometimes seems to have believed, neither are they pure natural ventings of feelings as groans, shrieks, and peals of laughter are. They are linguistic performances or rituals instead. Even in groans, shrieks, and laughter there is (usually) an element of convention. If I smile to my tormentor, must he think that I am really not feeling the pain or that I am undaunted? If a smile were like a blush or reddening of the ears (not under one's control or at least much less so), he could only do the former. At any rate, we must draw a distinction between empirical laws as summaries of the causal conditions for the occurrence of a sign and the conventional rules by virtue of which a sign becomes part of language and by reference to which the correctness of its intentional use is judged. But the intentional and rule-governed use of language is not limited to reporting or describing features of reality, objective or subjective. To say 'Blast it!' is not to report my disappointment or annoyance or anything else, it is a way of being disappointed or annoyed. It is a part of and fits in as a link in the wider rituals of human behaviour. By it nothing is stated, something is only shown, but it is shown not through a mere symptom. Similarly, when I shout 'Hurrah!', I am neither describing my mental condition, nor simply giving it away through a symptom; I hurrah, that is perform my part in, say, celebrating a victory.

Stevenson's working model for the term 'good', we recall, was: 'This is good' means the same as '*I approve of this, do so as well*'. His claim was that the second part of the definiens 'Do so as well', approximates the emotive meaning of the term 'good'. Now 'Do so as well' is an imperative—not a statement but a linguistic performance of a different sort. By uttering these words I am normally not informing someone of my needs or desires nor am I bringing to bear psychological pressure on him; I am rather, as Hare pointed out, telling someone to do something. It is perfectly true that from my utterance the hearer can gather information about my needs and wants and I may even utter my words with the intention of giving him such information. But all this would be a roundabout way of getting and giving information possible only against the background of the hearer's psychological knowledge about myself. Similarly, by uttering the words 'Do so as well' I may be bringing psychological pressure to bear on my hearer, and with these words it is probably inevitable that this is always so to a certain extent; but here too, in doing this I would be relying on other things besides conventions or linguistic rules.

The difference between the utterance of the words 'Do so as well' as a linguistic performance, that is, as an order, request, or command, and the achievement of such effects as letting someone have some information or influencing him by that utterance can be brought out also in this way. I would have accomplished my purely linguistic act whether or not the hearer in fact followed the order or got the information about my wishes. But I would have accomplished my task of influencing him only if he in fact did what I wanted him to do. He can reject my order, but he cannot, properly speaking, reject my influence. With getting and giving information from my words the situation is somewhat more complicated. When I uttered the imperative with the intention of informing him of my state of mind, we should perhaps, strictly speaking, not say that I was giving him information but that I was intentionally yielding him information. Giving information is itself a linguistic performance, but for effecting it one would normally use an indicative locution. The kind of locution used is, however, itself not decisive: I can give an order by saying 'I want you to do so as well'. The decisive thing is again that you can reject the information someone gives you by not believing it or mistrusting it but you cannot reject the information that someone yields to you. I would have been successful in yielding information to my hearer about my wishes only if he in fact came to believe that I had them.

This should make clear the sense in which the utterance of the words 'Do so as well' is a linguistic performance. What interests us even more, however, is that the first half of Stevenson's working model for the term 'good' can be interpreted also as a linguistic performance of a sort different from statements.[1] There is a certain ambivalence about such interpretation since there seems to be a difference between 'I approve' and 'I approve of'. Only the former, as we have remarked before, seems to be a clear non-statement whereas the performative force of the latter seems to be sometimes equivalent to that of a statement. But sometimes they are probably interchangeable. To avoid this possible complication, I shall discuss mainly 'I approve' rather than 'I approve of', as Stevenson himself has it, since our task is now less to understand Stevenson's views than to see where they may lead us if we take them as clues.

The phrase 'I approve this' does not function as a description of the mind or actions of the speaker. To utter the words 'I approve this' is not to say *that* I approve a certain thing, nor is it, normally, to say that I find myself in a certain mental condition or possess a certain disposition; but is simply to approve it, that is, to put my stamp of approval on it. When I have said 'I approve X' I have performed a certain act, that is, endorsed or backed or vouched for something, which is quite distinct from *saying that* I was doing a thing of that sort or feeling in a certain way.

Can the words 'I approve X' as a linguistic performance different from a statement be defended by reasons and arguments? We might, especially when the locution used is not 'I approve' but 'I approve

[1] Here, and in the next section, I am making use, in a slightly modified form, of my 'Approvals, Reasons and Moral Argument', *Mind*, vol. lxxi, 1962.

of', try to show that the speaker was sincere, that he meant what
he said, that he really had a favourable opinion of X. In that case
we are probably considering the utterance of the words 'I approve
(of) X' as an act of giving information or making a factual statement
about the attitude of the speaker. This, as a matter of fact, is how
Stevenson did conceive of it. But normally an utterance of this
form constitutes a linguistic performance such that in trying to
show that the speaker was sincere and meant what he said, we
would be merely concerned with what is implied by it and not
with what it directly says. When somebody says 'I approve X', he
may legitimately be taken to have a favourable attitude towards
X, to be willing to do something on behalf of X, and so on.
And of course, in a given case, all these things may be untrue:
the person in question might not at all be reacting favourably
towards X within himself. But all that would do is to make his act—
—his linguistic performance—insincere; it would not make it
invalid or void nor indefensible in other respects. Whether sincerely
or not, I will have approved the thing in question and can be asked
to defend my approval by reasons. In saying 'I approve X' I have
given my approval, I have not described my mental state. Therefore,
no statements concerning my attitudes, feelings, intentions,
decisions, opinions, or what-not, could serve as arguments, pro
or con, for my words, except in a special minimum sense which I
shall try to explain later.

What, then, is the nature of the reasons and arguments by
which a linguistic act of the form 'I approve X' may be defended?
Suppose I, say, issue the approval or endorsement, 'I approve Jones'
and am challenged. What form of defence may I give to my words?
Had I said 'Jones is intelligent' or 'I have known Jones for many
years', the appropriate kind of thing to do would have been to try
to show that what I said was true, that is, to give evidence for
Jones's intelligence or for my long acquaintance with him. In our
case, however, that would not do: if 'I approve Jones' functions as
an endorsement, it is not in any obvious sense true or false. Nevertheless, my saying 'I approve X' *implies*[1] certain matters which are

---

[1] What is this sense of 'imply'? It will become clearer as we make use of it in our
subsequent discussion. We may circumscribe it roughly by adapting and generalizing

capable of being true and false—namely, certain statements about (*a*) Jones, the object approved, and (*b*) myself, the speaker. In defending my endorsement, 'I approve X', I am thus confronted with a double task: I must first show that the object of my approval possesses certain characteristics and therefore meets certain standards; second, I must show that certain things hold true of myself by virtue of which I am in a good position to issue the endorsement, that is, that I possess the appropriate competence and have exercised a due amount of care and acumen.

Whenever we approve somebody, some object, some practice, we always approve it as something of a certain kind and as playing a part in a wider context or serving some function or end. I approve Jones, as the captain, for the morale of the team; steel chairs, as furniture, for the new house; strawberries, as dessert, for dinner; baseball, as a sport, for children. Such specifications are always present; if not explicitly stated, then presupposed and supplied by the context. Another point about approval is that we typically approve in a certain capacity, role, or standing. I approve Jones (as the captain for the morale of the team) as the coach; steel chairs (as furniture for the new house) as the owner; strawberries (as dessert

---

some of the things Austin said about the sense in which statements (as well as other speech-acts) imply the truth of certain other statements. To say that a speech-act P implies a statement Q is to say that by performing P *I give it to be understood* that I believe Q. (Cf. *Philosophical Papers*, p. 32.) Depending on the sort of speech-act P is, there are very different things that I give it to be understood that I believe to be the case by performing it. It is of utmost importance to be clear about what these things are; otherwise we would not know what reasons, if any, are relevant for supporting a given linguistic performance, for showing that it can be defended by good arguments. P implies Q, if it is the case that if we perform P we cannot deny that Q. If I did deny or negate Q, my performance of P would be insincere since by performing P I give it to be understood that I believe that Q. However, the negation of Q does not cancel out P; to say that P implies Q is different from saying that P entails Q. If P merely implies Q, not-Q and P are not contradictory although when uttered in one breath they do not make good sense. P implies Q is also different from P presupposes Q. If P presupposes Q, then if Q is false, P will be void or empty. The question of P being right or wrong, being supported by good reasons or not, does not even arise. (Cf. *How to Do Things with Words*, pp. 46–52.) For our purposes it will be important to keep implication distinct not only from entailment but also from presupposition. This distinction is blurred by Urmson's remark which is otherwise succinct and to the point '. . . if there is a convention that X will only be done in circumstances Y, a man implies that situation Y holds if he does X'. (J. O. Urmson, 'Parenthetical Verbs', in *Essays in Conceptual Analysis*, Antony Flew, ed., London: Macmillan, 1956.)

for dinner) as the host; baseball (as a sport for children) as a father or as a teacher. To these two points correspond the two lines of defence incumbent on me when my utterance of the words 'I approve X' is challenged.

Since to approve X is to view X against the background of a wider context of functions, purposes, and ends, it makes reference to standards. By approving X I imply that I believe that X comes up to such standards. Suppose I serve on the Admissions Committee and say, 'I approve Jones (as a new student)'. If my utterance is challenged, I may therefore justify it by showing that Jones meets the requirements for admission of new students, that is, present an argument of the following form:

> If the applicant possesses qualifications A, B, and C, he may be admitted.
> Jones does possess qualifications A, B, and C.
> ∴ Jones may be admitted.

But this might not be the end of it; the case may be more complex. Often the standards and rules that guide the work of committees and juries go only so far: they only amount to laying down the necessary, but not always the sufficient, conditions for an action to be taken or a verdict to be delivered. It may be that everyone is agreed that Jones does have qualifications A, B, and C (those sufficient in normal cases), but still the question remains whether or not Jones should be approved for admission. Someone may claim that the rule 'If the applicant possesses qualifications A, B, and C, he may be admitted' is not enough to decide *Jones*'s case favourably. And suppose that, no matter what qualifications of Jones's and what rules or precedents I cite, my fellow members of the Admissions Committee insist that I further justify my approval. I am expected to do better, but how can I do better? Since I have tried all the recognized principles and rules, no clear-cut 'proof' is any longer open to me.

There are, nevertheless, several things that I might still try. I might say (1) 'I know boys like Jones'—claim to have special experience and insight relevant to the case; (2) 'I have known Jones since he was a child'—claim to have special familiarity with the case

being judged; (3) 'I have served on this committee for fifteen years'
—claim to have ample experience in my job; or (4) 'I had a talk
with his headmaster the other day and he concurs in my opinion'—
refer to the corroboration of someone else. These remarks are by
no means absolute clinchers, but they all carry some weight and
I can always think of other and better ones. What is important to
notice is that they are considerations relating directly to *me* and only
indirectly to Jones. In approving something we are, characteristically, doing a certain job, playing a certain role, serving in a
certain capacity. Therefore, once my impersonal "proofs" have
failed, I can further justify my approvals by showing that I am, in
the given case as well as in general, fully qualified to do that job, to
play that role, to serve in that capacity.

The difference between the two sorts of thing that it may be
appropriate for me to do by way of defending my approval of something can be brought out also as follows. By approving a given
object I imply, give it to be understood, that I believe that that
object is worthy of being approved—that, by virtue of its characteristics, it comes up to certain standards. Consequently, when
challenged, I must show why I believe this; I must exhibit the
relevant facts and principles or standards as the evidence on which
my belief rests. But by approving something I do more than imply
simply that I, for my part, believe that the object in question comes
up to par. I also give it to be understood that others too may
believe that the object is worthy of being approved and therefore
may, or even ought to, approve it. By saying 'I approve X' I have
entitled others to approve X also, if they are otherwise qualified
to do so.[1] Consequently, I may be challenged not only to show that
there is *some* evidence for believing that the object in question is
worthy of being approved but also that that evidence is reliable and
valid for everyone.

Now it may be that all I have to do in that case is to cite further
evidence, evidence of a second order. My belief that the thing in
question comes up to par may be based initially on the fact that
it possesses a certain set of characteristics by virtue of which it

---

[1] Cf. Austin's discussion of the difference between 'I believe . . .' and 'I know . . .'
and between 'I intend, hope . . .' and 'I promise . . .' (*Philosophical Papers*, pp. 67–68).

satisfies a certain set of standards. When these standards themselves are called into question, I may be able to show that they are good standards simply by citing further evidence. What would constitute such further evidence? Well, further statements of fact—statements about the effects of following these standards—and further, that is, higher order, standards. In other words, I may be able to defend my whole manner of presenting evidence or furnishing a proof by evidence of a more general sort. But eventually I may have to resort to a different kind of strategem. I may run out of general standards or principles and must then simply try to show that I am a kind of person who is well qualified to judge objects of the sort in question and that I am in a good position to judge this particular one under consideration. In other words, I must exhibit my competence in an area of human concerns and show that I have proceeded in the given case with care and circumspection.

The justification of a linguistic performance such as 'I approve ...' proceeds thus in two stages. There is first the matter of furnishing evidence, of constructing a proof. There is second the eventual need to exhibit competence and to show that one has been careful and circumspect. These two stages of justification are parallel to what we have called the two levels of meaning. Evidence and proof are a matter of sense and reference, or to speak with Hare, of the phrastic element of our speech-acts. To give evidence or to furnish a proof is to list a series of statements whose criteria of application are related in a certain way: the criteria of application of the conclusion must be contained in the criteria of application of the premises. Characteristically, this is accomplished by citing as the premises (a) one or more general principles, and (b) one or more statements of fact. In order to give evidence or furnish a proof we must have both a general theory and particular data.

But as we have pointed out earlier, sense and reference constitute only one element or level of meaning; our full speech-acts also contain performative force. Furthermore, sense and reference, we recall also, are ancillary to performative force: we correlate words with reality, we single out certain particulars and universals, in order to engage in acts such as stating, warning, promising, approving. Similarly, we try to give evidence and furnish proofs in order to support our statements, warnings, promises, approvals, &c. We observe the relations between criteria of application in order to show that a given speech-act was right or wrong, correct or incorrect, good or bad. A given effort, or a whole manner, of giving evidence can therefore itself be deemed adequate or inadequate, relevant or irrelevant, sufficient or insufficient, good or bad˙ depending on how well it accomplishes this purpose. What does and what does not constitute good evidence will consequently vary with the kinds of performative force of our speech-acts. Furthermore, how it is to be decided what is to count as good evidence for a given speech-act depends on the kind of performative force it has.

In science we make an effort to lay down rigid and objective requirements for what is to count as good evidence and very little is left to individual powers of perception and discernment. At the opposite pole lie the expressions of our experiences, intentions, hopes, and wishes. Here almost everything is left to the person who performs the speech-act in question. Some philosophers have therefore argued that with regard to speech-acts such as these the question of evidence does not rise at all. In these cases we seem to assume that the speaker, if he is in the full possession of his faculties and there is nothing in the circumstances to push him into perplexity and confusion, is quite capable of judging the matter without the aid of any machinery of theory and data. Sometimes when we try to communicate our inner life to others, we assume that there are very great differences indeed between the degrees of excellence which different individuals exhibit in their powers of non-theoretical or direct discernment, but here we are perhaps more concerned with the beauty and depth of our utterances than whether they are right or wrong.

In a large variety of cases, however, there is need for both a general conceptual framework, a set of principles which confer significance to particular data, and individual powers of discernment. Often we must venture out on ground not covered by well-established standards of evidence, although we feel at the same time that we cannot leave the matter merely to our senses and sensibilities; we start out looking for evidence but this may take us only so far; after that competence and ability to judge without theory come into play. And we may then wonder what exactly constitutes such competence. Evidence and proof depend on general principles but we may run out of such principles. A complete ethical theory would describe the respective roles of moral principles and moral competence and how the two interact. It would further list and systematize these principles and explain what moral competence consists in. How much completeness can be achieved in these matters is a moot point. I shall argue that a certain open-endedness lies in the nature of the case. At any rate, an effort towards completeness would involve going beyond the neutral questions of language and logic. In this book we can only take some preliminary steps towards the fulfilment of this task.

It is time to return to our investigation of the different ways in which a linguistic act of the form 'I approve . . .' may be supported by reasons. The rather speculative remarks on the last few pages can be substantiated only by paying close attention to how real cases may develop in practice. We said that after my effort to give evidence for or prove my utterance 'I approve Jones' has failed, I can resort to a second line of defence and try to exhibit my competence to judge the case without the benefit of general principles. We can now bring out another important point. Suppose that I finally did succeed in convincing my fellow committee members through my second line of defence. My success would then have created a precedent, or even a new rule. Some points about the character, history, and achievements of Jones (P, Q, R) which until now had gone unnoticed might hereafter become *qualifications* for admission. Jones would have become a test case for the principles guiding the work of our committee; what was at issue was no longer just whether or not Jones was to be admitted, but also what should be the requirements for admitting new students in general. And my endorsement 'I approve Jones' would have had, for all intents and purposes, the force of 'I hereby subscribe to or enunciate the rule, "If the applicant possesses qualifications P, Q, and R, he may be admitted"'.

We may sum up the situation concerning the defence of utterances of the form 'I approve X' as follows. To say, to issue the endorsement, 'I approve X' is not to describe my attitudes or feelings, nor is it to describe X. As an endorsement it contrasts with such utterances as 'X is intelligent' or 'I have known X for many years' or 'I like X' and its justification does not, therefore, in any straightforward sense concern its truth or falsity. To say 'I approve X' is like saying 'I endorse or certify X is a qualified so-and-so'. If I am called upon to defend that linguistic act I may, therefore, have to show (1) that X meets certain requirements, that is, deliver an evaluative "proof". But since to say 'I approve X' is not just to state that X meets such requirements, this first line of argument might not be enough. I might have to go on and show (2) that I myself have certain qualifications, that I possess and have made use of abilities which make me competent to issue such an endorsement or certification.

3. *Reasons and Linguistic Performances II*

It may be objected that the procedure which we have just described could never *really* justify an approval or show that it was really right or well advised.

If we take this objection to mean that it can never be really shown by this method that in a given case the approval was justified, right, or well advised, it has already been amply answered. If after having said 'I approve admitting Jones' I show that Jones fulfils requirements A, B, and C—those sufficient in normal cases—and/or that I possess the experience and competence for doing my job well and that in the given case I have exercised the proper amount of care and acumen, have not been blinded by personal prejudice, &c., what further justification can be asked for?

If I say 'I approve of admitting Jones' I imply that Jones is worthy of being admitted. If after I have shown that Jones is gifted and industrious, possesses good character, has a good scholastic record, is an outstanding athlete, &c., &c., I am still told, 'That does not prove it', I would no longer know what to say. Or, supposing the case is in some way unorthodox and does not come under the established rules, if after I have shown that I have studied Jones's record carefully, had a long talk with him, his father, and his principal and, further, that I have done my job for many years with admirable success, &c., &c., I am still told 'You are nevertheless not competent to judge this case', I would again lapse into a puzzled silence. If my endorsement is challenged, that challenge is meaningful only if there is some indication of a more or less definite defect in my case end, hence, of how the challenge could be met. If there is no such indication, then (rational) justification of any kind has come to an end.

On the other hand, the above criticism may raise the question whether or not there is a way in which practices such as judging college applicants by boards, of which endorsements like 'I approve X' are parts, can themselves be justified. Now, in one sense, it may be said, there clearly is not. There is no way *within* a practice. In our case, what can be discussed within the practice is the justice or advisability of individual cases of approval and not the justice or advisability of the whole practice of judging college applicants by a committee. The fact that there is such a barrier comes out when, in discussing the Jones case, my recalcitrant colleagues make me blurt out 'I am a member of the committee, am I not?' The exchange between me and my fellows has then, in one sense, come to an end: I have invoked the very existence of the Admissions Committee as an institution. But in another sense we could still go on. Suppose that in answer to my last piece of rhetoric someone remarks 'Yes, but these things (admissions) are better judged by lot anyhow'. He has now moved the discussion to a different level—to a level, perhaps, where there would be a way in which the justice of the practice of judging college applicants by boards could be decided had the occasion been the meeting of the whole governing body of the college rather than that of the Admissions Committee. Though the justice of a practice cannot be discussed within that practice, this does not mean that there cannot be other practices in which it can.

The last paragraph contains an oversimplification. We have omitted the important point, mentioned before, that there are test cases. We may now elaborate on it. Practices like admitting new students through committees have a self-modifying or self-corrective character. Within such practices there are performances which shape the character of the practice itself. In discussing the nature of the justification of the endorsement 'I approve X' we said that often that justification takes the form of showing that the object approved fulfils the requirements laid down by certain accepted rules. In those cases 'I approve X' is justified if X satisfies the rules or requirements $r_1, r_2, \ldots r_n$. But we also saw that there are unorthodox cases where X does not come under any such existing rule. In such unorthodox cases the force of the words 'I approve X' goes beyond being an endorsement of just the object in question and amounts to subscribing to or enunciating a new rule or principle, r_{n+1}. We claimed further that a justification for the words 'I approve X' can also be given in these more consequential cases and that such justification takes the form of pointing out certain facts relating, at least directly, not to the object approved but to the speaker. It follows that if such justification is successful, then the whole practice of admitting applicants by approval of the board has undergone a modification: a new rule, r_{n+1}, has been added to the old ones, $r_1, r_2, \ldots r_n$.

Now one might claim that if the second type of justification—justification in unorthodox or test cases—is to count as justification at all, we need another pre-existing set of rules, $R_1, R_2, \ldots R_n$, in order to decide which facts are to count as the relevant ones when cited about the speaker, and that therefore the decision on test cases cannot really count as a modification or revision of the existing practice. But what would be this other set of rules? It seems that it would have to be a heterogeneous lot. When I am forced to take the second line of defence in justifying my endorsement 'I approve X' what I have to do is to show (1) that I am well qualified for my job, and (2) that I was doing it well in the given case. Under (1) we might thus list such things as past experience and success, integrity, loyalty, &c. Under (2) we might mention familiarity with and care in studying the particular case, impartiality, &c. That one could do any better, be more rigorous, in specifying the relevant matters is doubtful. There simply is no set of rules that lays down the necessary and sufficient conditions for members of college admissions boards to do their job well. In defending my endorsement I just have to wait and see what sorts of challenge are in fact raised and build my defences accordingly.

But a further complication must be mentioned. In the case of official practices such as judging college applicants by boards there are, nevertheless, some rules and requirements which in a minimum sense do lay down both the necessary and the sufficient conditions for the adequate defence of utterances of the form 'I approve X' in test cases. As we saw above, when driven into a corner or when encountering exceptional obscurantism, I might, in defence of my words, take the last resort and say 'I am a member of the Board, am I not?' With this move, as we mentioned above, the boundary of the whole practice of admitting new students by the Committee has been reached; any demand for a further justification would, in a sense, take us outside that practice. I have invoked the rules that define the whole practice we follow or make up the very constitution of our Committee, and I have pointed out that by virtue of these rules my words carry a certain ineluctable weight. If, at a meeting of the Admissions Committee, I say 'I approve admitting Jones', but it turns out that I was not really a member of the Committee as my appointment had not yet come through, my words would not have that weight. My endorsement of Jones would be null and void.

One way in which I can silence the criticism of my words 'I approve X' is simply to point out that the conditions which would make my utterance of them into a valid or bona fide endorsement do in fact hold. Besides uttering or writing the words 'I approve Jones', there are other conditions and circumstances which must be present before it can be said that there "really" was an approval at all. Perhaps it must be done on a certain form, or in red ink, or uttered when all, or the majority, of the members are present, or what not. And, of course, the speaker must be a regular member of the committee, duly appointed, &c. If such conditions are satisfied, my endorsement is in order or valid or legal. No matter what dissatisfaction my words may cause, in a sense, I am invulnerable. In particular, if I point out that I am the right person to approve applicants to our college, that by virtue of the constitutive rules of our committee it comes under my jurisdiction, the matter is closed. There is no longer room for argument.

But there is no longer room for argument not because I have now fully justified my words. Argument ceases at this point simply because authority has taken the place of reason. In a sense, all I have to do in order to defend my words is to exhibit the fact that I possess the appropriate authority and that I have, in the given case, exercised it in the proper manner. But this will not show that my approval was right or well advised. In a very important sense I have done nothing yet to justify it. As we have seen, the justification of a linguistic performance has to do with what is implied by it. But by uttering the words 'I approve Jones' I do not *imply* that I occupy a certain official position and that I have followed the appropriate procedures. Rather, my approval of Jones *presupposes* these things. If these things are not in order then it is, properly speaking, not the case that my words are unjustified or wrong. They are instead null and void. The question whether they are right or wrong, justified or unjustified, does not even arise.[1] That question arises only if, first of all, the conditions laid down in the constitution and the rules of our committee are satisfied so that my words can really take effect. The third line of defence which can be given to the words 'I approve X' which we have been describing is therefore not truly a method of justification at all. Once my words have taken effect, the task of justifying them still lies before me and I may be called upon to do so first, by reference to accepted norms and standards, through evaluative proofs and, ultimately, by more ephemeral or at least elusive and complex arguments concerning the qualities of the speaker himself, which derive their force not from a set of fixed rules but from the more general and unclassifiable fund of human concerns, ingenuity, and *ad hoc* inventions.

4. *Expressions of Feelings, Decisions, and Moral Argument*

According to Stevenson, everything in morality depends, in the end, on our subjective feelings or attitudes. General principles and standards do have their relevance, but they are not final. We recall that the question of standards or principles was dealt with by Stevenson in terms of what he called the second pattern of analysis. His main point was that moral standards, or the descriptive meaning

---

[1] Cf. Austin, *How to Do Things with Words*, pp. 48–51.

of moral terms that goes beyond reference to a pro-attitude of the speaker, are always specified by persuasive definitions which are themselves really one sort of moral judgement. What moral principles there are thus depends on what moral judgements of a more general sort we are willing to make. And a moral judgement is always really just an expression of an attitude.

In our analysis of approval as a linguistic performance we also said that principles and standards are not absolute. We claimed that the standards or rules in terms of which linguistic acts of the form 'I approve X' are justified in normal cases are themselves laid down by such performances in test cases. Approvals are typically parts of self-corrective practices. Nevertheless, our conclusions differ significantly from those of Stevenson. According to our analysis, approvals that constitute precedents and have the force of laying down new rules are themselves also open to rational argument. The test cases, any more than the ordinary ones, are therefore not arbitrary, unarguable ventings of attitudes and emotions. But if we did, in Stevenson's spirit, conceive of approvals as pure subjective expressions of attitudes, then, indeed, reasoning about them in any relevant sense would always be precluded.

Approvals as linguistic performances, we argued earlier, are not descriptions of our feelings and attitudes. To say 'I approve X' is not the same thing as to say 'I am fond of X'. Neither, as became clear in the previous section, are they in general what we may vaguely call expressions of our subjective feelings such as 'Hurrah for X!' or 'Blast it!'.[1] In general, but there may be marginal cases. 'I approve X', we said earlier, is like 'I endorse or certify X as a qualified so-and-so'. But to say 'I approve X' is also to back and take sides with X or simply to applaud and cheer it. Depending on the circumstances, its intention may come very close to that of 'Hurrah for X!'. If so, could 'I approve X', on such an occasion, be justified or defended by reasons?

[1] It is rather hard to decide what to call linguistic acts such as 'Hurrah!' and 'Blast it!'. I have chosen the term 'expressions of feeling' because of its vagueness. We might call them 'ventings of feelings', but there is no explicit performative formula 'I vent . . .'. Perhaps this does not, by itself, matter. Austin claimed that insulting is an illocutionary or performative act although there is no formula 'I insult. . . .' (*How to Do Things with Words*). The central point is again that in expressing my feeling there is an element of convention.

Perhaps I imply by an expression of a subjective feeling of mine that I do have that feeling and that I am a normal human being endowed with the ability to have feelings and to know what they are. Consequently, it would seem, the evidence or proof that can be required of me when I express my feeling is evidence or proof that I do have that feeling. But this is queer: my expressing a feeling is often the best "evidence" for others that I have it and I myself do not need any. Normally, if I ask someone to give evidence or prove that he has a feeling, I suspect that he is insincere. But of course, if he shows to my satisfaction that he does have the feeling and is therefore sincere, this does not in any way justify or give a reason for his having said or shouted 'Hurrah for him!', 'Blast it!', or 'I do approve it!'

I could give reasons for my expression of a feeling, and others could intelligibly ask for them, only if I imply by my words not only that I have that feeling but also that that feeling is somehow, in a more or less definite sense, appropriate to the situation, that the situation demands it in accordance with some more or less definite rules or conventions. But of course by expressing a feeling I need not imply anything of the sort, my act may be quite casual and inconsequential. To the question 'Why did you shout "Blast it!"?' I may simply answer 'I just felt like it' or 'I can't get this needle threaded for the life of me'. Since our linguistic performances are acts, the question 'Why?' is in a loose sense always appropriate. But if a request for reasons merely amounts to 'Give some reason or other' it is not very serious.

Furthermore, the request for reasons is only intelligible under the assumption that the speaker *is* sincere. By saying 'I approve Jones' in non-casual circumstances, we saw earlier, I imply that I believe that Jones satisfies certain requirements and that it is because of this that reasons can be asked and given. If it turns out that I do not believe anything of the sort, the whole process of asking and giving reasons is frustrated. My sincerity is a pre-condition for reasoning to develop; it is in these circumstances not itself an issue around which reasoning turns. If I am not sincere, I may be accused of attempted fraud, but that need not have directly anything to do with the question whether Jones ought to be admitted. Similarly, if there happens to be an issue concerning the appropriateness or rightness of my words 'Blast it!', it need not have anything to do with my sincerity. Even if we do say that the expression of a subjective feeling implies the having of that feeling, evidence to the effect that the feeling is in fact present does not really constitute a reason for the rightness of that expression, if indeed there happens to be an issue about its rightness on a given occasion. Evidence for the sincerity of what we do is evidence for the rightness of what we do only in a minimal sense.

Besides the question of sincerity there is, however, another sense in which it can be asked whether we really have the feeling which our expressing it implies. I may make mistakes about my own feelings. But of course, being right about my feelings does not justify my expressing them any more than being sincere about them does. Being wrong about them may *excuse* us in some cases. If we do not know what our feelings are, this may free us from responsibility.

These points lead us to the second thing that we said is implied by the expression of a feeling: the ability to have feelings and to know them. Earlier we had claimed that the defence of our speech-acts depends on what our words imply. We had also said that part of such defence consists of giving evidence or furnishing a proof. We have therefore looked for the sort of thing that could be regarded as the justifying evidence for expressions of feeling. We found that when we ask for evidence in this area, we are, characteristically, interested in sincerity but that sincerity is not a justifying reason in any serious sense. We recall, however, that the second part of defending a speech-act consists of showing the competence and ability of the speaker. Perhaps in this sense, then, expressions of feelings can be justified. What constitutes competence with regard to expressions of subjective feelings? Well, our ability to know our own feelings and, perhaps first of all, our ability to have them. When I express a feeling I imply that I am capable of having it and knowing it; in other words, that I am a normal human being. But really I do not imply these things; rather, they are presupposed. Expressing our feelings makes sense, can exist as a language-game or form of communication, only against the background of such normalcy. If I do not have feelings or do not know them, I cannot express them. I may use forms of words such as 'Blast it!' or 'Hurrah!', but they would be void and empty. Consequently, pointing out the fact that I am a normal human being does not, properly speaking, constitute part of the justification of an expression of feeling either. Or, it constitutes justification only in the third and attenuated sense which we described above as silencing criticism by referring to one's official status or authority. If we are normal, we have the inviolable and uncriticizable right to express our feelings—if nothing else hinges on them.

It should be clear then that if, as Stevenson's theory makes us believe, moral judgements can, at the end, be reasoned about only in the sense in which subjective expressions of feelings can be reasoned about, the possibility of reasoning in morals is very meagre. If, by following the spirit of Stevenson's working models, we conceive of moral judgements as subjective expressions of attitudes, we could not explain how moral reasoning in any serious sense is possible.[1] But moral judgements are surely not as impressionistic as some of our approvals may be and the reasons which we may be required to give for them go beyond showing that the speaker, a human being in full possession of his emotional capacity, happens to have a certain attitude or feeling. The mere existence of an attitude or feeling does not silence moral criticism. The point that moral arguments are sometimes designed to bring out is just that a certain attitude or emotion was all too human. Moral criticism may arise from the fact that moral judgements are passed by human beings; pointing to that fact can never justifiably silence it.

Hare's theory of moral discourse, despite its significant differences from Stevenson's, is subject to similar criticisms. For him, moral judgements are one type of value-judgement and this means, roughly speaking, that, although being in part descriptive, they

---

[1] Stevenson seemed to think of moral judgements as being, in part, not expressions of feelings, but statements about feelings or attitudes. The first part of the working model for 'good', 'I approve of this', was, as we saw, according to him a description of my attitude. If so, the consequences we have been trying to point out would follow even more obviously. All I can and need do in the process of giving reasons for my moral judgement is, in the end, to show that I do feel approval or disapproval.

entail imperatives. To assent to a moral judgement is, in the end, to assent to an imperative. Now Hare claimed in *The Language of Morals* that moral judgements, just as imperatives, can be supported by reasons because they follow from premises which consist of (*a*) factual statements, and (*b*) general principles of conduct. However, we saw that in Hare's theory the question of which general principles of conduct or standards—in other words which descriptive meanings or criteria of value-terms—one should accept turned out to be a question of decision for which reasons could no longer be given. Morality thus became a matter of sheer decision and serious moral criticism an impossibility: I decide what I decide, and this is the end of the matter.

Hare's insistence that besides evaluative or imperative (commendatory, prescriptive) meaning moral judgements also possess descriptive meaning does not really get us out of the difficulty of explaining how serious moral reasoning is possible any more than Stevenson's similar claim did. In Stevenson's theory, the descriptive meaning of moral terms rests, at bottom, on our subjective attitudes. In Hare's theory, it depends, ultimately, on our decisions. Moral principles are created by our decisions of principle. But decisions as such are no more capable of being argued about than expressions of subjective attitudes are. In his later book *Freedom and Reason* Hare had a great deal to say about how moral decisions are somehow special and therefore susceptible to reasoning, although the ideas he presented there were also, as we saw, ultimately unsatisfactory. But in *The Language of Morals* he suggested bluntly that what entitles us to make decisions that create moral principles is just the fact that we are human beings. According to him, the circumstance that we are human beings, that we have to make decisions, that we have to go on with the business of living, sums up our moral being. Thus he wrote:

We cannot get out of being men; and therefore moral principles, which are principles for the conduct of men as men—and not as poisoners or architects or batsmen—cannot be accepted without having a potential bearing upon the way that we conduct ourselves. If I say to a certain person 'You ought to tell the truth', I signify my acceptance of a principle to tell the truth in the sort of circumstances in which he is; and I may find myself placed unavoidably in similar circumstances. But I can always choose whether or not to take up poisoning or cricketing as a profession. (*LM*, 162.)

But this is clearly inadequate. In connexion with Stevenson, we pointed out that our human prerogative to have likes and dislikes does not justifiably silence moral criticism. We may now add that our human predicament as described in the passage above does not silence it either. Once I have shown that I decide to accept and subscribe to a general moral principle as a man—and not as a poisoner, architect, or what not—who constantly and inescapably finds himself faced with these and similar decisions, it can always be asked of me: 'Yes, but was it (morally) right of you to subscribe to that principle?' The human faculty of having feelings and attitudes and the human need to make decisions indeed give rise to moral problems, but they do not solve them.

It seems that what both Hare and Stevenson have really done is to view morality as a kind of all-embracing institution, as a popularized Kantian Kingdom of Ends perhaps, made up of men "as men". And therefore, to them moral reasoning had to appear to be basically similar to what we have described as the third type of argument by which utterances of the form 'I approve X' sometimes may be supported—the argument from authority or official status. When my moral judgements are challenged, then, in the end, all I can, and need, say is 'I am a human being, am I not?'—that is, invoke the "authority" and status which I possess as a member of humanity by virtue of the sheer fact of being a creature endowed with sentiments and confronted with the necessity of having to make decisions. But certainly, this will not do.

Invocation of authority may be, as we saw, looked upon as a reason or argument only in the tenuous sense of showing that a certain legislative act, enunciation of a principle, is formally valid and legitimate, that it does come under the jurisdiction or office of the person in question; it cannot show that that legislative act was in any further sense right or well advised. Furthermore, since in the type of institution that both Stevenson's and Hare's analyses of moral language make us think of, the judge and the legislator can be any human being whatever, it would seem that when in doubt about what is the morally right thing to do or what moral principle to adopt, I can ask any man and get the final answer. But, of course, I do not ask just any man; nor do I need to think that the answer I get is final. I want to make sure that the person in question possesses enough wisdom, intelligence, and experience and that in the given case his judgement will not be a mere whim, prejudice, or blunder. Hare himself, we have remarked, takes notice of this point but he does not pay sufficient attention to its relevance to the nature of moral reasoning and justification (*FR*, 47).

There is an element of truth in Stevenson's and Hare's views. We saw that there is no set of rules or standards which specify what must be the course of argument in defence of an approval in a test case, that is, in a case where the force of the utterance 'I approve X' becomes 'I hereby subscribe to or enunciate the principle P'. The nature of such arguments, we found, was best described by saying that here the speaker must answer any specific challenges that are in fact brought forward. There is no way to tell, no general formula for telling beforehand and for certain, what these challenges ought, or are going, to be. The burden of proof lies, as it were, with the challenger rather than with the speaker. In a minimum way we all, as human beings, are qualified moral judges and legislators; prima facie, that is unless we are challenged, we are all free, have the right, to prescribe to our fellow beings. To speak of the human prerogative to have emotions and attitudes and of the human predicament of having to make decisions is to point out the two aspects of this freedom. But we must not be carried away. Our ability and competence to enunciate norms is often challenged and many of these challenges are obvious and always in the air. As human beings we have a certain right to determine how others should act. In a minimum, and rather special, sense the justification of our moral judgements therefore consists simply in insisting on our feelings, attitudes, and decisions. But as a human being I have the right merely to have my conscience *heard*; in that capacity I can claim nothing more. With a moral judgement I enter my case: to this, as a human being, I have the right. In the further task of defending it, it is no longer sufficient merely to appeal to that right. I must, when challenged, go on and try to justify my judgement by a moral "proof"; and if that fails, by showing that I was in the position, had the competence, to pass it.

In *Freedom and Reason* (see especially chapter 9) Hare paid much more attention to what we have called the question of moral competence than in his earlier book. He claimed, as we have seen earlier, that it follows from the logic of moral terms that moral judgements are universalizable. If I claim that it is right for me to perform a certain act in certain circumstances, I have said that it is right for anyone to perform that act in the same circumstances. Consequently, I am competent to pronounce an act right only if I am impartial and do not consider myself an exception. Furthermore, Hare argued, I must be sympathetic and imaginative and be able to view a proposed action from the point of view of others. I must be able to put myself in other people's shoes and regard their interests as mine. If I do not possess these abilities, or do not make use of them, I am what Hare calls a fanatic. Fanaticism does not, however, disqualify a man as a moral legislator, according to Hare. This is due to his rather broad notion of fanaticism. It almost seems that, for him, a fanatic is any man who in the name of an ideal of human excellence is willing to disregard some of the inclinations, desires, or interests that people, including himself, may happen to have. What is needed, and what a complete ethical theory would offer, is a narrower definition of moral fanaticism which *would* disqualify a man from enunciating moral principles; but it is quite possible that such a definition would involve us in taking a normative stand.

5. *Criteria, Evaluative Proof, and Moral Reasoning*

Toulmin, in effect, attempted to develop an ethical theory which was not based on the analysis of moral terms. Moore's effort to analyse ethical terms had led to the conclusion that at least one type of moral judgement is intuitive and incapable of being supported by reasons. This conclusion, as Toulmin rightly pointed out, was due to Moore's too strict standards concerning what are to count as reasons for a moral judgement. Moore had assumed in *Principia* that before we can tell whether a given statement can serve as a reason or as evidence for a moral judgement, we must know the correct analysis of that judgement. And, he assumed further, a statement can be given as a reason for a moral judgement only if that statement constitutes (part of) the analysis of the moral judgement in question. But since he came to the conclusion that the term 'good' and statements of the form 'X is good' are unanalysable, it followed that moral judgements of that form are incapable of being supported by reasons. Questions of intrinsic value are decided by intuition and there is therefore nothing which would (logically) prevent me from being a Humean moral solipsist and preferring the destruction of the whole world to the pricking of my finger.

Moore's conclusions were clearly paradoxical. In everyday practice we do reason in support of moral conclusions. Thus Toulmin proposed that we begin, not with an analysis of ethical terms and concepts, but by going directly to the question of moral argument and reasoning. There are indications that Moore himself came to view the analysis of ethical terms and concepts as an unworkable basis for a theory of moral discourse. His later theory, we recall, was that there are a number of logically equivalent pairs of propositional functions such that in each pair one of the functions expresses the concept of intrinsic value, and the other the concept of moral obligation. Moore would not have called these equivalences analyses of the terms 'good' and 'ought' or 'duty'. They were merely two-way general hypothetical statements on the basis of which certain statements of moral obligation could be inferred from certain statements of intrinsic value and vice versa. Similarly, what Toulmin sought was not an exact analysis of ethical terms but a formula that could serve as an inference licence between descriptive statements of fact and judgements of moral obligation. He thought he had found such an inference licence in the principle of social harmony. But the question arises: what makes that principle into an ultimate or even acceptable warrant for such inferences from facts to moral obligation? How are we to decide that this, and not some other principle, ought to be accepted as the rule of moral inference? Toulmin's answer seems to have been that this principle is, *as a matter of fact*, accepted as the inference licence in the practice of moral reasoning. He claimed that his theory was no "theory" at all, but a description of the facts of usage (*PRE*, 144). But, as we have now repeatedly pointed out, harmonization of interests is itself just one fact among others. We were therefore obliged to interpret Toulmin as recommending the adoption of the principle of harmony as the supreme moral principle. It would seem natural to interpret Toulmin's claim as a recommendation. To speak of harmony of interests is clearly to speak of an ideal. If we interpret Toulmin's claim as a descriptive generalization it becomes a sociological remark about a typical aim of human societies. If we take it as a recommendation, it belongs more properly in moral philosophy. In neither case, however, is it a logical doctrine about moral language.

Toulmin's attempt to explain the nature of moral reasoning without paying attention to the analysis of ethical terms thus ended in a moral ideal dogmatically put forth. Why should moral reasons be limited in such a way? Once it has been proved to me that a contemplated action, X, is conducive to the harmonization of interests in my society, why could I no longer ask the Moorean question 'Yes, but is X (morally) right?' We can refrain from asking such questions only if we are singularly blind to what Stevenson and Hare (misleadingly) called the emotive, evaluative, or prescriptive meanings of moral terms. Toulmin himself had to admit that

'This practice would involve the least conflict of interests attainable under the circumstances' does not *mean* the same as 'This would be the morally right practice'. (*PRE*, 224.)

But if the principle of harmony does not specify the whole meaning of moral judgements, there must be moral questions to which that principle does not provide the full answer.

We saw that Stevenson and Hare, in effect, looked at moral reasoning as having the pattern of what we have called the third kind of defence that can be given to our speech-acts—defence based on our own authority and status—although they conceived of such authority and status in an extremely liberal spirit. What Toulmin did was to conceive of moral reasoning as having the nature of what we have called the first kind of defence of our normative speech-acts—giving evidence or furnishing an evaluative proof. What he offered us was allegedly the supreme principle in terms of which such evidence or proof can be given. This too is one-sided and mistaken.

To give evidence or deliver a "proof" in defence of a moral judge-ment may never be enough, since which rules of inference may be legitimately used, or, to use Hare's way of putting it, which major premises may be cited in a moral syllogism, may itself be a moral question. A moral "proof"—an argument attempting to show that an evaluative conclusion follows from a set of factual premises—is only a part of the total activity through which moral judgements are supported by reasons. In order to have a proof I must have major premises. Therefore, by delivering a proof I have committed myself to certain general principles, and I may have to be prepared to show that I had the required competence for choosing these principles rather than others. Furthermore, there may be un-orthodox cases which do not come under any pre-existing principles and where offering a proof is therefore impossible. I must then show that I am well qualified to enunciate new principles so that a proof can be constructed. In either case I must thus ultimately resort to what we have called the second line of defence.

Toulmin, we saw earlier, concentrated on the criteria of applica-tion of moral terms and neglected their performative force. The study of the latter is, however, indispensable for a sound ethical theory. Whether a proof is valid or not depends on the criteria of application, the sense and reference, of the terms involved. But how fixed the criteria of application of a given term are, that is, whether and how much doubt and dispute there may be concerning its application in a particular case, depends on the kind of linguistic act in which it characteristically figures. Those terms the natural role of which is to figure in describing, giving information, pre-dicting, &c., may possess rather fixed criteria. There is hardly ever any doubt whether something is or is not a table, book, dog, &c. (that is, apart from situations where conditions of observation are not favourable). But even here doubtful cases arise which call for a decision. (Do the Japanese sleep in beds?) We do not have criteria ready for all eventualities and we may have to decide in a given case whether from the fact that a thing possesses certain properties it follows that a word applies to it.[1] But of course with a vast number of descriptive words this hardly ever occurs and their normal criteria are found to be perfectly adequate and beyond dispute.

On the other hand, terms which have the tendency to appear in less neutral or theoretical speech-acts possess criteria of application which are less fixed and with regard to them the necessity to make decisions is a rule rather than an exception. Stevenson's theory of Persuasive Definitions, in its own way, makes us aware exactly of this fact. When a term, such as, to use Stevenson's example, 'democracy', functions as a commendatory or prescriptive term, its criteria of application are likely to be in flux and dubious cases abound. It is characteristic of such terms to function in both neutral and non-neutral contexts and the degree of fixity of their criteria varies accordingly. How fixed the criteria of 'democracy' are, depends on whether it occurs, say, in a treatise on political theory or in an international political debate. Whether or not it follows from the fact that a form of government or social practice has certain characteristics that it is 'democratic', often calls for decision. And such decisions may of course conflict. In order to escape deadlock, one would have to try to defend such decisions by reasons. And eventually such defence may have to consist of the speaker exhibiting his competence to enunciate the criteria of application, that is, the standards of 'democracy'.

Finally, there are terms the whole nature of which is made up by their role in normative speech-acts. Of these the so-called moral terms 'good', 'right', 'ought', and 'obligatory' are the most conspicuous ones. These terms possess, by themselves, no criteria of application at all. All they have is their commendatory or prescriptive force. Let us single out 'good' for a more detailed examination. To say that the term 'good' has, by itself, no criteria of application is to say in a less misleading way that goodness is a supervenient property. It makes no sense to say that this is good and that is not but in all other respects they are exactly similar; it does make

[1] Cf. Waismann on 'open texture' (Friedrich Waismann, 'Verifiability' in Antony Flew, ed., *Logic and Language*, first series, Oxford: Basil Blackwell, 1955).

sense to say that this is yellow and that is not but in all other respects they are exactly similar. In other words, 'a good something' and 'a bad something' do not differ in their criteria, whereas 'a yellow something' and 'a non-yellow something' do. The phrase 'a good something' does not single out anything specific in the universe any more than the word 'something' does. Goodness has no general criteria, there are criteria only for types of goodness.

Does it follow then that whether something is good is always, in the end, a matter of decision or attitude, as Stevenson and Hare have it? It does not. In our discussion of how the performance 'I approve X' may be supported by reasons we pointed out that one always approves of something as something of a certain kind or as serving a certain purpose. Owing to this fact, we said, approving something makes reference to standards and we are able to furnish evaluative proofs in support of our approvals. The same is true of speech-acts involving the use of the term 'good'. We always claim that something is good as a thing of a certain kind or as serving a certain purpose. Correspondingly, calling something good always involves criteria although the word 'good' has, by itself, no criteria. There are no criteria for being good *tout court*, but there are criteria for being a good table, book, dog, man. And again evaluative proofs are possible. However, since such criteria are not fixed, such proofs are not always available. Often these criteria must be fixed by decisions and by offering a "proof" we will have committed ourselves to novel criteria. There are orthodox cases where doubt and dispute do not arise concerning the criteria of 'good table', 'good horse', and even 'good man' any more than concerning the criteria of 'table', 'horse', and 'man'. But the unorthodox or the test cases are vastly more common when the question is not just whether something is a table, horse, or man but whether it is a good table, horse, or man. And in those cases the criteria and standards, and eventually the men who enunciate them, may themselves have to be tested. Similarly, there are situations in which to refuse to dispute further the question of whether an action was really right or wrong, once the facts of the case have been settled, is no more dogmatic than to refuse to dispute further, once the facts are determined, whether an action was *really* swift or

slow. But there are many other cases where to refuse to dispute
over criteria of rightness would be unwarranted dogmatism.
Toulmin claimed that all rational argument about right and wrong
comes to an end once it has been shown that an action or practice is
or is not conducive to social harmony. But it is possible that there
are instances in which the criterion of social harmony will itself
need defence.

6. *The Variety of Performative Force and Moral Reasoning*

Ethical theorists in the twentieth century have striven towards
neatness and conclusiveness. This aim has proved to be neither
warranted nor constructive. In Moore's writings it led to the
unhelpful notions of intuition and non-natural properties. In
Toulmin's hand it led to the identification of one moral ideal with
the whole logical structure of moral language. It forced Stevenson
and Hare to make it seem that morality is merely an expression of
our unarguable decisions and attitudes. I will try to show that we
can do justice to the richness of moral language only if we study it
in terms of a number of models. To make a start, let us return to
Stevenson's discussion of what he called the emotive meaning of
ethical terms.

According to Stevenson the term 'good' "has no exact emotive
equivalent" (*EL*, 82). We can never *give* an expression which has
the same emotive meaning as the term 'good'; the best we can do
is to "characterize" or describe its emotive meaning. What, then,
can be said about the emotive meaning of 'good' by way of charac-
terization and description? Stevenson said that the *amount* of
emotive meaning the term 'good' has in a given case depends on
the "attendant circumstances" of its utterance. Sometimes 'good'
only "indicates" a favourable attitude, while on other occasions
it is "strongly hortatory". But again, there are cases when the
emotive content of the term 'good' sinks to a practical zero (*EL*, 83).

How then, on the basis of its emotive meaning, can we distinguish
the term 'good' from other, non-moral terms? It would seem that
in the case of any term there is a considerable range of intensity
in the accompanying emotions. The degree of this intensity depends

on the context and on the peculiarities of the speaker and the hearer. Stevenson *could* say that on the whole, or normally, ethical terms are charged with more emotion than other terms. But to say this would be misleading. It would obscure the fact that the emotional reactions which accompany the use of words are variegated in many different dimensions. In order to make the study of emotions and attitudes useful to the study of moral terms, we must pay attention to the different kinds of emotion that may be involved.

Moreover, what do we mean by the degree or amount of emotion? In common parlance we know well enough what we mean when we say that someone is experiencing a strong emotion, or that someone is feeling a stronger emotion than someone else. But in such cases we are usually making comparisons within a relatively limited context or situation. When, at a political convention, we say that A feels very strongly about a given proposal, then perhaps all we mean is that A spoke longer and more loudly about it than did any other delegate. If I say that I do not feel as strongly about tennis as I used to, all I might mean is that I do not play as often or get as keen a pleasure out of it as I did in the past. In other words, we understand phrases like 'feels strongly' from their context and it is doubtful whether there is any single thing which they mean in all contexts.

Anyone who is sufficiently familiar with a language can easily tell what words in that language are emotionally stronger than others. This is perhaps part of what constitutes knowing a language. But here again other things enter in. When we say 'You ought not to have used such a strong word', we do not mean 'You ought not to have used a word of such high degree of emotional intensity'; what we are more likely to be pointing out is the type of emotion which that word might have evoked or been taken to express. Some words are vulgar, some delicate; some are kind, some cruel. Perhaps if we concentrated on such emotional connotations of words, and tried to describe and analyse them, we might be embarking on a very illuminating study. If we succeeded in bringing out the characteristically moral emotions, we might have discovered a way of distinguishing moral terms from others and saying something important about them.

What Stevenson had to say along these lines is disappointingly meagre. The following passage comprises practically all that can be found in his book:

> The peculiarly moral attitudes, associated with the moral senses of the ethical terms, are not easily described, but can roughly be marked off in this fashion. ... Suppose that a man morally disapproves of a certain kind of conduct. If he observes this conduct in others, he may then feel indignant, mortified, or shocked; and if he finds himself given to it, he may feel guilty or conscience-stricken. But suppose that he dislikes this conduct, as distinct from morally disapproving of it. He may then be simply displeased when he observes it in others, and simply annoyed with himself when he finds that he is given to it. Similarly, if he morally approves of something, he may feel a particularly heightened sense of security when it prospers; whereas if he merely likes it, he may feel only an ordinary sort of pleasure. These differences in response, given similar stimuli, help to distinguish the attitudes which are moral from those which are not. The full distinction, should occasion require it, could be made by supplementing these remarks by others of a similar kind. (*EL*, 90.)

These remarks may be a first beginning but as they stand they are clearly inadequate. It is even doubtful whether "other remarks of a similar kind" would be more useful. They would not provide the differentiae of moral emotions. To say that one morally disapproves of something simply if and only if one is "indignant", "mortified", or "shocked" is simply false. Moral indignation is one sort of indignation among others. Further, why cannot there be "mere displeasure" or "annoyance" which is moral? Terms like "guilt" and "conscience" are more to the point, but they are complex phenomena and would require a detailed analysis.

Stevenson seems to have felt that although the moral emotive meanings of terms like 'good', 'ought', and 'right' could be identified through psychological description of the specifically moral emotions attending their use, such an attempt would be immaterial for the purposes of logical analysis. And in one sense, although not in his own, he was right. We have seen that a moral judgement as a linguistic act is *psychologically* compatible with *any* emotions which might attend it. Moral judgements are not symptoms or causes of emotions. Nor are they statements about emotions. Nevertheless, as we have seen, they imply the presence of certain emotions and attitudes. A person cannot normally without oddity claim in the same breath that a thing is good and he despises it or that an action is wrong and he has no aversion against doing it. Therefore, it is quite possible that a closer study of the sorts of emotion and attitude to which we commit ourselves in making moral judgements would be illuminating for the purposes of the analysis of moral language. Earlier, by taking a clue from Stevenson's notion that the use of the word 'good' is accompanied by the feeling or attitude of approval, we found it possible to use the linguistic performance 'I approve X' as a model for investigating how moral judgements can be supported by reasons. Further light may be thrown on the nature of moral reasoning if we can succeed in bringing out the character of specifically moral approvals. A detailed study of the kinds of emotion implied by the use of words like 'good' may be useful in such an investigation.

Stevenson admitted that his working models did not identify the specifically moral meaning of terms like 'good' although he thought that they could be modified in such a way that they would do so.

When "good" is assigned a descriptive meaning that refers, generically, to the speaker's favorable attitudes, and an emotive meaning that may serve to evoke the favor of the hearer, it does not become a peculiarly *moral* term. It is no less suitable for the context, "He is a good fellow", than for the context, "He is a (morally) good man". This broad, generic sense can readily give place, of course, to two or more specific ones, each of which will still fall within the first pattern. We may recognize a sense where "good" abbreviates "morally good", and refers not to *any* kind of favor that the speaker has, but only to the kind that is marked by a special seriousness or urgency. And we may recognize another sense, similar to that of "swell" or "nice", which refers descriptively to attitudes of the common-garden variety. (For each of these more specific senses, in appropriate contexts, there will be differences in emotive effects.) Thus "good", within the limits of the first pattern of analysis, can be given either one broad sense or several specific ones. (*EL*, 90.)

But Stevenson contended that it is immaterial whether or not we try to identify the specifically moral meanings of words like 'good' in the first pattern of analysis. He believed that to do so would not affect our views on the nature of moral reasoning: "the moral senses of the ethical terms", he wrote, "raise no special problems of language or methodology" (*EL*, 92). The main idea contributed· to Stevenson's total conception of moral reasoning by the working models was that, in the end, any moral argument has to appeal to subjective attitudes. It is not at all clear, however, that finer discriminations within the first pattern of analysis, or the working models, would not affect our views on moral reasoning. For example, if instead of saying,

(1) 'X is good' means 'I approve X, do so as well',

we substitute for approval some other attitude and said,

(2) 'X is good' means 'I respect (or reverence, or love, or admire) X, do so as well',

the reasons which we would bring forth to support an assertion of the form 'X is good' would not be the same as the ones which we would regard appropriate had we adhered to (1).

In order to make good the claim that as long as we confine ourselves to subjective attitudes, variations within the first pattern would not affect our views on moral reasoning, should we then eliminate "descriptive meaning" from the working models altogether? Stevenson claimed that the working models *could* have contained only an imperative.

The first pattern would remain roughly acceptable (though only as one type of analysis, to be supplemented by the second pattern) if descriptive meaning were eliminated entirely. "Good" would then *suggest* that the speaker approved, simply because of its laudatory emotive meaning; but it would not *descriptively mean* anything about his approval. (*EL*, 95–96.)

But even this would not do. Presumably, by eliminating the descriptive meaning from 'I approve of this, do so as well' it becomes 'Approve of this'. But to say that the emotive meaning of 'This is good' is 'Approve of this' is also to choose one among possible alternatives. Instead, we might propose, 'Respect this', or 'Please approve of this', or 'Admire this'. And surely, all these alternatives could make a difference with regard to the kinds of reasons by which an assertion of the form 'X is good' may then be supported. It is far from clear that finer discriminations within the first pattern would not raise any "special problems of language or methodology".

What Hare called the evaluative meaning of moral judgements has a great deal in common with what Stevenson called their emotive meaning. And it too has allegedly nothing to do with the sorts of reasons by which such judgements may be supported. According to Hare, the moral sense of words like 'good' is to be distinguished through their descriptive, rather than through their evaluative, meaning. The word 'good' is always used for commending, but in moral contexts its descriptive meaning, that is, its reference to characteristics which make a thing good, is different. And it is the descriptive meaning of the term 'good', and it alone, that determines what will count as reasons for saying that something is good (LM, chapter 9).

There is a curious asymmetry in conceiving of the matter in this way. The descriptive meaning of 'good' varies with the context, but its evaluative meaning does not. But surely we may wonder whether moral commendation differs from commendations of other sorts simply in that the objects commended are different. 'He is a good man' and 'That is a good fire-extinguisher' are vastly different and it does not seem possible that the difference lies only in the descriptive meaning, that is, the criteria of application, of 'a good man' and 'a good fire-extinguisher'. It seems that the difference lies also in the evaluative meaning, that is, the performative force of these two speech-acts. In commending a person I am reacting to him as a person, not as a thing. When I say that he is a good man it is significant that I am a creature like him and I imply something concerning my own future conduct. By commending a person I further imply that I respect him, but can I respect a fire-extinguisher?

Even if we did not question Hare's contention that the evaluative meaning, or as we should rather say, the performative force, of judgements of the form 'X is good' consists solely of their commendatory function, we thus find reason to doubt that the performative force of such judgements always remains the same regardless of context, and that the only difference between 'He is a good man' and 'That is a good fire-extinguisher' lies in their respective criteria. But it is extremely doubtful that 'X is good' always has the same force as 'I commend X as. . . '. May it not also have the force of, say, 'I grade X as . . .' or 'I assess X as . . .' or 'I estimate that X . . .' or 'I proclaim X . . .' or 'I choose X . . .' or 'I nominate X . . .' or 'I promise that . . . X' or 'I intend to . . . X' or 'I propose to . . . X' or 'I guarantee that X . . .' or 'I pledge myself to . . . X' or 'I favour X for . . .' or 'I compliment X for . . .' or 'I pay tribute to X for . . .' or 'I applaud X for . . .', &c.

When we realize this, it becomes evident that the peculiar moral sense of the words 'X is good' is not determined solely by their criteria. It will then also become evident that the nature of reasons that can be given in support of a moral judgement is not solely dependent on and at the mercy of what Stevenson and Hare called their descriptive meaning. The vicissitudes of the criteria of goodness are not, fortunately, the final decisive factor in moral reasoning.

In the last pages of *The Language of Morals* Hare adumbrated a view concerning the evaluative force of moral judgements which, had he developed it fully, would have been far more subtle and adequate than the oversimplified notion that in so far as moral judgements are evaluative judgements, they are always very much like imperatives or commands. The gist of the matter is contained in the following two passages:

Instead of 'You ought to tell him the truth', let us write 'If you do not tell him the truth, you will be breaking a general *"ought"*-principle to which I hereby subscribe'.

· · · · · · · · · ·

If I say 'I hereby subscribe to such and such a principle', that is as good as actually enunciating the principle; the words 'hereby subscribe', as it were, cancel out the inverted commas, in the same way as 'I hereby promise that I will obey, serve, love, etc.' would have the same force in the marriage service as 'I will obey, serve, love, etc.' Thus in the sentence 'If you do not tell him the truth, you will be breaking an '*ought*'-principle to which I hereby subscribe' . . . there is a live imperative element. (*LM*, 194.)

These remarks remind us of the distinction between phrastics and neustics. It seems that here Hare *is* applying this distinction directly to moral judgements. Instead of saying that the moral judgement 'You ought to tell him the truth' contains and therefore entails an explicit imperative, Hare seems to be saying that it consists of something like the phrastic

(*a*) 'If your not telling him the truth, then your breaking the principle P'

and the neustic

(*b*) 'Hereby subscribed to'

rather than of the complete indicative sentence

(*a'*) 'If your not telling him the truth, then your breaking the principle P, yes'

and the complete imperative sentence

(*b'*) 'P being kept, please'

as the rest of his theory would demand. If we looked at the matter in this way, the "live imperative element" of a moral judgement would no longer be the simple 'please' appropriate to plain imperatives. This would have the advantage of recognizing clearly that moral judgements are not really like imperatives at all and allow us to abandon the dogma of two types of meaning of such judgements.

Hare insisted that moral judgements must provide genuine answers to questions like 'What should I do?' With this, as we have argued, one must agree. But his insistence on this point created the impression, at least in his earlier book, that moral judgements are very much like imperatives or commands. Moral judgements and commands are typically different. If I say 'X is good', I am not merely urging you to choose X. In saying 'X is good' I entitle you to say, on your part, 'X is good' in very much the same sense in which I would, if I were to say 'X is red', entitle you to say 'X is red' also. If I say 'X is good', I cannot object to your saying 'X is good'.

'Choose X', on the other hand, does not entitle you to say, on your part, 'Choose X'; X might not, for one thing, be yours to let me choose it. Similarly, in saying 'Y is right' or 'You ought to do Y' I am not merely trying to influence your pending decision, I am saying something which is universal and does not depend on its authorship. A command, on the other hand, is not universal, and whether it may be objected to may depend a great deal on who its author is. We saw that all this is really recognized by Hare himself particularly in his later work where he emphasized that a moral judgement, or for that matter any value-judgement, unlike a plain imperative, is "universalizable". With *that* part of Hare's theory we found no reason to disagree. The thesis that moral judgements entail imperatives was even in his earlier book hidden behind many qualifications. Obviously he himself did not think that this thesis did justice to the whole nature of moral judgements. It is therefore surprising that Hare kept insisting that moral judgements always have in common with imperatives a kind of meaning or performative force.

That the performatory force of moral judgements is variegated and cannot be brought under one formula becomes evident when we reflect that societies and times differ in their moral tone and character; the moral temper of places and times is not always the same. And these dissimilarities are reflected in language in two dimensions and not merely in one. For example, there may very well be two societies where men are morally praised or blamed for exactly the same reasons. In that case the moral criteria of the term 'good man' would be the same in both of them. Nevertheless, moral praise or blame may have a much more rigid, institutionalized, dogmatic, authoritarian character in one of these societies than in the other. In such a case the differences in morality between the two societies are reflected not by the criteria but by the evaluative meaning, that is, performative force, of moral terms. It is exactly here, in the character of the performative force of moral terms, that the difference between what has been called "catholic" and "protestant" morality lies.[1] A moral judgement is never just a

[1] Cf. Aiken, 'The Authority of Moral Judgments', in *Philosophy and Phenomenological Research*, June, 1952.

personal act arising from the innermost recesses of an individual soul. But neither is it an act the authority of which is derived solely from its ceremonial setting. A moral judgement is neither a purely personal voicing of a conviction nor a totally impersonal verdict delivered by an institution or tradition. In moral judgements both of these aspects are present, but, depending on the kind of moral conscience of the person or community in question, one or the other has greater relative weight. Differences of this sort may make a difference with regard to what will count as a valid moral argument or justification. But, at the same time, differences of this sort need not be reflected in our moral standards. No matter whether our morality be "catholic" or "protestant" in the above sense, we can still agree, for example, that murder is (morally) bad and loving our neighbour (morally) good.

7. Conclusion and the Task Ahead

Stevenson, we recall, argued that to specify the descriptive meaning, or as we have preferred to say, the criteria of application, of terms like 'good' is to take sides with respect to a normative issue. If our reasoning has been correct, then to specify the evaluative meaning, or, properly speaking, the performative force, of such terms is also a normative issue. In so far as moral philosophers are concerned with the neutral task of analysis, it seems that they cannot determine the meaning of moral terms on either one of its two levels. Neither does it seem possible that the neutrality of ethical theory, or meta-ethics, can be preserved by proceeding directly to questions of moral argument. To say that such and such are the criteria of validity of an evaluative argument is no different from enunciating evaluative standards and principles. This, I think, is the truth in Moore's contention that the term 'good' is indefinable. If moral philosophy is not to degenerate into the making of dogmatic normative claims, it is therefore clear that we must avoid anything like the giving of definitions. Moral philosophy should be instead a gradual exploration of the criteria of application and the performatory forces of moral utterances. Even then we may not be able to escape normative issues. But I am not sure whether the point is really to escape such issues rather than just to escape being dogmatic about them.

Twentieth-century moral theory got a fresh start when Moore's effort to discover the nature of moral terms through a study of the properties to which they allegedly refer was found to be wrong-headed and futile. By splitting the meaning of moral terms and judgements into two elements, descriptive and evaluative, philosophers believed to have made the problem at last manageable. We have seen, however, that the distinction between descriptive and evaluative meaning was, in the end, a misfortune. Where Moore had seen one difficult question, subsequent writers tended to see two (or three) deceptively easy ones. Where Moore had asked, 'What is the definition of the term "good"?' others came to ask (1) 'What is the descriptive meaning of the term "good"?' (or 'What are good reasons for saying "X is good"?'), or (2) 'What is the evaluative (emotive) meaning of the term "good"?' The result was, as we have seen, one-sidedness and oversimplification. The radically new approach to problems of ethical theory which was foreshadowed in some of Moore's writing and came to its first full expression in Stevenson has not yet fulfilled its promise.

Anti-descriptivism has been the most marked thing about post-Moorean ethical theory. That moral judgements are not wholly descriptive but have a kind of meaning peculiar to them has become almost axiomatic. The initial plausibility of this notion had much to do with the fact that it could be used as a device for preserving what was considered the truth in Moore's views and, at the same time, avoiding the difficulties into which Moore himself was led. Moore's central thesis that the term 'good' is indefinable has, we saw, two interpretations. On the one hand, it can be taken to be an assertion to the effect that goodness, a certain non-natural property, is simple and unique; on the other, it can be regarded as saying just that the concept of goodness is simple and irreducible. We have seen that the first of these alternatives brings with it a number of difficulties. The notion of non-natural properties is hopelessly obscure. How non-natural properties differ from natural ones, and how the presence of a non-natural property in an object depends on the presence of natural properties in that object, are questions to which no one has been able to give a satisfactory answer. Furthermore, if Moore's thesis that the term 'good' is indefinable is taken to be an assertion about the simplicity and uniqueness of goodness as a property, it boils down to a tautology: goodness is what it is and not anything else. If the so-called Open Question Argument—the most important argument that Moore gave in defence of his thesis—is supposed to prove just that goodness is what it is, it cannot be a useful tool in ethical theory.

But Moore himself did not always, in practice, conceive of ethical theory as a study of a non-natural subject-matter. And indeed it need not be supposed that by the claim that the term 'good' is unanalysable anything is said about the nature of a special kind of entity. The concept of goodness, no more than, say, the concept of negation, need be thought of as a concept of some entity. In interpreting Moore's views in this way we also found it necessary to reject Moore's claim that any definition of the term 'good' is absolutely and in principle impossible. If his Open Question is to be a meaningful question, it cannot support such a sweeping and universal claim. Nevertheless, we saw that the Open Question is a useful method for criticizing any ethical theory of a descriptivist bent which in fact is or may be offered. We made use of it ourselves, particularly in criticizing Toulmin's views.

The third difficulty to which Moore's views led was the absurd consequence that in so far as moral judgements are capable of being supported by reasons, they cease to be practical. We saw that, according to Moore, we can defend a moral judgement by an argument only if that judgement concerns either merely cause and effect relations or the obligations of a purely hypothetical or ideal agent.

These three vexing points, (a) the obscurity of the notion of non-natural properties, (b) the tautological character of the claim that 'good' is indefinable as a term referring to a property, and (c) the paradox involved in the position that in so far as moral judgements can be reasoned about they cannot be practical, brought about a change in the whole manner of approaching questions of theoretical ethics. Instead of non-natural properties and the indefinability of the term 'good' philosophers started to talk about

a special kind of meaning or function that moral judgements have and to cast about for a different mode of analysis which would explain the nature of reason in ethics. But all this did not turn out to be an easy task.

Moore's notion of non-natural properties was intended to help to show that moral terms differ in significant respects from other terms in language. Stevenson and those who came after him tried to make the same point by saying that moral terms and judgements have two types of meaning: evaluative and descriptive. But this bred new difficulties. If a moral judgement has two distinct meanings, it must somehow contain two speech-acts. How, then, can it be supported by reasons? An utterance can be a reason for another only if there is an appropriate relation between their criteria of application. But one of the speech-acts which was said to be incorporated in a moral judgement—the act of suggesting, commending, prescribing, or what not—was allegedly not governed by criteria at all. Criteria went only with descriptive meaning or with the act of describing which was also said to be part of passing a moral judgement. How evidence or reasons can be given for a moral judgement as a whole therefore remained a mystery.

Among the writers who followed Moore, Stevenson and Hare were impressed by the evaluative and practical aspect of moral judgements. But since they thought of this evaluative aspect as a totally separate kind of meaning, it became impossible for them to explain how it is related to the sense and reference or the criteria of application which are also embodied in those judgements. Toulmin, on the other hand, concentrated on the descriptive element or, more properly, the criteria of application of moral terms. It seemed to him certain that these terms are used according to criteria. But he imagined that these criteria can be determined once and for all. This resulted in neglecting the evaluative aspect, or, properly speaking, the performative force, of moral judgements.

Has the air of progress in twentieth-century ethical theory then been totally deceptive? Not necessarily. We have argued that a more satisfactory view of the nature of moral language and reasoning can be developed if we realize that the evaluative aspect of a moral judgement does not constitute a separate kind of meaning.

Rather, the evaluative aspect of a moral judgement is made up by its performative force or forces which are different from the performative forces of statements, descriptions, predictions, &c. Nor does the descriptive aspect of a moral judgement constitute a kind of meaning. The proper thing to say here is that moral judgements, like all speech-acts, have sense and reference, that is, are governed by criteria of application. Instead of two kinds of meaning, we should speak of two different levels or elements of meaning. We have seen that if we do that, it becomes possible to interpret at least some of the doctrines of our three latter authors as parts of a more comprehensive and unified theory of moral language. It is in this direction that progress in twentieth-century ethical theory must be sought. Each of these authors managed to suggest only fragments of the total performative nature of moral judgements. Their theories were one-sided in one way or another and provided only partial answers to the problem of how moral judgements can be supported by arguments.

This one-sidedness can be avoided if we realize that moral judgements, like all speech-acts, involve both criteria of application and a characteristic performative force. Owing to their criteria of application, moral judgements are capable of being supported by evaluative proofs. But because the performative forces of moral judgements are non-descriptive, the relevant criteria are never fixed. Evaluative proofs require that the criteria of application of value-expressions be held constant. But in many cases there is nothing but our decisions to lend such constancy. In offering an evaluative proof we have often, in effect, fixed the criteria ourselves, or, what amounts to the same thing, subscribed to a moral principle. However, such decisions need not be arbitrary. They themselves can be supported by arguments although in their case the argument is no longer an evaluative proof but an attempt to establish the competence of the person making such decisions.

We saw that in ordinary or normal cases a linguistic performance like 'I approve X' can be defended by arguments which consist in showing that X comes under the recognized rules $r_1, r_2, \ldots r_n$, and that therefore a certain action, Y (e.g. admission to college), is permitted or even well advised. In these cases the justification of that linguistic performance takes the form of a "proof". Let us suppose now that I utter the words 'You ought to tell him the truth' instead of 'I approve Jones'. The structure of the relevant "proof" would then be the following:

I. A general principle or rule, r, is cited:
   Whatever is A, B, and C is obligatory.

I then add a minor premise and draw the conclusion:

   Telling him the truth is A, B, and C.
   ∴ Telling him the truth is obligatory and 'You ought to tell him the truth' that is, my urging you to tell him the truth, is justified.

In the unorthodox or test case there is no ready-made principle, r, available. Let us assume that the moral judgement in one such case is 'You ought not to tell him the truth' which amounts to an effort to establish a precedent or to lay down a new rule, say, 'Discretion is obligatory'. How could that moral judgement be "proved"?

II. First, we may imagine, a higher rule, R, is cited:
   Whenever a rule is X, Y, and Z, then observing it is obligatory.

And again, we may think, one adds the minor premise and draws the conclusion:

   The rule of discretion is X, Y, and Z.
   ∴ Discretion is obligatory and 'You ought not to tell him the truth', that is, my enunciating the rule of discretion, is justified.

But this is not plausible. What are we to imagine as capable of being put in the place of X, Y, and Z? 'Is conducive to social harmony', one may suggest. But would not that, as we have argued, amount to just enunciating a further normative principle? Eventually one would run out of such principles and would have to use other means, other modes of reasoning, if the whole argument is not to remain inconclusive. What are these other means? Well, we have suggested that one can try to show that a principle or rule is final because it is enunciated by someone who is in the position to do so.

But what is to count as being in the position to enunciate moral principles? Suppose a father tells his son 'You ought to stop seeing Jane' and is asked 'Why?' As his first line of defence the father can refer to rules and standards. But there might not be any set of existing rules which fit the case exactly. In the course of their argument both the father and the son might come to feel that therefore the judgement 'You ought to stop seeing Jane' really amounted to laying down a new rule for the conduct of young men in similar circumstances: the son's courtship of Jane may come to be viewed as a test case.

Consequently, the father must now take the second line of defence. He must show that he is in a good position to do the job of a parent or of anyone whose business it is to guide the conduct of the young and that in the given case he has performed this function intelligently, conscientiously, with understanding, and in familiarity with the facts. There is no longer the possibility of delivering a "proof". The father must merely answer the challenges and questions which are in fact brought forth. Speaking roughly, very roughly, we may say that the circumstances and powers one may have to exhibit in establishing one's competence are always those relating to (1) the intellect and (2) the will. Under (1) a man must show that he is familiar both with cases of a certain kind and with the particular case in question, that he is capable of finding the truth and has taken care to find it now. Under (2) he must exhibit his integrity of character and show that he has been impartial, honest, disinterested, and scrupulous. But we must remember that there are no necessary and sufficient conditions which make a man succeed in this form of justification of his speech-acts. For this line of argument almost everything in heaven and on earth may be relevant and we must simply wait and see which things we are required to establish as the discussion proceeds and specific challenges are brought forward. Furthermore, although the second form of defence goes beyond the first, there is an intimate connexion between the two. We have argued that the first line of defence goes with sense and reference, the second with performative force. But we also argued that sense and reference, on the one hand, and performative force, on the other, are inseparable and function together in a full speech-act. Similarly, the unorthodox cases, the cases in which the question of competence becomes relevant, are intelligible, can arise, only with reference to and in contrast to orthodox and normal cases. The standard rules serve a double task. The speaker uses them in his first line of defence for giving evidence, for conducting his "proofs". But his manner of doing this, the degree of familiarity, efficiency, and acumen exhibited in judging normal cases, can count as a test of his ability to handle the unorthodox cases as well and to lay down new rules.

Earlier, after having presented the outline of how linguistic performances of the normative sort can be supported by arguments, we went on to consider a possible objection. The objection was that our account is insufficient to explain how such linguistic performances can be *really* justified. We saw that in one sense this objection was quickly answered: if what is to be justified is my performance as it is related solely to a given individual case, then by delivering an evaluative proof I have given all the justification that may be (reasonably) desired. If, however, my linguistic performance constitutes an unorthodox or test case and has implications going beyond the individual case at hand, the above objection was seen to introduce two complications. And we discussed these complications under the headings (1) 'the self-corrective character of a practice', and (2) 'the defining or constitutive rules of a practice'.

By the 'self-corrective character of a practice' we meant that within practices such as admitting new students through admissions boards, there is room for performances that shape, regulate, and correct the whole character of those practices themselves. We saw that in test cases a performance like 'I approve (admitting) Jones' acquires the force of 'I enunciate the principle P (for admitting new students)' and is thus capable of modifying the whole procedure of admissions. We saw also that we can conceive of moral language in a similar way. Following Hare, we may say that in uttering the words 'You ought to do Y' the speaker either just issues a singular prescription or performs in a more far-reaching manner and subscribes to or advocates a general principle. And by taking a clue from Stevenson, we may say that in uttering the words 'X is good' the speaker either just approves X or lays down for all objects like X a general standard (or, more closely in Stevenson's own words, approves approving objects like X).[1]

In which of these capacities a moral judgement is used becomes clear from the context: it depends on whether these judgements are uttered in ordinary or in test cases. Morality is thus also a practice that is self-corrective or self-regulative and that has room for performances capable of modifying its whole structure. If I utter the moral judgement 'You ought to do Y' (or 'X is good') in a test case and am able to justify it, I have established a new moral principle of conduct (or a new standard of moral appraisal). And I have justified my performance in such a momentous case, if I succeed in what we have called the second type of argument, that is, in showing that I am well qualified as a moral legislator.

The point of our imaginary objector thus becomes that the 'second type of argument' is insufficient for establishing my right as a moral legislator. You have the right to enunciate, you are justi-fied in enunciating, a principle of conduct only if that principle is a right principle, and in order to show *that* you need further, higher principles. You must *prove* that you are a well-qualified moral legislator, show that your performance has the backing of the Moral Law.

There are three points to be mentioned in answer to this criticism.

I. The Moral Law is either (*a*) a description of a non-natural world of values, or (*b*) an empirical generalization, or (*c*) itself enunciated by a legislator. It cannot be (*a*) since this is, essentially, the Moorean view and is, as we have seen, refuted by the argument that the description of a non-natural world can create only an "ideal" obligation but cannot serve as a practical guide concerning what we ought to do here and now. It cannot be, or at least very likely is not, (*b*), since we have seen that no formulation of the Moral Law as an empirical generalization has yet been given with regard

---

[1] The second of these types of jobs that moral judgements do is pointed out also by Ryle, when he talks of moral judgements as "warrants" or "licences" addressed to "any potential givers of behests and reproaches". (Gilbert Ryle, *The Concept of Mind*, London: Hutchinson, 1949, p. 128.)

to which we cannot ask, *à la* Moore, 'Ought we always to obey it?'
We are thus left with the third alternative, that is, that the Moral
Law itself exists only so far as it is enunciated by a competent
moral legislator.

II. You could *prove* that you are a well-qualified moral legislator
only if there were a clear set of principles in terms of which such a
proof could be conducted. But, as we have argued, to show that
one is well qualified as a moral legislator is to show that one is
wise, intelligent, understanding, careful, possesses insight, is not
prejudiced, &c. The concept of being well qualified as a moral
legislator, or the concept of moral competence, is thus a concept
with "blurred edges".[1] First, wisdom, intelligence, understanding,
insight, integrity, impartiality, &c., are themselves qualities for
the presence of which there are not always any necessary and
sufficient conditions. Aside from certain obvious requirements for
the possession of these qualities in general, there are no tests,
no clear-cut criteria, for determining whether a person possesses
them in a degree sufficient for an occasion. Second, it would
be unrealistic to hope for an exhaustive list of the qualities which
make up moral competence. There is no such list for all cases.
The colour and feel of morality is variegated and the sizing
up of a given concrete moral situation may demand a kind of
talent, experience, and attention which might not at all be suited
for a different kind of case. Moral competence is what has been
called a defeasible concept.[2] There are some obvious requirements
which are prima facie necessary and sufficient for being morally
competent, but there are many cases in which, although these
requirements are satisfied, one's pretension can nevertheless be
defeated. We saw that in a minimal sense *all* that is required is the
possession of a sound mind and body, but that, characteristically,
we are asked to go beyond that. However, what exactly are the
additional things the lack of which can defeat one's claim to moral
competence cannot be determined once and for all. Therefore,
there is no general formula for the second type of argument by which

---

[1] Cf. Wittgenstein, *Philosophical Investigations*, sections 71–78.

[2] Cf. Hart's discussion of defeasible concepts and utterances in H. L. A. Hart,
'The Ascription of Responsibility and Rights' in Antony Flew, ed., *Logic and
Language* (first series).

moral judgements can be defended. Impersonal procedures of giving evidence and proof cannot be substituted for competence in personal decisions. Showing that someone is a well-qualified moral legislator must always fall short of proof; it must consist merely in answering specific challenges, charges of certain lacks and inadequacies, that are or may be in fact made.

III. If morality were an institution, and this brings us to the second complication that we mentioned earlier, then there would be a further sense in which enunciations of moral principles could be defended with the finality of a proof. If morality were an institution, then when justification of the words 'I enunciate (the moral principle) P' is demanded, the speaker might be able by citing the defining or constitutive rules of morality to show that under these rules, enunciating P comes under his authority and jurisdiction. But we have seen that reference to official status is not truly a justification at all. That the speaker does in fact hold the proper office makes his performance legal, but it need not make it well advised. Furthermore, we have seen that if morality is an institution at all, it must be a kind of Kingdom of Ends in which all of us hold equal office and are, at the same time, both legislators and subjects. And in such an institution, if we wish to call it that, all authority is shared, being thus responsibility as well as right. Having this authority, office, or status is best described as having the right or freedom to make one's moral voice heard, coupled with the responsibility or obligation to listen to that of others. Whose voice should prevail cannot be decided by reference to our "status" as human beings; for deciding this we must return to arguments of the first and second kind. What Dewey called "reflective", as opposed to "customary", morality cannot be said to be an institution in any more full and rigorous sense.

We have seen that by conceiving of moral judgements as possessing both criteria of application and a non-descriptive performative force a satisfactory explanation can be given of how these judgements can be supported by arguments. In other words, we can give an adequate account of the place and nature of reason in ethics. But there still remains the task of giving body to this doctrine. In terms of what performatory models should moral language then be studied? The expressions 'X is good' and 'You ought to do Y' are more protean than is perhaps generally supposed. Philosophers have been engaged in an unprofitable and misleading search for their *generic* emotive meaning (Stevenson), for their *common* evaluative use in all contexts (Hare), or for their *ultimate* use and purpose (Toulmin). The only safe, short, and comprehensive way to specify the meaning or use of moral judgements is to say that 'X is good' is used for saying that X is good and 'You ought to do Y' is used for saying that you have an obligation to do Y. If we want to go beyond this, we must delve into detail and be ready to qualify our assertions at every step. Certainly, 'X is good' is used for approving and commending. But it is also used for laying down and subscribing to standards, praising and blaming, giving one's word, grading, ascribing and accepting responsibility, affirming solidarity, applauding, casting out of or accepting in a group, paying tribute, congratulating, guaranteeing, &c., &c. Certainly, 'You ought to do Y' is used for prescribing. But it is also used for enunciating and subscribing to principles, placing demands, taking sides, licensing, advocating a course of action, transmitting authority, invoking sanctions, overruling, restricting, instructing, &c., &c. A fully adequate ethical theory would analyse and systematize the whole variety of linguistic performances and commitments that are embedded in the use of moral language. Only in this manner can we hope to reach a full description of reason in ethics. And since, as we have seen, reasons in ethics eventually lead to the person who gives these reasons, in analysing moral language our final concern would be with the moral agent, judge, and legislator, in short, with the moral person.

A full ethical theory would move in the direction of comprehensiveness and systematization. But we must shun *a priori* arguments. What is needed instead is what Austin has called "field work". If we stop too soon we lay ourselves open to the charge of circularity. We have said that in order to support a moral judgement, we need moral principles; but then if we went on and specified such moral principles, we would be passing moral judgements ourselves. We have also said that we can justify a moral judgement, if we can show that we are competent to pass it; but if we then went on to say what moral competence is, we would be putting forth a moral ideal. We have avoided circularity *in theory* by saying that no moral principles are final in practice and that the concept of moral competence is, in practice, a defeasible concept. But there is also, of course, a different and equally legitimate concern that the moral philosopher may have: he may want not just to generalize *about* practice, but also to generalize *for* practice. He may *want* to say what moral principles there are and what constitutes moral competence. However, when he undertakes this task, he must first of all be clear that he is leaving pure theory behind. Furthermore, his theory must remind him that his conclusions cannot be timeless and are, in principle, open to criticism.

INDEX

Aiken, H. D., 93, 238 n.

Approving, 79, 119, 121, 205 f., 206, 208, 212, 217.

Aristotle, 9, 94.

Attitudes, 73–76, 78, 88, 92, 95, 99 f., 100, 186 f., 192, 217, 220, 232–4.

Austin, J. L., 3, 27 n., 28 n., 29 n., 48, 117 n., 123, 140 n., 149, 157, 168 n., 201, 205 n., 208 n., 216 n., 217 n.

Broad, C. D., 11–12.

Competence, 205, 209–12, 219, 224, 245, 248, 251.

Criteria of application, 150–60, 166–9, 209 f., 224–30, 235, 239, 242 f. *See also* Sense and reference.

Decision, 68, 81, 105, 169, 170, 175–82, 186, 192–4, 216–24, 243.

Definitions, 5–8, 18, 21, 64, 66, 101. *See also* Persuasive definitions.

Descriptive meaning, 2, 32, 42–47, 50 f., 53, 58 f., 61, 63–73, 93, 122, 135, 143, 151 f., 156 f., 160–70, 182, 221, 234, 236, 239.

Dewey, J., 94 f., 249.

Duality of meaning, 3, 31 f., 40–45, 51 f., 143, 145 f., 149–60, 165, 169, 182, 240, 242 f.

Emotions, *see* Feelings.

Emotive meaning, 42–45, 47, 49, 51–64, 69 f., 89 f., 122 f., 139, 141, 143, 146, 151, 186, 200, 202, 230, 232, 235, 250.

Ethical theory, 1–2, 4, 10, 15 f., 27, 101, 127, 145, 197, 201, 211, 230, 239–41, 243, 250.

Evaluative meaning, 2, 32, 151 f., 164, 168 f., 182, 221, 235, 239.

Evidence, 23–24, 32, 156, 180, 209–11, 249.

Feelings, 129, 132, 134, 136, 216–24, 231–3.

Function, *see* Use.

'Good', 15, 21, 27, 31, 35, 40, 60, 65, 68 f., 110, 150 f., 159, 203 f., 225, 228, 230, 233, 235, 239; Indefinability of, 5–9, 16, 21, 30, 32, 53, 239, 240 f.

Goodman N., 135 n.

Goodness, 8–16, 33, 37, 53, 108, 150, 200, 229, 240; Simplicity of, 9, 16–22.

Hampshire, S., 132 n.

Hare, R. M., chapter iv *passim*, 2, 40, 63, 67, 86, 92, 104 n., 119 n., 199–201, 203, 209, 220–4, 226 f., 227, 229 f., 235–8, 242, 246, 250.

Harmonization of interests, 104, 111, 114 f., 118, 121 f., 126, 136, 187, 189, 193–5, 201, 226, 230.

Hart, H. L., 132 n., 248 n.

Hume, 95–96, 108, 225.

Ideals, 188–95, 251.

Illocutionary force, *see* Performative force.

Imperatives, 83, 85–87, 95, 99, 138–51, 157, 161 f., 164, 170 f., 184, 190 f., 200, 236 f.

Inclinations, 184–9, 191–3.

Incorrigibility, 128–31, 133 f.

Interests, 92, 113, 126, 186, 189–91, 194 f.

Intrinsic value, 12–13, 15, 22, 32 f., 35–37, 75, 98, 225.

Intuition, 23, 33, 91, 225.

Kant, 85 f., 88, 222.

Linguistic performance, 3, 7, 25, 45, 93, 117, 140, 148, 202–16. *See also* Speech-act.

Linguistic rules, 29, 44–47, 49–52, 55, 59 f., 68–70, 99, 119, 124 f., 155, 200–2.

Meaning, 25, 29–31, 42–52, 55, 63, 66, 122–4, 143 f., 146, 148–50, 153, 159, 197, 209.

Meta-ethics, 1–2, 70, 239. *See also* Ethical theory.

Moore, G. E., chapter i *passim*, 2, 40, 53, 66, 75–77, 94, 97–102, 108 f., 136, 150, 156, 197–9, 201, 224, 226, 230, 239–42, 247 f.

Moral reasoning, 3, 32–39, 53 f., 72–91, 97 f., 106, 110 f., 132, 136, 165, 170–5, 182–96, 216–30.

Naturalism and non-naturalism, 11–16, 22 f., 40, 53, 94, 150, 172 f., 183, 185.

Neustics, 142–52, 157, 159 f., 162 f., 172, 237, 240.

Open Question Argument, 16–21, 40, 241.

Performative force, 3, 25–32, 146, 150–60, 163, 172, 204, 209 f., 230–9, 243, 246.

Persuasion, 77, 81, 88–91, 139–41, 148, 187.

Persuasive definitions, 64–73, 103, 217.

Phrastics, 142–52, 156, 159 f., 160, 162 f., 167, 171 f., 209, 237.

Plato, 9, 94.

Prescriptivity, 93, 139, 141, 151, 166, 169, 183 f., 194, 221, 228.

Principles, 64–73, 103–7, 111, 125, 161, 164, 169, 174–82, 192 f., 207, 209–11, 214–16, 221, 244 f., 251.

Proof, 84, 88, 98, 118, 207, 211 f., 216, 224–30, 243 f., 246, 249.

Purpose, 112–14, 119–22, 124, 127, 137, 250. See also Use.

Reasons, 77 f., 82–88, 93, 95, 100–7, 119, 121, 123, 125 f., 160–70, 178, 182 f., 202–16, 218 f., 221, 224, 235, 242.

Reference, see Sense and reference.

Rules, see Linguistic rules and Principles.

Ryle, G., 247 n.

Science, 124 f., 127–37, 156, 183–5, 210.

Sense and reference, 2, 7, 25–32, 141, 145 f., 149, 153 f., 156, 158, 160, 168, 209, 242 f., 246.

Speech-act, 7, 25, 27, 37, 47 f., 123, 141, 143–5, 147, 149 f., 153, 155–7, 159, 209 f., 243. See also Linguistic performance.

Standards, see Principles.

Stevenson, C. S., chapter ii passim, 2, 14, 97–103, 105, 108 f., 116, 117 n., 118, 122 f., 138 f., 140 n., 141 f., 145 f., 148–51, 155 f., 159–61, 165, 182, 186, 197, 199–205, 216 f., 220, 222 f., 226, 229–36, 239 f., 242, 247, 250.

Supervenience, 14, 21–24, 32 f., 53, 108, 228.

Test cases, 105 f., 176 f., 211, 213 f., 217, 244, 246 f.

Toulmin, S., chapter iii passim, 2, 40, 140 n., 170 f., 173 f., 176, 187–9, 199–201, 224, 226, 230, 241, 250.

Truth, 97–102, 107–112.

Universalizability, 161, 165, 183 f., 188–93, 238.

Urmson, J. O., 205 n.

Use, 25–32, 52, 113–15, 117–23, 140, 146, 157, 159, 199, 202, 250.

Utilitarianism, 126, 183, 187–9, 192 f.

Validity, 72, 76–83, 97–102, 107–12, 138, 170, 193.

Waismann, F., 228 n.

White, M., 17 n., 94 n.

Wisdom, J., 17 n.

Wittgenstein, L., 117 n., 123, 124 n., 148 f., 154, 201, 248 n.